THE DUMBEST KID IN THE THIRD GRADE

By
Robert V. Broughton

Benson Smythe Publishing
Wellsville, New York

Copyright©1999 by Robert Broughton
All rights reserved. This book may not be
reproduced, in whole or in part, or in any
form without written permission
from the author.

The Dumbest Kid in the Third Grade
ISBN 1-888911-12-3
Library of Congress Number
98-61286

Cover Design by Bruce Broughton
Cover Photographs by the author, Bruce Broughton
and Annie Graham

Book Design by Benson Smythe Publishing

To order this book you may contact the author:
Robert Broughton
321 Farnum Street
Wellsville, NY 14895
Telephone: 716-593-1309

Published by Benson Smythe Publishing
3052 Palmer Road
Wellsville, NY 14895-9746
Telephone: 716-593-6145

Printed in the USA by

3212 East Highway 30 • Kearney, NE 68847 • 1-800-650-7888

This book is written to reflect events as the author has recollected them. Recollections, opinions, ideas, or theories expressed in the book are those of the author's and do not reflect those of the management of Benson Smythe Publishing. Many names have been changed for the sake of privacy. Any resemblence to actual persons, living or dead, is entirely coincidental.

An Amateur's Point of View

I suppose I could have been a bit more elegant in my style of writing, if I even have a style. For example, in describing how the girl I fooled around with down by the creek in Almond, looked after I hadn't seen her for an extended period of time. I could have said something like.... "Nature had taken command of an awkward, adolescent body, and through her wondrous ways, had transformed her into the glorious dawn of womanhood." But it's simpler for me to write the way I talk.

The book is languaged to reflect life in the Service and certain events. Its wording is not meant to offend any of its readers.

Writing elegantly and using imaginative sentences, I think, takes the skill of talented people, and the readers of these talented people must possess an equal skill and talent, to understand what the writer is trying to convey.

There's a huge pile of books out there I would never attempt to read, as they are much too deep for me. On the other hand there must be a lot of people who do read, understand, and enjoy these books as they just keep coming. What I'm trying to say is I think there should be something for everyone. I think there should always be a *Romeo & Juliet*, a *Tom Sawyer*, a *Bambi*, and even a book by Bob Broughton, who never wrote much more than a post card, but thinks that he has a little story to tell. This way everyone can enjoy reading books, and maybe try a little writing if they get the notion and if they stay within their abilities they won't make a fool of themselves. A short, fat, three hundred pound man doesn't make for a good pole-vaulter.

Introduction

About a year before the nineteen twenty-nine stock market crash and the great depression, my father lost his job at the Erie Shops, in Hornell, thus giving us a head start at being poor and destitute.

This picture of my brother Jim, myself, and my sisters, Alice and Eva, was taken in nineteen twenty-eight on Aunt Bertha's farm in Middleberry Pennsylvania. The shed-type building at the far right was Aunt Bertha's ice house. They cut ice from their pond in the winter and stacked it in the shed with thick layers of sawdust sandwiched in between for insulation. She had ice all summer long.

Aunt Bertha is standing in the doorway of her woodshed. The little dog in the picture was Teddy. We had him nearly sixteen years.

In nineteen twenty-eight about all I owned was one-fourth interest in a little dog, a dirty shirt, and a pair of slightly used diapers and by the looks of the picture, I was about to lose the latter.

TABLE OF CONTENTS

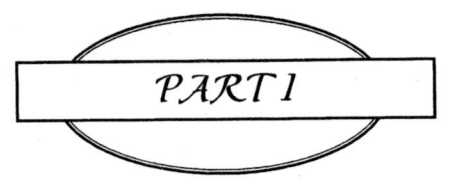

PART 1

Canisteo	1
Clayton Henry	3
Aunt Bertha's Farm	5
Aunt Bertha's Boys	10
The Fast	13
The Party	15
Some Day	18
Wellsville	19
Rhythm Band	21
Birdsall	23
A Birdsall Christmas	29
A Christmas Play	33
Mother	36
Harold	38
Shawmut	41
Dad and His Brothers	44
The Dumbest Kid in the Third Grade	47
Mrs. Bensen	64
The 1930's	66
Fourth of July	68
The Cannon	70
Mort	72
The Old Stone House	77
A Place of Higher Learning	79
Ncay Ouyay Alktay Iggpay Atinlay	84
The New Deal	86

PART II

Wellsville 1940	92
Signing the Papers	94
The Weidrick Bridge	97
Camp	97
Navy Boot	101
Songs	104
USS Arkab	105
Praise the Lord	121
In Defense of the Four Letter Word	122
San Francisco to Pearl Harbor	124
Christmas Eve in the Crows Nest	128
Armed Guard - Treasure Island	129
The Day Our Leader Died	132
A Hug and A Kiss	134
Harry	140
Welcome Home?	142
Last Hunt	149
Religion	152
A Bad Fire	154
Maria	161
On the Great Lakes	165
Slim	172
One Bad Apple	179
Ve Gonna Make You a Veelsman	184
Bartender, We'll Have Another Round	187
The Little Pilot	189
I Youst Touched Da Piers	192

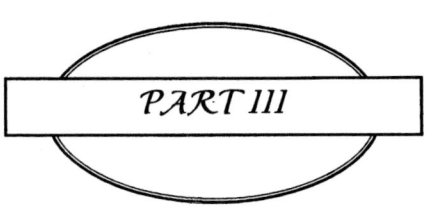

PART III

Beulah	196
A Real Steamboat Man	201
Lake Superior's Wrath	204
The Shipkeeper	207
The Winter Gang	208
The Shipkeeper's Wife	210
Where Did All the Boats Go?	211
Anna III	212
A Champion Falls	217
Beulah, Bonnie and Bob	221
Beulah, Bonnie, Barbie and Bob	224
Beulah, Bonnie, Barbie, Bruce and Bob	227
Beulah, Bonnie, Barbie, Bruce, Billy and Bob	230
The Machine Shop	233
The New Stone House	237
Boatswain Kelly	239
Boat Trip	242
Remembering Kelly	245
A Theory of a Lowly Wheelsman	248
The Wellsville Dry cleaners	256
Family	258
The Pink House	262
The Texas Hot	267
House Number 3	273
Where Did All the Trains Go?	276
Dreams	278
Florence	283
Friends	284
An 'Ol Man's Chat With Time..	286

Someone Once Said... 287
Quarry Farm 291

Part 1

Canisteo

"Push him in," my cousin Regis whispered. So I did. A bunch of us kids were standing on the creek bank watching the high water from the spring run off and I pushed Clayton Henry in. By all rights, Clayton Henry should have drowned that day; but someone must have been watching over him. The fast water carried him to the low end of the bank where he was able to drag himself out of the freezing water. It still haunts me thinking about it. To this day I can see in my mind Clayton Henry struggling to get out of the water and up the slippery creek bank, clawing at the tree roots and brush, muddy brown water running out of his heavy coat, none of us kids helping him. We all just stood there watching except for Regis' big German shepherd, who we all called Big Ted. Big Ted was running back and forth along the creek bank where Clayton was trying to get out. He was upset and barking non-stop. He seemed to know the peril Clayton was in better than any of us. I honestly think Big Ted had the intelligence to go into the water and pull Clayton out, if he had not been able to get out by himself.

Big Ted loved kids, as they loved him, and he was very protective of them. Aunt Margaret, Regie's mother, had to shut the big dog in a room if she had to punish Regis or Duane, her younger brother, with a spanking. When Clayton finally got out and up the bank, he never yelled or even cried, he must have been in shock. He just staggered home, his heavy wet coat and clothes weighing him down. I knew I had done something very bad. I was scared and sorry I had done such a bad deed, not sorry for Clayton, but for myself knowing some kind of punishment was sure to come.

That event is as far back as I can remember. It must have been in the Spring of 1930. I was four and a half years old. The mean streak was showing up at an early age.

The great depression must have been an invention of Satan himself, no money, no jobs and worse of all, no hope. Talk about "The Grapes of Wrath", at least the "Oakies" had a dream, they were going to California for a chance of a better life. We did not have anything, not even a dream, just despair.

I remember my older brother Jim and I used to meet the bread truck when it pulled into Kellogg's store. Sometimes the driver would give us some cookies that were too stale to sell. Once they put free balloons inside the bread wrappers, and I conned old man Kellogg into giving me a loaf of bread so I could get one of those balloons. I told him that Dad would come up to pay for the bread later. I opened the bread under the porch, ate what I wanted and left the rest there. Not acting too bright, I walked into the house blowing up the balloon.

"Where did you get that balloon, Bobby?" my dad asked. I got my little rear blistered harder for that caper than I did for pushing Clayton into the water.

I never got too many spankings when I was little. If my shenanigans were weighed on the scales of justice against punishment rendered, the scales would have been heavily out of balance in my favor. My father had other ways of punishing me.

Once he caught me taking a leak in the middle of the street. "If I ever catch you doing that again, I'll take you down to old Dr. McCarty and have that thing cut off," he threatened. The threat was very effective. I never relieved myself in the street again. From then on, I hot-footed to the privy out back, no matter how busy I was playing. I was quite sure my dad wouldn't do such a thing, but was not about to take the chance that he might.

F.D.R. was president. He said he was going to turn things around, and he did. I don't see how he could have missed. Any change would have been for the better.

Clayton Henry

"Get lots of spit on your tongue, Clayton, and stick it on the rail and hold it there for a little while." Regis, Duane, and I were standing on the bridge near where I pushed Clayton in the spring before. It was bitter cold out. Clayton did what Regis told him to do, he stuck his tongue on the frosty iron rail and it stuck there. Frightened, Clayton jerked his head back, leaving a small patch of skin on the rail. It must have hurt like mad. Clayton ran home bawling.

It seems just about every kid in upstate New York has participated in that little trick; half of them perpetrators, like my Cousin Regis, the other half, victims - like Clayton Henry.

***

If I take the nickel, Ma will miss it, I reasoned, so I'll just take the penny. There was six cents in my mother's pocketbook. I took the penny and headed for Kellogg's store. On the way I met Clayton riding down the street on his big, shiny, new red tricycle.

"Where ya going, Bobby?" Clayton asked.

"I got a penny," I bragged. "I'm going to Kellogg's and buy me some candy. Can I have a ride on your new tricycle?"

"No. My mother told me not to let anyone take my new tricycle, but if you give me half of your candy, I'll give you a ride to the store on the back of my bike." I think the kids were a little jealous of Clayton. He always had nice warm clothes and things to play with. He and his mother lived alone. She must have had some money stashed away.

There was a steep hill behind Kellogg's store.

"Why don't we push your tricycle up that hill Clayton, you could coast down and have a nice ride." At the top of the hill I held the tricycle while Clayton got on. When I let go, Clayton took off like a shot. He was going so fast he couldn't keep his feet on the pedals. Halfway down the hill he lost control, the tricycle flipped over, landed upside down and stopped. But Clayton kept going. He ground cinders into his face and hands, and once more Clayton went home bawling.

I went in the store, bought my candy and then walked Clayton's bike the rest of the way down the hill. I had a big, shiny, new red tricycle to play with and a penny's worth of candy. Clayton didn't come back for the tricycle until late in the day. It must have been the best day I had during the whole depression.

"Whose been in my pocketbook?"

"Not me Ma," I lied.

"Get lots of spit on your tongue, Clayton, and stick it on the rail."

Aunt Bertha's Farm

In the summer, when school was out, Mom and Dad shipped us out to Aunt Bertha's farm in Middleberry, Pennsylvania "To fatten us up, so we would make it through the winter," Dad told us.

Aunt Bertha was a Cherokee Indian. I don't see how she could have been any relation to the Broughtons, but we called her Aunt Bertha anyway. Her husband was gone. She had two boys, Karl and Mort, who did the chores, but Aunt Bertha was boss. She made all the decisions. She was the most self-sufficient person I ever knew. She managed her farm with the skill of a high-powered executive, but I don't think she could read or write. Neither could Karl. Mort could read a little. On Sunday mornings, Mort would read comics to his brother. Mort read slowly and deliberately, causing Jim, Alice and Eva to snicker when Mort labored over the words, reading aloud to Karl.

Aunt Bertha was also a big woman. She had straight black hair and a red face. Looking at her, there was no denying she was Indian. She had a violent temper, and was a sight to behold when her dander was up. Aunt Bertha never talked much; she didn't have to, she communicated with her facial expressions better than most do by talking. When she smiled at you, it was warm and sincere, and you knew she meant it. If she frowned you knew you better stop irritating her. When her black eyes snapped, and she set her jaw and doubled her fists up you knew well enough to get the hell out of her way, as the nearest object she could reach was coming at you, be it a kitchen chair or one of her big butcher knives.

Sometimes Aunt Bertha would ask me to go out in the meadow and find what she called a "puff ball," a large round fungus with insides that were grayish white in color, similar to a mushroom. Aunt Bertha sliced them up and fried them in homemade butter. She put maple syrup on mine. She and I were the only ones who ate them. You had to pick them early in the morning, before the sun dried the dew. As they turned powder dry in the hot sun by day's end. If one gave a puff ball a kick in late afternoon, it disintegrated into a cloud of brown dust.

I loved my Aunt Bertha. Although the last time I saw her was in nineteen forty-two, to this day my image of her is clear in my mind. She was always good to me and my brothers and sisters. She assigned chores to them, but I was to stay in the kitchen with her most of the time. I never had to do much, maybe just go with her to gather eggs, or slop the hogs.

Aunt Bertha let me drink coffee with her. Hers was black and strong. Mine she fixed with one-third honey, one-third pure cream, and one-third coffee. It tasted sweet and good, and it made me feel grown up. She was always giving me a hug or some maple sugar she had stashed away in her cupboard.

Listening to Aunt Bertha and the boys, I learned to swear well. If I told Aunt Bertha I was going to go out and see if I could find her a "damn 'ol puff ball," she didn't bawl me out, she only chuckled a little.

When she saw I was getting a little bored, she let me go into her parlor. It was cool in there. The shades and curtains were always drawn, and it took a little while for my eyes to get accustomed to the dim light. Aunt Bertha would get out her huge old Bible, and I would sit on the floor with the Bible in my lap. Aunt Bertha went back to her kitchen, and I leafed through the big Bible looking at the many full-page pictures letting my imagination run wild. I was very impressed with David holding up the severed head of Goliath. I thought Eve was pretty neat eating her apple without any clothes on and those mean guys driving nails in that other guy's hands and feet - "If I could have been there with one of Karl or Mort's guns, I would have shot them," I thought.

I knew I was special to my Aunt Bertha when she let me in her parlor. Aunt Bertha's parlor was never, ever used, except when special company was visiting, or when someone was being laid out.

*Mom and Dad shipped us out to Aunt Bertha's farm
in Middleberry, Pennsylvania
"to fatten us up, so we would make it through the winter."*

"This picture of Jim, myself, Eva and Alice in the background was taken in nineteen-thirty. The picture shows us all fattened up after a summer on Aunt Bertha's farm. Mom told me that Aunt Belle and Uncle Rob Pye bought us all new clothes and took us to Hornell to get our picture taken. In the picture we all looked well nourished and healthy, but the winter in Canisteo would be long, lean and cold.

Dad told me we lived well in the early twenties, but in nineteen twenty-eight he lost his job, along with a lot of other people. At one point during the depression, he thought he would have shot himself if he'd had a gun in the house. My mother once told me a story about my dad:

***

"Some sort of charity was giving out free food to poor people. So I went down to get some of the free food. I knew George wouldn't go, his pride wouldn't let him. While I was picking up the food, the man in charge, who knew George, asked, 'What's the matter with George, is he too lazy to come down to get his free food?' I left the food there and went home crying. When your father found out what happened he went down to the place where they were giving out the free food. He was in a rage. He swore and cursed at the man in charge and was about to attack him when they dragged him out of the place, tears of rage, hurt and humiliation streaming down his face. That's the way it was during the depression, a lot of meanness, and sad times."

She told me that during the depression, doctors made house calls, but there was little incentive for a doctor to make calls to poor people when they knew there would be no pay for their services. Kids would get sick and die from relatively minor diseases because they were malnourished and it didn't take much to do them in. Many never saw a doctor until it was too late. *"George and I were in constant fear one of you kids would get sick."* She told us.

Aunt Bertha's Boys

Aunt Bertha's son, Karl, had black curly hair and dark banjo eyes. He wore a constant grin on his face and would terrorize us kids. I was scared of Karl and always gave him a wide berth. Once Karl chased Eva and Alice to the top of the hay loft where they were forced to jump to the hay wagon below. Alice suffered a nasty cut to her lip. If one of us kids had told Aunt Bertha about his actions, she would have probably killed him, but we never did.

Karl's brother, Mort, was a good man, kind and always good to us. Karl always took advantage of his brother's good nature. It was Mort who always cleaned the drop in the cow barn, and it was Mort who pitched the hay in the wagon while Karl drove the team. Mort loved his little brother anyway.

Aunt Bertha had a good-sized dairy farm. She made her own butter, and she had a bee hive where she got honey to be used in the place of sugar. There were peaches, apples, cherries and berries on the farm, and there was a natural gas well for heat and cooking. She butchered her own beef and pork, and she had a flock of chickens and ducks for meat and eggs. She used ice from their ice house for refrigeration. She made the best homemade ice cream I ever had, using her own ice, milk and eggs.

The boys made homemade brew which sometimes they overindulged in. When the boy's drank too much home brew, even Aunt Bertha couldn't handle them. Sometimes they would butcher a cow, take it to Elkland Pennsylvania and sell it to the local butcher. The boys would take the money and go out looking for women while continuing their drinking binge. Jim told me about one time when he was reading out on Aunt Bertha's front porch:

***

"Karl and Mort drove in the driveway in their old pickup, after one of their binges was over. Aunt Bertha was there waiting for them. Mort got out of the truck first, his head lowered and hands in his pockets. Aunt Bertha gave him a few swats beside his head, and

told him to get his ass to the cow barn. 'Those cows haven't been milked in two days,' she yelled. Mort shuffled off to the cow barn, his head still down and his hands in his pockets. Aunt Bertha headed for the other side of the truck where Karl was sitting with his banjo eyes nearly bulging out of his head and that eternal grin on his face. Karl quickly got out of the truck and made a bee line towards the barn. Aunt Bertha couldn't catch him so she picked up a rock and flung it at him. Karl picked up the pace a little.

From left to right: My Dad, Karl, Mom holding Maggie, Grandma Pitts, myself and Aunt Bertha on Aunt Bertha's farm about nineteen thirty-two.

From Left to right: Grandma Pitts, Aunt Mildred and Aunt Bertha. I don't know who the old gent is, but he must have put on a necktie special for his picture. Back then, taking a picture was a big deal and serious stuff. Grandma Pitts never smoked or took a drink, but could swear a little when she was worked up.

The Fast

We had an uncle who lived on Aunt Bertha's farm by the name of Vern Dodge. Vern was Grandma Pitts' brother. Before Uncle Vern came to live on Aunt Bertha's farm he was working his small farm up on Karr Valley Road outside of Almond. I was told that Vern's wife, Aunt Rose, had died and Uncle Vern's health had started to go. He was very lonesome so he turned his livestock and equipment from his modest farm over to Aunt Bertha in exchange for his keep.

Uncle Vern was a little man. He shook all over, especially his hands. He couldn't walk very well, just shuffled along, his shoes never quite losing contact with the ground. When shuffling, his upper torso pitched way forward as if defying the law of gravity. One would swear he was going to fall flat on his face. Basically, Aunt Bertha was good to old Vern, but sometimes her patience wore thin. One morning at the breakfast table old Vern shuffled over to the stove to get his coffee.

"Don't you fill that cup full," Aunt Bertha commanded.

Vern paid her no mind, filled his cup until it was full to the brim. He spilled some from his shaky hands, causing a puff of steam to rise from the hot stove. On his return trip to the table he slopped more along the way. After he got sat down, he slopped still more trying to get the cup to his lips. The coffee spilled onto Aunt Bertha's new oil cloth. Fire leapt from her eyes. She gave Vern a whack on the back of the head, and what was left of the coffee spilled on the table. Poor old Vern slowly got up, left the table and shuffled off to the sanctuary of his old rocker on the front porch. Jim, Alice, and Eva were upset. They all liked old Uncle Vern and felt sorry for him. Me, I thought the incident was a little funny, but I sure as hell knew better than to laugh.

I could see Aunt Bertha wasn't going to be in a very good mood, so when Jim and my sisters went out in the vegetable garden to weed, I went with them. They were mad at Aunt Bertha for being so mean to old Uncle Vern. It was decided we should go on a hunger fast. That would make her sorry, we all agreed. At lunch time we hid in the apple orchard, and tried to fill up on summer apples, but the apples were too green and hard. That evening at the supper table Aunt Bertha scolded us for not being around at lunch time. She had a big iron skillet full of chicken frying on the stove. While Aunt Bertha had her back turned getting the chicken off the stove I whispered to Jim, "Would it be okay if I had just one little piece of that chicken?" Jim shrugged his shoulders. I took that for a yes. I put a drumstick on my plate and the vow was broken. Everyone ate a hearty supper, even old Uncle Vern. The fast was over. Later, Jim and my sisters all said it was my fault the fast didn't work out. I put food on my plate first.

The Party

In late summer Mom and Dad would come to take us back to Canisteo and the depression. As bad as things were in Canisteo, we were all homesick, and our reunion was a joyous thing for everyone. Aunt Bertha would insist Mom and Dad stay a few days. Then the home brew flowed like the Johnstown flood. Chickens had their heads chopped off, little pigs had their throats cut and took turns being stuffed whole in Aunt Bertha's big oven. The neighbors came with banjos, guitars, harmonicas and mandolins. Mom sat down at the old pump organ while Dad tucked his fiddle under his chin. Aunt Bertha's old house trembled from the do-se-dos, alaman lefts, and the stomping of many feet keeping time with the music.

For a while, there was no depression, just laughing, dancing, drinking and maybe a little hanky-panky behind the milk house. A fist fight broke out in back of the granary, caused by someone getting too friendly with someone else's wife or girl friend.

The next morning I was the first one up. I went downstairs and surveyed the aftermath of the party. People were sleeping on the floor, in the yard and on the front porch. The kitchen table was full of glasses and bottles. The floor of the kitchen was sticky when I walked across it in my bare feet. The screening was gone from the kitchen door. Someone must have fallen through it, I thought.

Back in those days, people used fly stickers to get rid of flies. They were a strip of sticky tape that hung from the ceiling. When the flies landed on the tape they were doomed. The stickers hanging from Aunt Bertha's ceiling were completely black with flies, struggling in agony, giving off eerie, high-pitched little buzzing sounds as if crying for help. The stickers could accommodate only a fraction of the flies as there were swarms everywhere.

I thought I would like to know what kind of magic was in those bottles, that caused people to have such a good time. I started draining out the bottles into a large water glass, and managed to get the glass full. I took a taste, liked it, and drank it all. That's about all that this five year-old remembered of that incident. Dad liked to tell about the time little Bobby got drunk. Dad said I was talking 'Dutchy' and staggering around Aunt Bertha's kitchen bumping into things yelling, "Gimme some more, somma dat stuff, dat stuff makes me sing." Then I went out in the front yard and started doing somersaults. After a few somersaults, I sort of passed out.

"About then, I got concerned," Dad said. "But when I picked Bobby up, he had a big grin on his face, so I figured he was okay. I put Bobby to bed, and he slept most of the day."

Sometime in the early seventies, my Aunt Bertha died. Karl and Mort were living in the house and it burned to the ground. I sure would have loved to have that big old Bible she let me look at, but it must have burned up in the fire that they had. Too bad every little boy couldn't have an aunt like Aunt Bertha.

Photo by Milt Pitts

Uncle Howard and Aunt Bertha. There was a long span of time when I didn't see Aunt Bertha. I don't remember her the way the picture portrays her. I remember her with straight black hair and heavier, rather than the frail old lady shown here.

It must have been one of the last pictures taken of her.

Recipe for Home Brew

1 Can Malt. 1 Yeast Cake. 5 gal. Water. 3 lb. Sugar
Dissolve sugar in hot water, let cook and add malt and yeast cake. Pour into crock and keep warm. Let stand 3 days or until ready to bottle. Keep outside as it is liable to blow up.

Someday

I recall one time my father was sitting on the broken steps in front of our rented house on Taylor Street, in Canisteo. The house was sided with black tarpaper and was little more than a shack. A few days back he had gone through an appendicitis operation. Earlier in the day I had heard him talking to my mother. He had said something about a doctor saving his life and that he was 'the best damn doctor in Canisteo' and he didn't have one red cent to pay that good man with. I remember I was playing in some loose dirt close to the steps where my father was sitting and I happened to look up at him. I was only five years old, but I sensed that awful sadness in him and I wanted to go to him and sit on his lap, but I was dirty and didn't know if he would want me to or not. So I just sat there in the dirt looking up at him. He looked back at me as if he had just discovered I was sitting there.

"Hi ya Bobby," he whispered softly, as if the greeting was a special secret between he and I that no one else should hear. Then he got up and went back into the house.

I picked up my toy car and went back to building roads in the dirt, running my car over them making motor sounds like my Dad's old car did whenever he could scrape up the nine cents for a gallon of gas. My little cast iron car had a chunk missing out of one of it's wheels and it bumped as I pushed it along. The broken wheel sometimes would dig in the dirt and stop the car. I pretended it had a flat tire.

When my Dad gets a job someday and buys me a new car I'm gonna keep this 'ol car, too. I got the best damn Dad in Canisteo. "Brummm, Brummm, Brummm."

Wellsville

Dad landed a job at the Moore Steam Turbine in Wellsville. We moved out of the shack in Canisteo, to a house in Wellsville. The house had electricity, gas, a coal furnace and a real bathroom. We had a radio so I could listen to Jack Armstrong and Buck Rogers. There was even a movie theater to go to if you had a dime. Once Tarzan was playing at the show. I just had to see this movie, but I didn't have a dime. I was a good con artist so I walked up to the kid taking tickets and told him my folks were good friends of the owners and that I had permission to get in free. After that, whenever I wanted to see a show, I just walked right in. This worked for awhile, until a new kid was hired.

I had a gift for conning people. I knew what I was going to say, and got to the point quickly. I conned my parents by always telling the truth about little things, but lying about big things like the dime missing from my mother's pocketbook. My grandma used to brag, "Bobby always tells the truth, he never lies."

It was great in Wellsville. On summer evenings Dad, Mom, and my uncles and cousins would gather on the big front porch and have jam sessions. Dad played the fiddle, Mom the piano, Uncle Mort the banjo, Uncle Howard the xylophone, cousin Charlie the guitar, and cousin Leo the drums. They were all good musicians. They played popular songs of the thirties like; "Has Anybody Seen My Gal", "Old Shanty Town", and waltzes, and fox-trots. It was great music and you don't hear it much anymore. Maybe I'm just out of style, but today's music just doesn't cut it with me. When they played, half of the neighborhood gathered in the front yard to listen. I was very proud of my mom, dad and all my uncles and cousins.

Now, that big old house on the corner of Cusick and Pine is gone. The neighborhood said it was an eyesore and indeed it was, but the last time I saw the old house it looked restorable to me. The siding was bad, the porches were rotting off and the place looked a little trashy, but the ridges were level and the house looked plumb and square. They tore it down anyway.

Though the house is gone, Eva and I still have the memories of the good times we had there, before we had to move out. I bet if I were to stand on the corner of Cusick and Pine some quiet, warm summer night and shut my eyes and listened, I could still hear the music coming from where the big old front porch used to be, and I bet the song I would hear in my mind would be that haunting and beautiful "Missouri Waltz" they used to play so well. It was my favorite when I was a little boy. They always played the "Missouri Waltz" last. I liked to think they played it special for me because they knew how I liked it so.

Rhythm Band

In nineteen thirty-two, I started school in Wellsville. It's strange how I can't remember as much about my first year in school as I can about things that happened before that, but some things stand out in my mind. I remember my mother talking to some people from school about whether I was going to be placed in kindergarten or the first grade. It was decided that I should be placed in kindergarten. My mother reluctantly agreed as my birthday was going to be a week after school started, and I was already five. It would make me six years old and the oldest in the class. With such a late start, I was almost always the oldest kid in class, all through school. I always tried to conceal my age and never told anyone how old I was unless I had to. The other kids must think I'm pretty dumb, I used to think.

One thing I can remember about kindergarten was what the teacher called a rhythm band. The band consisted of about twenty sets of round red wood dowels about a foot or so long. These were called rhythm sticks. We also had two tambourines and a shiny metal triangle, held by a string and a little rod to strike it with. The teacher would wind up the old victrola, put on a marching record and twenty kids would bang the rhythm sticks together, two would pound and shake the hell out of the tambourines, and one would whack away at the triangle. When it came time to play the rhythm band, right after our ten minute nap, I would sit at my little table in great anticipation, "maybe this time I'll get to play one of those tambourines or better yet, maybe that shiny triangle," but alas it never happened. Some well-dressed, snotty little girl with curly hair and glasses always got the triangle and two "sissy boys" got the tambourines. I always wound up with those "damn 'ol rhythm sticks."

One of the little boys that got to play the tambourine the most often, lived on Pine Street, the same street I lived on. When I caught him walking home I would beat up on him with a vengeance. I was bigger than he was and it was easy to do as he never fought back. Then one day after school I went after the kid as he was walking up Pine Street. The kid took off running until he reached his house.

Then he stopped, turned and faced me. This surprised me so I cautiously approached him. When he was just a few feet away he came at me swinging his arms like a windmill. He must have hit me a half dozen times without me ever laying a hand on him. The boy's mother was watching all this from her doorway.

"You boys get in this house," she yelled. I started to run. "Right *now*," she yelled. The authority in her voice convinced me to follow the kid inside. Once inside she made us shake hands and promise not to fight each other anymore. She sat us down at her kitchen table, got out a tin container of milk from her ice box and poured out a tall glass of milk for each of us. She disappeared into her pantry just off the kitchen for a moment and came out with a dish of cookies. She sat them down on he table between us. I can't remember what that little boy looked like, but I still can envision his mother leaning back against her kitchen wall, her arms folded in front of her, a little half smile on her face as she watched the two of us drink the cold sweet milk and eat fresh homemade sugar cookies. Walking home after leaving their house I surmised it must have been the boy's mother who taught him to stand up to me and come out swinging his arms like a windmill.

Birdsall

People started to garnishee Dad's wages from the debts built up during the depression. We couldn't pay the rent half of the time so we moved in with my Uncle Nate in Birdsall, New York. Back to square one; no electricity or gas, just wood cook stoves for cooking and heating, an outhouse and an outside water pump. We used to joke, "We have five rooms and a path." It wasn't as bad as Canisteo. We were used to it, and this time we had a little money coming in.

We attended a one-room school house; also with no utilities. Jim and a kid named Johnny O'Conner did the chores and helped the teacher. There were sixteen kids in the school and six of them were Broughtons. Miss Gregory was a no nonsense teacher, but all the kids loved her and respected her. No one failed their grade that year. Miss Gregory made you work. She would hammer away at you until you got it right, and you didn't mind because you knew she cared. Not many Miss Gregory's around today, too bad. Jim skipped ahead a grade that year.

***

"Shut the door Duane, the girls are coming." Duane and I shared a room together. We were more like brothers than cousins. Our bedroom door adjoined the girls' room. We would slam the door shut which never really shut tight and always left a crack. We would make a big deal about shutting the door so the girls couldn't see us get ready for bed, as if they would have given a damn. Then we blew out the oil lamp and watched them get undressed for bed through the crack in the door. "I wish we had electric lights," Duane whispered, "so we could see better."

Watching Cousin Regis, just before she slipped her night gown over her naked body, was the first time I ever gazed upon the developed body of the opposite sex. She was full-figured and beautiful. Her long black curly hair fell past her shoulders, framing her breasts. I remember her skin shined and glowed in the dim yellow light of the oil lamp. At the time, Cousin Regis was the most gorgeous and exciting thing I had ever seen. If anyone thinks little boys don't have lustful thoughts, they had better think again, I would have given anything to have crawled in bed with Cousin Regis that night, even though I wouldn't have known what to do after I got there.

My uncle dreamed of having a farm, but his place in Birdsall just didn't work out. The garden didn't grow well and his young stock kept getting out. Even Miss Spotty, his milking cow, let him down. She got in the grain barrel and killed herself from overeating. Jim did all the chores. He never complained. His pay was gratitude from Uncle Nate and Aunt Margaret. They truly appreciated Jim and that was pay enough for him.

After a few months in Birdsall my sisters, Alice and Eva, were ready to leave. They were at the age where they noticed boys and there were few boys in Birdsall, although Alice did have a boyfriend which Duane and I kidded her about to the point of tears. I don't know if little Eva had a boyfriend or not. She was always secretive and quiet. Sometimes I would look at her and she would have this little smile on her face but she would never reveal what she was thinking. Maybe some knight on a big white horse was taking her out of Birdsall. (Eva loved books, she was always reading.)

Most of today's poor would be considered pretty well off if you compared them with the very poor in the late twenties and early thirties. We had no food stamps or welfare. Most had no bathrooms, telephones, radios, running water, electricity or gas. If you were to transplant "poor" families of today into places like Birdsall, into drafty, uninsulated houses with no utilities of any kind, give them a bucksaw and a water pail, I doubt if most would make it through a winter. Looking back on it, I doubt if I could make it through a winter like we had in Birdsall, anymore.

A typical winter day in Birdsall started out early. To get to work Dad had to drive about twenty miles to Wellsville. It wasn't the distance of the drive that took the time, it was getting the old Essex to start, it was more stubborn than a mule. Dad called it his "ass-ache", a more suitable name than Essex, he said when it wouldn't start.

When we woke up in the morning it would be freezing cold in the house. Jim and Dad would get up first and get a fire started in the kitchen wood stove. Mom put the teakettle on, sometimes the water was frozen. The rest of us kids would crawl out from under a mountain of blankets and dash downstairs to the now warm kitchen stove, where we would finish dressing. When the water in the teakettle was scalding hot I took it outside to thaw out and prime the pump. Then I'd pump the water pail full and take it in the kitchen to warm on the stove so we could wash our hands and face. In the winter our hands and faces were about the only parts of our anatomy that got washed during the week. Sunday night we took turns bathing in a wash tub behind the kitchen stove.

Breakfast was always the same, toast and cocoa or postum. Sometimes, though, on a Sunday morning Uncle Nate made a pile of pancakes with sausage. They were delicious. In the morning the first one out to the two-holer would brush off the snow that had blown through the cracks of the privy during the night. I liked to be the last one out to the outhouse as the seat would be warmer after the others got through.

The Broughton kids didn't have it too bad walking to school. We lived closer to the school than the others, about a mile or so. In the winter sometimes it was fun to go to school if there was enough snow to ride our sleds. But you don't get something for nothing. When school was out we had to drag the darn things back up the hill. I had a little secret I never told Dad about. I always hoped the Essex wouldn't start too soon. That way we could ride to school. If the car started right off Dad would leave too early to take us to school. After school I would have to fill a bushel basket full of kindling wood. There were a lot of sumac trees behind the house. The wood was dry and brittle and easy to break off. The first few pieces of sumac I would break off long enough to catch on the sides of the basket. This way the pieces wouldn't go all the way to the bottom, leaving an empty space. I would form a crude grid and pile more sumac on top. This gave the appearance of a full basket. Once when Dad saw the full basket he told me, "Good job, Bobby." My mother looked at me and gave me a little knowing smile. I couldn't con her. She knew her Bobby like a book.

Sometimes while playing on weekends, Duane and I were out in the cold from dawn to dark, never taking time to button our coats, and half of the time with no mittens. We always lost them. Sometimes while playing in the snow and nature called we would try to write our last name in the snow while peeing. Duane would write BROTN as he couldn't spell too well. The letters he didn't know he simply left out. I never had enough pee left to cross the "t" in Broughton. We had runny noses most of the time, which we wiped on our coat sleeves, giving our mothers fits. But we never got sick. All the time I was in Canisteo, Birdsall and Wellsville I never was taken to a doctor, nor were any of my brothers and sisters except for Maggie when she got pneumonia, but that was in Almond.

It was a hard life in Birdsall but we were family, and we got along very well with each other. We had much more happiness than sorrow and we had our humor. I kind of feel sorry for anyone who never went through hard times. I think hard times builds character, appreciation, compassion and humor. I'm glad I wasn't born rich and never sat a pampered little rear end on a cold outdoor privy seat, but I sure wouldn't mind being rich right now.

My Uncle Nate and Aunt Margaret.

At the time Cousin Regis was the most gorgeous and exciting thing I had ever seen.

"Alice has a boy friend...Alice has a boy Friend..."

A Birdsall Christmas

"Please, Maw, can I go with you?"

"No Bobby, we're going Christmas shopping for you kids. You stay home with your brothers and sisters."

"Please Maw, I'll stay in the car while you and Dad are in the store." I won out, as I knew I would. I could go to Hornell with them if I stayed in the car while they bought us kids our Christmas presents.

I loved riding in our old Essex. I always demanded a seat next to the window so I wouldn't miss any of the sights along the way. It was near dark when Dad and Mom finished their shopping. then we paid a visit to Aunt Nell and Uncle Preston, Mom's brother that lived in Hornell. Aunt Nell suggested we bring in the gifts from the car.

"We can take them in the kitchen and wrap them. That way they'll be all ready to place under the tree when you get back home," she said.

"Maw, I can help with the presents," I offered. They vigorously rejected my offer. They wrapped all the gifts, then took them back to the car and piled them on the car floor in the back. It was getting pretty late when we left Uncle Preston and Aunt Nell's house so Mom told me to lie down in the back. Then she covered me with an old laprobe we carried in the car. Dad made a pillow for me out of his old mackinaw that he wore when working out in the cold, cutting wood. I had my mother and father all to myself. I didn't have to share them with my brothers and sisters. Dad's old mackinaw smelled of wood smoke and kerosene oil. Not an irritating smell, but one that made me feel close to him. It made me feel safe and secure. As we passed under each street light, driving through Hornell a flash of bright light flooded the interior of the car. I could get a quick glimpse of the red and green wrapped gifts piled on the car floor. The light reflected off of the silver and gold ribbons they were tied with and I wondered which gifts were mine.

Soon we were out of Hornell and all alone bounding down the

dark narrow dirt road that led to the tiny settlement of Birdsall. The inside of the car was dark except for the dim yellow glow from the dash lights silhouetting my mother and father sitting in the front seat of the beloved old Essex. The confinement and closeness in the car just added to the warmth of it all. Mom was sitting close to Dad and they were talking. The growling sounds coming from the rear end of the old Essex were drowning out most of what they were talking about, but I was able to catch a few words like "Good kids...Alice...Eva...Jim...Maggie" and once in a while the word I liked to hear most, "Bobby." Every once in a while Mom would look back to see if I was sleeping. The growling sounds and vibrations coming from the rear end of the Essex were hypnotic and were putting me to sleep, but I didn't want to go to sleep. I wanted to stay in that state of being half awake and half asleep, drifting in and out. I wanted the ride to last forever. I didn't want to miss one moment of it, but the old Essex was persistent and won out. I fell fast to sleep.

"Bobby...Bobby...wake up, we're home," my mother was calling. I woke up, but I kept my eyes shut, pretending I couldn't wake up.

"Why don't you carry him up to bed, George," my mother said. Dad carried me up to bed, took off my shoes and covered me up. Then he blew out the oil lamp and went downstairs. I had squeezed every last drop of pleasure there was to be had for me out of that little trip to Hornell and back. I don't recall, but I bet there was one little boy who had some very pleasant dreams that Christmas Eve.

No matter how hard up we were, my folks always managed a Christmas for us. Sometimes not much, but always something. That year, Dad was working; so Mom and Dad told us that each of us could have two gifts. I wanted a flashlight and a jackknife, and I got both. The jacknife came in a little knife holder on the outside of a brand new pair of high top leather boots, something I really wanted but knew my folks couldn't affort. They must have borrowed money for that Christmas

Dad could only dream of owning a new car like this one. Our Essex was old and beat up, but Dad was a good mechanic and kept her running.

They must have borrowed money for that Christmas.

A Christmas Play

I remember one time Miss Gregory decided to put on a Christmas play. Every kid in the school was to have a part in the play. We were all happy with the parts we had until it came time for someone to play Scrooge. Miss Gregory informed Howard O'Donal that he was to be Scrooge. Howard was the biggest kid in the school. He had fiery red hair, and a fiery temper to match. When Miss Gregory informed Howard that he was to be Scrooge, he was furious. He picked up his big orange colored geography book and slammed it down on his desk with all his might. "I AIN'T GONNA BE IN ANY DAMN PLAY," he swore. The room turned deathly quiet. Miss Gregory slowly walked over to Howard's desk, stuck her face in his and whispered just loudly enough for the whole school to hear. "YOU..WILL..BE..IN..THE..PLAY," she hissed. Then with her head held high, she walked briskly back to her desk, sat down and surveyed her flock with a stern and determined look, leaving no doubt as to who was boss in the Birdsall School. Howard just sat at his desk, his face as red as his hair. He knew he was beat. He knew he would have to play Scrooge.

When it came time to put on the play, all the desks had to be moved to make room. The dads sat on the floor, with the moms sitting on benches in the back and the play was on. Well, as I remember, the play was a great success, except for the youngest kid in school, Duane. He pretty much screwed up his one liner. I can remember you could hear the wood fire pop and crackle whenever there was a pause while saying our lines, and the oil lamps gave off just enough light so I could see the smiles on the faces of the proud mothers and fathers watching. I was thinking the hot fire in the pot belly wood stove could have completely gone out and the room would still have a glow and be warm on that Christmas Eve in the Birdsall school.

Howard O'Donal did the best job of all the kids in the play and we told him so, but he just gave dirty looks to anyone who complimented him. Howard was the biggest kid in the school, and we were a little scared of him because of his bad temper; but he wasn't a bully. I can't recall him ever hurting any of us, and it was Howard and my brother Jim who always kept the fire in the wood stove going and always brought in two buckets of fresh water from the pump. One bucket was for drinking and one for washing our hands. Miss Gregory always insisted we kept clean. Every morning she made us put our hands on our desk and checked our fingernails and behind our ears for dirt. I had no fear of bees so it was my job to shoo out the yellow jackets and hornets in the privy out back during warm weather.

This one-room school house located in Alma, New York is almost exactly like the Birdsall school I attended when I was a lad. Even the setting looks the same. I was elated when I found it. Beulah and I were just out riding one day and there it was! Later we drove over to Birdsall to see if my old school was still there. It was, but only the back part resembled the school I remembered, and someone was living in it. Too bad it wasn't preserved like the one in Alma. My brother and sisters and I only spent one semester there, but oh, what a bunch of memories we have of that school! I wonder how one little one-hundred-ten pound school teacher was able to handle sixteen farm kids and teach first through eighth grade without a union. Not one of Miss Gregory's pupils left her school without knowing their three "R's".

She would start off each school day by reading a few chapters from a story. I always looked forward to the story. She read "Heidi" to us and "Bambi." I was completely captivated by "Bambi." I was awed by the old stag in the story and I loved Bambi, but them damn 'ol hunters! I wished they would all get lost in the woods and freeze to death.

Mother

My mother hated this picture. My father and all of us kids loved it. Despite Mom's objections it always hung on our living room wall.

Shortly after my mother and father were married, they were driving along a road south of Wellsville. It was dark and snowing and hard to see. There was a farmer who lived along the road. He raised horses and some of them had gotten out and were in the road:

***

"I saw the horses in the road, but in the snow storm, they looked like people," Dad told us. "I didn't have time to slow down much. I swerved to miss a horse on the right side, but crashed into one on the left side of the road. "We hit hard," Dad said. "After we stopped it was quiet and pitch black. I was holding a piece of the broken wooden steering wheel in each hand. After a few seconds one of the horses we hit started screaming and making noises like no other ani-

mal can make."

"I lit a match to check your mother," Dad told us. "She was crying and holding her face with her hands, blood was coming out between her fingers. I was shaken, but unhurt, except for a cut lip," Dad said. "Finally a car came along and took your mother and I to Jones Memorial Hospital in Wellsville. I was okay, but they took your mother into a room and examined her. After a long time a doctor came out of the room."

"I have some bad news," the doctor told me. "Your wife has lost her right eye, she will have to stay here for a while. We will have to operate."

"It was one of my worse times of my life," Dad said.

Looking at the picture, it's pretty obvious my mother's right eye was glass, but dad knew it would take more than a glass eye to destroy her beauty. Especially the beauty she had inside.

(Photo by Shirley Case)

"Finally a car came along and took your mother and I to Jones Memorial Hospital in Wellsville."

Harold

I know of no one who had a better sense of humor than my mother. She could find humor even when things weren't going well for her. She was a very good musician and would play a number on the piano reading the sheet music only once; from then on she could play the song without it. My father played the violin, or "fiddle", and was good at playing square dance music, Irish reels, and jigs, but my mother could play it all. In fact, all the Pitts' were good musicians. One of her brothers, Harold, played piano for silent movies at the Hub theater in Rochester, before the theater acquired talkies.

When I was a little boy, I loved to listen to my Uncle Harold play the piano. I guess of all my uncles, Harold was my favorite. I worshipped him, maybe because he paid so much attention to me. One time, while Uncle Harold and Aunt Irene were visiting for a few days, Uncle Harold and I got up early one morning and took a walk in the woods below the house. The woods had a small creek running through them. When we came across a spot where the creek formed a small pool a couple feet deep, Uncle Harold took off his shoes and socks, rolled up his pant legs and started wading in the pool, bent over with his hands in the water. He slowly walked over to a tree growing on the creek bank whose roots extended into the water. Then he extended his hands under the tree roots and he just stood there not moving. Suddenly he let out a yell and flung his hands in the air. I was astonished he had a fish in his hands. I didn't even know there were any fish in the little creek.

"It's a horned dace," Uncle Harold told me. He pointed out the rough little bumps protruding from the fish's head. Part of the fish's body was bright orange.

"I didn't know there was any fish that pretty," I told my Uncle. After we examined the fish, Uncle Harold gave the little fish a little toss back in the water.

"Why'd ya throw the fish back, Uncle Harold?" I asked. "Now we can't show it to anybody."

"Well Bobby, he's kind of a pretty fish. If we had kept him, we would have to kill him, then clean him, and your Aunt Irene would have to cook him. You and I would have to eat him, and he probably would have a lot of bones; besides, he's so small there wouldn't be much to eat after we split him between us."

"Not only can my Uncle Harold catch fish with his bare hands, he's awful smart." I thought.

At the time I thought it was a very nice day that my Uncle Harold and I had together. Now when it comes to mind it seems it was a pretty special day.

From left to right; my Uncle Harold, looking uncomfortable in his too small suit and high collar. Notice the long slender fingers that could span past an octave with ease on the piano. Next Uncle Preston, the banjo player, he married his music teacher, Aunt Nell. Next Uncle Howard, the xylophone player and my mother, who played the piano. The proud looking lady sitting in front is Grandma Pitts, who played a mean harmonica. Grandpa Dumont, not shown here, made a living playing the violin. Grandma Pitts had good reason to be proud of her kids. They were such fine people. They were gentle people who never hurt anyone, they were honest, but never cared about making a lot of money. Their ambitions never went beyond making enough money to live comfortably. They didn't go to church much, they didn't have to.

Shawmut

The Pittsburgh, Shawmut and Northern Railroad ran through Uncle Nate's cow pasture and in front of his house in Birdsall. We always referred to it as the Shawmut. In fact, I never knew that Pittsburgh and Northern were part of its name until I did a little research on the railroad. The Shawmut never made much money. It operated less than fifty years and about forty years of its life it was in receivership. But the Shawmut wasn't a failure for me considering the wealth of boyhood memories it gave me, memories I never tire of; especially the vision I still have of the Shawmut struggling to haul a string of cars up the Canaseraga grade late at night.

At one time my sister, Eva, told me that one of the engineers tossed a comic book to her as she stood by the railroad tracks watching the train go by. It was the first comic book she ever saw. What a treasure it must have been to her, given her love of reading! I never saw the comic book. She must have hid it from the rest of us kids, her little secret.

In the winter Duane and I used to take our sleds down along the tracks and pick up large lumps of coal that the fireman tossed out because they burned too slowly in their fire boxes. We would haul the lumps up to the house and try to bust them up so we could burn them in our heating stoves. After a while, we gave it up. The soft coal smoked like hell and stunk up the whole house. It plugged up the chimneys with black soot, and it was just too much work. Sometimes when Duane and I had a penny, we would place it on the rail and let the train run over it. The train would flatten out the penny to about twice the normal size. We would always have a long discussion about whether to place the penny on the rail or take it down to Mapes General Store where, for a penny, you could buy two of those round, pink peppermint candies that tasted so good and made your tongue and mouth bright pink when you ate them. But it was a country mile down to the store, so most of the time the train had the last word.

One time Duane and I went into Mapes' store and asked for two of those peppermint candies. When Mr. Mapes gave us the candy, Duane handed him one of our squashed pennies.

"What's this?" Mr. Mapes asked.

"It's a penny. We let a train run over it."

"It's no good now," Mr. Mapes told us. "I'll give you your candy this time, but don't do it again," he scolded.

"Why?" Duane asked. "It's a lot bigger penny than it used to be," he reasoned.

Sometimes late at night we would hear the whistle of a train coming far off and lonesome sounding. It seemed as if it took forever for the freight to reach the farm, but when it did what a commotion it caused. Duane and I would get out of bed and go the bedroom window to watch. There was a steep grade from Birdsall to Canaseraga. The Shawmut had smaller engines than the big powerful Erie freight trains, and it took three engines to haul their string of cars up the Canaseraga grade; two pullers and a pusher. One old steam engine going by would be quite intrusive to a calm summer night, but three would absolutely destroy the tranquillity.

***

The first thing that came into view was the lead engine's headlight invading the night with a long narrow shaft of light that reached far up the tracks. Then came the black smoke and red sparks belching from the stacks. The smoke billowed straight up into the starry night sky. You could make out plumes of white steam shooting out of the relief valves of the pistons driving the connecting rods. The driving wheels slipped and raced demanding that the engineer throttle down and run sand on the rails until the drivers could get a new grip. Then the cycle started all over again. Each engine huffed and puffed independently, with their own rhythm, out of sync with the other. The noise echoed and rumbled through the woods behind the house making it sound as if you were surrounded by trains. When the fireman opened his fire box door to shovel in more coal the cab of the engine burst into a yellow glow silhouetting the engineer leaning out of the open cab window. The light reached up into the bedroom causing shadows and reflections to dance off the ceiling and walls. The vibrations made the house tremble causing the windows to rattle.

The train melted away in the same manner it came, slowly, until after a long time all you heard was a lonesome whistle far off in the distance. Duane and I went back to bed. The man-made intrusion was gone and the night fell back to the business of being peaceful and natural with only the sounds of the crickets sending their soft symphony riding through the open window on the gentle summer night's breeze.

Duane and I use to poke fun at the Shawmut railroad, saying things like, "If it was the Erie going by the farm it would take only one engine to haul an even longer string of cars up the Canaseraga grade. We oughta know, Uncle George used to work for the Erie, and my Dad still does," Duane used to brag.

Fact was, Duane and I loved the Shawmut and the engineers and firemen who always returned our waves. They always had big grins on their faces when they did. I think their feelings would have been hurt if we didn't wave. We had to wave first of course, sort of like showing a little respect from us, like a private saluting his superiors. The private is supposed to salute first. Duane and I were young, but we knew no manmade machine ever worked harder than the little Shawmut locomotives hauling their string of cars up the Canaseraga grade.

No manmade machine ever worked harder than the little Shawmut locomotives hauling their string of cars up the Canaseraga grade.

Dad and His Brothers

    My Dad is on the left and that's Uncle Nate on the right. Dad was a Machinist and Uncle Nate was a Railroad Man. This picture was taken in nineteen thirty-three. Dad's holding a part off the old Essex. He did all his own mechanical work.

    He liked to tell us kids how he and my mother took out a motor of a Model T Ford and dragged it into the kitchen to work on because it was cold outside.

***

    "Your Mother and I started in the morning and had the Model T running with a complete engine overhaul by night fall," he bragged to us kids.

    Dad and Uncle Nate were close, they sometimes would spend a whole day just talking and walking around Uncle Nate's two hundred acre farm. Their father, my Grandpa James Broughton died at the age of twenty-nine. Uncle Vern was seven years old at the time, my dad was four years old and Nate was just a year old. They were split up, Vern and Dad going to my Uncle Rob Pye and his wife, Belle (Broughton). Nate and their infant sister, Velma, went with Grandma VanZile. Uncle Nate was working in the silk mills when he was fourteen while Dad started his machinist's apprenticeship at the age of sixteen. Neither finished high school.

Dad, and Vern must have been close, too. Dad told me about the first time he ever had a treat in the local drug store, which had an ice cream parlor.

***

"Vernie told me to wait outside while he went into the drug store for a moment. When he came back out, he told me to go in and sit at the counter. He said he had something to do and he would be back in a little while. I went into the drug store and sat down at the counter. The soda jerk was making an ice cream sundae." Dad said, *"When the soda jerk finished making the ice cream sundae he sat it in front of me and told me it was all paid for. I didn't know that Vernie didn't have enough money for two sundaes. He waited outside until I had finished my first treat in a drug store soda fountain."*

Dad's voice choked a little with emotion while telling the story.

Uncle Nate was a crane operator. What a hell of a man he was. When it came to character and class, he beat most men hands down and so did my dad. I miss them both.

*Dad with a rotor wheel
from a Moore steam turbine about 1932.*

   Dad started his machinist's apprenticeship at the age of sixteen. He became one of the top machinists at Moore Steam Turbine and taught others the intricacies of the craft.

The Dumbest Kid in the Third Grade

It was kind of hard having two families living in one house, so Dad decided we should move to Grandma's house in Almond. The house had just gone through the big flood. The cellar was full of water and the first floor was full of mud. What a mess. We cleaned it up, but it was still a dump with only gas for utilities. To this day, I appreciate bathtubs and flush toilets and don't take them for granted.

There were some positive things about Almond. The people were great. The town fathers hired a steam shovel to deepen the creek for a swimming hole and they made the kids a ball field. When my sister, Maggie, almost died of pneumonia they took up a collection for her. The people didn't look down on you even if you lived in a shack. Like all towns, there were a few exceptions.

My friend, Raymond, and I were walking by the boarding house where our teacher roomed. As we were going by we noticed a car parked in the driveway and we could make out people sitting close together. The back of the car faced the street. Being a little leery yet curious of what we might find we walked down the long driveway until we could get a better view through the back window of the car. Our suspicions were confirmed. Our teacher and a gentleman friend were sitting in the front seat. Two cigarettes were smoldering in the ashtray.

By today's standards they were not doing anything wrong, but in the thirties school teachers just weren't supposed to be carrying on like that. School teachers were expected to have the morals and discipline of devout nuns. The rules generally allowed for no entertaining of mixed couples. If a couple wanted a little extra social life, they did it out of town or in a car. If they were desperate, they took a chance in a secluded place in the great outdoors.

Raymond and I were watching through the back window of the car for a little while when suddenly Raymond started yelling. "We see you, we see you," he taunted.

"Shut up, Raymond," I told him, "yer gonna get us in a lotta trouble," But it was too late. Raymond took off running down the street with me hot on his heels.

When I took my seat in the class the next morning, I glanced up at the teacher sitting at her desk, her icy stare was directed at me and she was tapping her pencil rapidly on her desk.

"Dorothy, watch the class for a few moments. Robert, go out in the hall and wait," she ordered.

When she came out in the hall where I was waiting she spun me around and pushed my back against a row of lockers, then she grabbed the front of my shirt and held me there. She was so close I could smell stale tobacco smoke on her breath.

"I didn't like what you did yesterday, that was a nasty thing you did, spying and yelling at me."

"I didn't yell at you, honest. Raymond did," I tattled.

"It was you, she insisted. "I saw you and don't you ever pull a stunt like that again, and you better keep your mouth shut. Now get back to class, and tell Dorothy to send Raymond out here."

Well, the rest of the school year went by pretty much uneventful until the last day before summer vacation started, the day I loved more than Christmas or even the Fourth of July.

"Class, you are excused for summer vacation, all except for you, Robert. I want to talk to you," the teacher announced.

After all the kids had left the room, and I was sitting alone at my desk, the teacher got up from her desk and slowly walked over to mine. For a long moment she just stood there, standing close with her arms folded in front of her, not saying anything. It seemed she was ten feet tall. She consumed the whole room. I was scared, I must have done something bad, I thought. When she finally spoke it was more like a loud whisper.

"Robert, I didn't pass you, I feel you are too immature to advance to the fourth grade. You're excused, you can go now."

This was totally unexpected; I had no idea I wasn't going to pass my grade. I was shocked, hurt, and ashamed all at the same moment. All I wanted to do was get out of that room. It seemed the door was a mile away. I wanted to run towards it, but I didn't. You didn't run in school, if you did you had to go to the principal's office. Big boys like myself didn't cry, but the tears started coming before I could reach the door.

Holy cow! I'm the only kid in the whole third grade that didn't pass. I'm the dumbest kid in the whole third grade, maybe the whole school. Aw, Geeze! I'm even dumber than Raymond 'cause Raymond passed and I didn't and Raymond's the dumbest kid I ever knew. Aw, geeze! What am I gonna tell Mom and Dad? Mom won't say much, but Dad's gonna be awful mad and the other kids are gonna call me dummy. I don't ever wanna see any of 'em anymore. Aw geeze! So no one would see me, I slowly walked home up the creek bed, picking up stones and throwing them in the water as hard as I could, trying to work off my hurt and shame. Aw geeze…

"Robert, I didn't pass you."

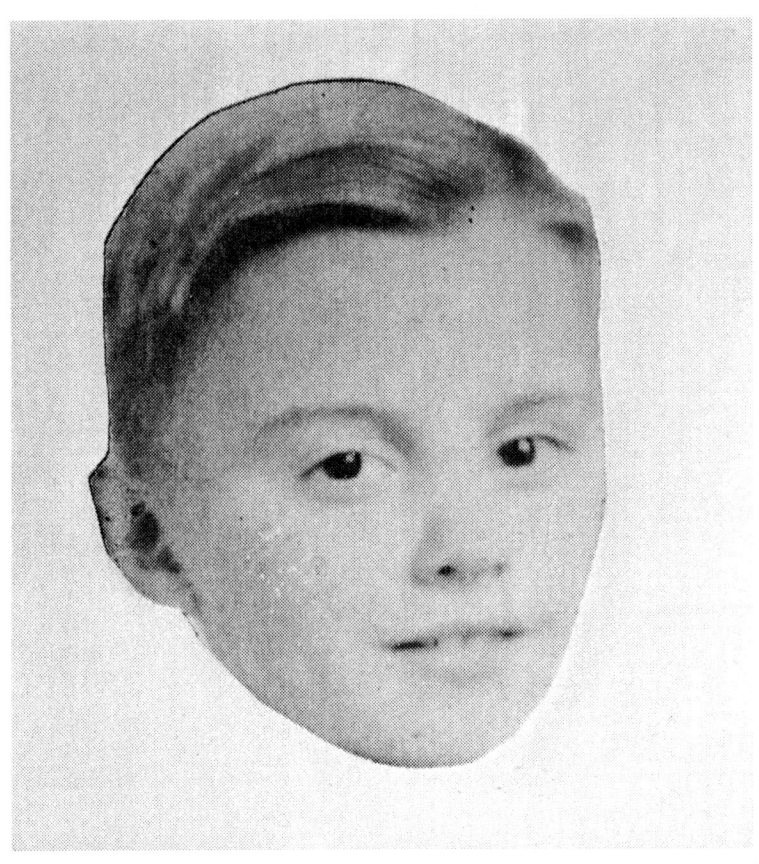

Maybe I was the dumbest kid in the third grade, but that's better than being the second dumbest. I bet everyone who is still alive and was in that third grade class in almond with me remembers the dumbest kid, but who in hell remembers the second dumbest or for that matter the second smartest.

Myself, Jim, Mom, Dad, and Grandma Pitts

The picture shows everyone but me ready to tackle the big job of cleaning up after the flood. I wanted to go fishing, but Dad said I had to help clean up. I wouldn't look up to have my picture taken. The structure behind me was the two holer that the flood tipped over. When we lived in Almond, the Broughtons seemed to be a little worse off than most of the poor people in Almond, maybe because Dad's paycheck had to take care of ten people, counting Grandma.

I remember I never let any of my friends inside our house. I was embarrassed because all the kids had to walk by Grandma's rundown house on their way to the swimming pool, and the third grade teacher drove her car past the house on her way to school. I used to wonder what she thought when she drove by. Sometimes she drove by slowly, her stare locked on the house, her head turning as she passed, her stare still locked on the house after she was well past.

The old Almond School had a large wooden flagpole in front of the school. One day a bunch of us kids were playing around the swing. We would grasp the rope, getting a running start and swing out as far as we could. One of the bigger kids got an extra good running start, swung out and the pole snapped off at its base. It must have been rotten there. The heavy pole fell on a young boy by the name of Bradley. His sister, Ann, was there.

"Oh! I'm dying, I'm dying, kiss me, Ann, I'm dying!" He screamed.

I sure didn't want to see anyone die. I got the heck out of there! I ran home as fast as I could.

Well, the Bradley boy didn't die, but he did get a broken leg out of the incident.

***

"Gee, look at that," my friend Bert whispered. We were on our way to go fishing and we stumbled on a sight to behold. A young couple was making out in the bushes, not too far from our fishing hole. For Bert and me this was a very exciting spectacle to witness. We kept down and watched until they were finished, and we savored every second of their performance. Bert handled the event with much more finesse than Raymond did, except for some heavy breathing brought on by the excitement of it all. He never let a peep out of him.

After witnessing the young couple, I thought I would like to try doing what they did. One of my friends knew a girl (a friend of the family) who came from out of town to spend the summer, so I asked him if he thought she would let me "spend some time in the bushes with her," and would he mind. He said he didn't care. In fact, he set it up for me. He told me she liked the little root beer barrels that you could buy for a penny. He told me to buy some and go down to the fishing hole. He would tell his her I was down there and had some root beer barrels for her.

Sure enough, she came down and asked for the candy. I told her first she had to take off her clothes and lay down on her back. She did this without hesitation; in fact she seemed to know precisely what to do. About one and a half minutes later she got up, put her clothes back on, grabbed the sack of candy, and yelled at me, "You don't do it good like your friend does!" This was all very hard on my ego, but I guess you get what you pay for, and it only cost me four cents worth of root beer barrels.

***

I was sitting on the steps of Whitters Feed Mill, and Allen walked up and introduced me to his friend that was with him.

"This is one of my relation, and I don't like the son-of-a-bitch." With that he hauled off and hit me square in the face and gave me a bloody nose. He and his friend then walked off like nothing happened. I didn't do anything about it because Allen was one tough guy, even meaner than I was. I knew I couldn't lick him.

Weeks later we were playing softball in the park. Allen was at bat. He hit the ball and threw the bat while running to first base. The bat hit me a glancing blow to the side of my head and cut my ear lobe. I wasn't hurt, but I played it up big. The location of the cut caused it to bleed profusely. I laid down on my back moaning and carrying on, and then I closed my eyes and lay still, letting the blood run down my neck. Allen thought he had killed me. He ran home, one scared kid. I told Bert to go to Allen's house and tell him he didn't kill me, but I might have to go to the hospital, as I was in bad shape. The idea behind this was I hoped Allen's Pa would find out and beat the hell out of him. Later, Allen really got his.

***

My brother's two-dollar pocket watch was missing from the china cabinet where he kept it. Jim told Allen, "I lost my watch, Allen, if you happen to find it I'll give you some money." Next day Allen came up to Jim. "I found your watch, Jim." He handed the watch over to Jim, and asked for the reward. The watch wasn't Jim's it was Dad's gold Elgin railroad watch, Dad's prized possession. It wasn't running and the hands were off. Allen's father, found out about the incident and dragged Allen down to our house. First he made Allen tell Jim and Dad how sorry he was for stealing from them. Allen was scared. His father told Allen to lay down on his belly, and then he pulled off his belt and proceeded to beat Allen. He was like a crazy man. My Dad told him to stop, but Uncle Sherman just kept beating him. Allen was screaming, "I'm sorry. I'm sorry!" Finally my Dad got a full nelson on his dad. It was the only way to stop him. Allen got his, but somehow I didn't enjoy it. Allen had an excuse for being like he was.

***

Geez, now I've had it. I was just approaching the house, coming back from swimming, and there was Mr. Spratt, our neighbor, knocking on our door, holding a dead chicken at his side. Earlier in the day I had shot one of Mr. Spratt's chickens with my Daisy BB gun, just for the hell of it. I had hit the chicken in the neck, and it was bleeding. Another chicken took a peck at the bleeding chicken, then another did the same, pretty soon the whole flock was after the bleeding chicken. The flock must have killed the hapless critter. I thought Mr. Spratt must have seen me shoot his chicken and was coming over to tell my Dad, but I heard him say, "One of my chickens got hurt, so I killed it. I thought you might like it for supper."

At the supper table that night my mother asked, "What's the matter, Bobby, don't you like the chicken?"

Sometimes people act just like that flock of chickens did. When a person is hurting, someone steps in to hurt them some more, then another and another until everyone around gets their licks in. Sometimes it's verbal; sometimes it's physical.

My friend Bud and I were not always friends. We were only friends after one hell of a fistfight. Bud and I didn't know each other very well, but well enough to know we didn't like each other. Once Bud came up behind me and gave me a shove.

"Do it again and I'll hit ya," I told him. He did it again. I kept my promise and the fight was on. This time my adversary was bigger and stronger than I was, and the first blow bud landed gave much cause to regret hitting him in the first place. After taking some hard licks, I had had enough and wanted to quit; but I knew the kids who gathered around to watch the fight would yell, "Coward!" My pride wouldn't let me quit. We were on the school grounds and the kids wouldn't let me quit. We were on the school grounds and the kids had formed a circle around us and kept working us to the back of the school so no one would see us and stop the fight. Bud and I were bleeding at the nose and mouth, and I kept hoping one of the older kids would step in and stop it, but none did. They just cheered along with the younger kids.

Neither Bud nor I were skilled fighters. Neither knew how to cover up or ward off blows to keep from getting hurt. Not knowing how to protect ourselves resulted in making the fight much more brutal. We just stood toe to toe and slugged it out almost as if we were taking turns hitting each other. Every time I struck Bud he would go into a rage, as a bull goes into a rage when he feels the sting caused by the dart from the matador. I stood my ground in dread, knowing Bud's avenging blows were inevitable. Even though I knew the consequence of hitting bud, I just kept hitting him and he kept hitting me back. We hit as hard as we could, full on the face. When we paused for a little while, the kids yelled insults at us until we started in again.

When I look back and think about the fight, the picture of bud's face always comes to mind, tears running down mixing with the blood on his face, his eyes red and starting to swell. I had told myself, "He ain't gonna make me cry like he's crying, no matter how much he hurts me," and he was hurting me plenty! I hated him and was scared of him, yet somehow, through all the hate, fear, and pain, I was starting to feel sorry for Bud. Feeling sorry for someone was foreign to me. I couldn't understand how I could feel sorry for someone I hated and was scared of and who was doing his best to hurt me.

At first I thought the ringing in my ears was caused by Bud's blows, but no; it was for real. The school bell was at last our excuse to stop fighting. I let my arms fall down to my sides, unclenched my fists and turned my back to Bud. Slowly I walked over to a nearby tree and sat down by its base for a long moment. Then I headed for the boy's room. My whole face felt numb and my swollen lips felt huge. One eye was almost shut, and I could taste the warm salty blood coming from a gash inside my mouth. I didn't have a handkerchief. I had to keep wiping my bleeding nose on my shirt sleeves.

When I went to the boy's room, Bud was already there sobbing and trying to clean up. I approached Bud with my hand held out. I was scared. I didn't know if Bud would hit me or take my hand. Bud took my hand, and instantly we were best friends. There was no animosity between us. Somehow, as soon as the fight was over, a bond was created between us.

We were late getting back to the sixth grade class.

"You two have been fighting!" The teacher yelled at us before we had a chance to sit down. I told the teacher that Bud and I were riding double on his bike, and we took a real bad spill coming down Karr Valley Hill. Bud managed to grin a little and shook his head in agreement. I couldn't con this sixth grade teacher, however, and she didn't buy my little fib. With head tilted back, she looked down her nose at me and ever so slightly shook her head. I think she thought Bud and I weren't worth much. If we wanted to fight, so what? Why worry about it?

"Robert, you're a mess. Go to the boy's room and clean yourself up. And take off your shirt and rinse it out in cold water. You'll have to put it back on wet." There was a tone of contempt and disgust in her voice. "Martin, you wait here until Robert gets back. Then you do the same," she snapped.

When I looked at myself in the mirror in the boy's room, I was shocked. "Holy cow! Bud did all this to me? But by damn he did not make me cry!" I gazed at the battered image of myself in the mirror and painfully grinned at it. Never in my young life was I more proud of myself.

The next day the kids analyzed the fight. They unanimously decided bud was the winner, but I was a winner, too. Bud had knocked a lot of meanness out of me. I thought about the kids who watched the fight and yelled degrading and insulting words at Bud and I when we paused during the fight. They wouldn't have cared if one of us had killed the other. I decided I didn't like those kids anymore and I didn't want to be like them. I also decided I didn't want to beat up on Donnie anymore, the kid who lived across the street and was smaller than me. Later Donnie and I became good friends. I looked out for him and treated him like a younger brother.

***

Donnie and I became partners in crime. When Donnie's mother sent Donnie to Fenner's General Store with her grocery list, Donnie would come and get me to go with him. I would put on an old leather jacket someone had given me. It was about three sizes too big for me, and the only time I wore it was when Donnie and I went grocery shopping for his mother. The old jacket had deep, loose pockets. When we were inside the store, Donnie would go to the end of the long counter and give old man Fenner his mother's grocery list. Near the other end of the counter was a tub of chocolates old man Fenner sold in bulk. I would stand at that end. Donnie would joke and laugh with old man Fenner's and try to stand in such a way as to block old man Fenner's view from me. Me, I was just browsing. While old man Fenner had his back turned making out the order, and conditions were right, I would make a quick grab at the chocolates with my greedy, grubby little hands and stuff the loot in the deep loose pockets of the old leather jacket. On a good day I would get in two grabs. When we got outside I would share the loot. If I got seven chocolates, Donnie got three and I got four. My job was the most dangerous, I would tell him.

Almond was too small for a movie theater, so on occasion some people who traveled from town to town with a movie projector would stop and show a movie in the town library. The fee was a dime. One time while standing in line for a show, I reached in my pocket for my dime to pay for my ticket. The dime was gone! It must have fallen through a small hole in my pocket. I started looking for the dime, but couldn't find it, and it was getting dark. Old man Fenner was waiting in line behind me.

"What's the matter Bobby?" He asked.

"I lost my dime. I guess I might as well go home," I sadly answered him.

Old man Fenner reached in his pocket, and got out his change purse. Looking over his spectacles, he poked around until he found a dime. "Here's a dime, Bobby. Maybe in the morning when it's light you can find the dime and pay me back."

Well, I never did find that dime, and I never paid Mr. Fenner back, but I never stole any more chocolates off Mr. Fenner again.

Fenner's General Store

In the town park was a bandstand. My friends and I used it for sort of a club house. When it was too hot to play ball, we sat around the benches built around the inside perimeter and talked, using all the swear words we knew. We practiced swearing in pig Latin, so we could swear in front of our folks and they couldn't understand what we were saying.

Another favorite pastime was reading and swapping Big-Little Books and comic books. The big maple trees in the park kept it shaded and cool. We spent a lot of time there.

One time one of my friends discovered one of the lattices that went around the outside of the bandstand was loose, and by pulling on it one could get in the crawl space under the bandstand. Once inside all we had to do was pull the lattice back in place and we were hidden from the watchful eyes of the grownups. We had a secret place right in the middle of town. We could see out, but it was very difficult to see in. It was roomy inside and high enough so we could almost stand up, but it was a little too dark, so we got candles for light. It was a wonder we didn't burn the place down. It was a safe place to learn how to smoke cigarettes and look at those little Popeye and Mutt and Jeff cartoon books with dirty pictures in them, showing all the things grown-ups do. But we were not supposed to do it because it was nasty and God would punish us if we did.

One of my friends had an almost endless supply of the Dirty Little Books. He took them from his father's dresser drawer, one at a time, always replacing the one he had taken previously. This way his father never knew. We always looked forward in great anticipation to viewing a new book hoping the new book would be more explicit than the last. Little did we know each one was the ultimate in sexual explicity as far as pictures were concerned.

Just the word "sex" was taboo in school. There were no sex education classes, but us boys learned most of the various ways to perform from the Dirty Little Books. Later in life most of us found out the actual acts were a totally different concept from what the books taught us, which in reality, wasn't all that much.

Some of us boys coaxed two local belles into our hideout, which didn't take a hell of a lot of coaxing. There was also one little boy who was somewhat retarded. We usually let him hang around us, but right then we didn't want him around, as we had some serious business with the girls. We didn't want him to see as he might tell his dad, and we would be in big trouble. We told him to beat it, but he wouldn't budge. He was a frail lad and I remember he had a pale complexion and white hair. Finally one of my friends told him, okay, you can stay, but if you do, you have to pull your pants down and show the girls your peter." Well he did just that. He dropped his pants and stood there with a big grin on his face. One of my friends said, "Holy cow!" Another said, "Geeze!" He was a little boy with man-size equipment. The rest of us boys decided we did not want to play doctor with the girls after all. I felt nature had cheated me and right then was unsure of myself. My friends and I left, while the two girls and the kid stayed behind.

There was another mentally impaired lad in town who must have been about eighteen or twenty years old. He was short and heavy set. He had a big jaw and thick lips. When he walked down the street he took short, quick steps and pumped his arms back and forth very fast. With all his erratic motions it appeared as if he was almost running, when in reality he wasn't covering much ground at all. My friends and I didn't feel sorry for him, maybe because he was older and much bigger than we were. In fact, we were always taunting him and calling him dummy. When we taunted him, he would stomp his feet up and down, jut out his big jaw at us and shake his fist. Then we would cower in mock fear and he would continue up the street with a big smile of satisfaction on his face. Looking back on it, I think he enjoyed it all.

One day, Al Palmer, the owner of the local pool hall caught us taunting the poor guy.

"Ya know, ya better watch out for that guy," he told us as he scraped out his pipe with his jackknife. "Those kinda people are stronger than a gorilla and if they want ta, they can run real fast. If he ever catches one of ya and squeezes ya, he'll break every bone in yer body." Then he fished a flat tin of Prince Albert pipe tobacco from his hip pocket, filled his big kaywoody pipe carefully and tamped down the tobacco with his forefinger. He flicked his thumbnail across the head of a wooden match, lighting it on the very first try, as I had seen him do a hundred times before. I always marveled at his skill. Out of the whole pool hall gang, Al was the only one who consistently lit a match in this fashion on the very first try. He held the flame close to the top of the pipe bowl and puffed until the pipe was well lit, almost obscuring his face in smoke. After the smoke had cleared a little, he sternly looked each one of us straight in the eye, holding the stare until we each in turn looked to the side or down to the ground. Satisfied he had gotten his message through; he hobbled off towards his pool hall.

Well now, my friends and I had hitchhiked to Hornell a while back and we had seen the movie King Kong. We knew what a gorilla could do. For awhile Al's little story worked, and for a few weeks we quit taunting the poor fellow. But, after a spell we started again, but from across the street just in case.

A few years back, I chanced upon Doris and Lillian, Donnie's two sisters, whom I hadn't seen in many years. I was shocked and saddened, when they told me my old partner in crime, along with his son had been killed in an automobile accident while living down in Florida.

It was Donnie's family, the Guthrie's who started up a collection for my sister, Maggie, whom we almost lost from pneumonia. They collected twenty-seven dollars, about five dollars more than my Dad made a week. Most of the money was in nickels, dimes, and quarters. The Guthries were such fine people. In fact, most of the seven hundred people in Almond were fine people. In the late thirties we were all like one big family in Almond, New York.

Mrs. Bensen

A little ways up from our house sat a large white house with a picket fence around it. A lady by the name of Mrs. Bensen lived there. We kids figured Mrs. Bensen had a lot of money, at least a zillion dollars, we speculated. Mrs. Bensen hired kids to do chores for her and mow her large lawn. It took three of us to mow the lawn. Back then, no one owned a lawn mower with an engine on it. You did the job with a reel type push mower, it was hard work.

Mrs. Bensen had two large overly friendly St. Bernard dogs, who mauled the hell out of us while we tried to mow the grass. The big brown mounds in the yard were proof that the dogs were well fed. When we came upon one of the large mounds, we mowed around them coming as close as we could without hitting them. The smaller mounds, we got a running start, shut our eyes and plowed through. All things considered we did a good job except for the tall clumps of grass surrounding the big brown mounds.

Sometimes on a Saturday afternoon after we finished mowing Mrs. Bensen's lawn, she got out her huge old touring car from the barn, took us kids to Hornell and dropped us off at the show. Mrs. Bensen drove and had a lady friend of hers ride up front with her in the big old open car. Both ladies were dressed to kill wearing large black hats with wide brims, long strings of beads and bracelets. I remember thinking they looked like two old gals out of Hollywood. The car's interior was all rich brown leather. It had a spare tire mounted on each side. My friends and I sat in the back seat. The dogs sat on the floor. What a thrill it was riding in that big old open car, even if there were two big old St. Bernards drooling all over you.

When we arrived at Hornell, we had a big decision to make as to which movie to see. Hornell had four movie theaters, the Strand, Majestic, Hornell and Steuben, all enticing the kids to spend their dime at their movie house. Most times the Majestic won out because we were hooked on the weekly serial shown there.

With the twenty-five cents Mrs. Bensen gave each of us, we

were able to see a show, buy a nickel's worth of candy, and have a dime left over to buy a model airplane. We spent a long time selecting which model plane to buy. I bought a lot of model airplanes, most of which I never finished and the few I did finish didn't fly too well. There was, however, one particular model that flew fairly well. It would climb quite high until the rubber band motor ran down, then go into a slow lazy spiral, and glide gracefully to the ground. I decided this model was worthy of a glorious ending. Scenes from the movie, *"Wings"* and *"Hell Angels"*, showing World War I biplanes being shot down and falling from the sky in smoke and flames fascinated me. I had visions of my airplane ending in such a grand manner.

I emptied the contents of an oil lamp over the model, wound up the rubber band motor, lit a match to the craft and, at the same time, launched the airplane. Whoomp! The airplane burst into a ball of flame and black smoke. The kerosene, balsa wood, paper and glue was totally consumed before the craft had flown much more than four or five feet. I was fortunate, I escaped with only singed hair. The flight didn't pan out at all like I had envisioned.

At Christmas time my friends and I used to scour the woods, anybody's woods, for Christmas trees to sell. One Christmas Mrs. Bensen asked us to get her a tree, so we did. It was a fine tree, shaped and filled out just right. Mrs. Bensen was so pleased with the tree she gave us a dollar, instead of the fifty cents we asked for. There was one thing we neglected to tell her. We had cut the tree from a secluded place in the back of her large lot.

1930's

With no television, kids in the thirties spent most of their time outside playing. The boys all had cap guns and one of our favorite pastimes was playing cops and robbers. I always wanted to be Dillinger. In my mind he was the badest of the bad. We had some bloody shoot-outs and I must have been shot at least a hundred times a week. It always took at least ten shots to kill me and I always took at least a dozen G men with me before I took my last gasp.

"Hey Bobby, come on over," my neighbor called from across the street. Donnie was all excited, he had just gotten the first issue of Superman and he wanted to share it with me. After reading about the strongest man in the universe all the rest of my heroes like Batman, Captain Marvel and all the others paled. They were nothing compared to superman, even my real-life hero, Joe Lewis, the brown bomber, who could knock out a man with a six-inch punch, was nothing compared to superman. If anyone ever told me back in nineteen thirty-eight that I would live to see Superman get killed in a fight with a huge monster called Doomsday, I would have thought them out of their mind, but alas, it really happened as I sat at my desk the other day reading about the death of Superman. I just can't believe a mere mortal like me would live to see the creation and death of Superman. Hell, he was only fifty-four years old. But we'll see.

Back in the thirties there was a lot of violence and killing in the big cities of America. It was mostly mobsters and bootleggers killing each other. I honestly don't think most people gave a damn. It was good reading and it took people's minds off the hard times of the depression, it gave people something to talk about when a bootlegger got caught killing another bootlegger. The philosophy in Al Palmer's pool hall was "That's one less S.O.B. we have to worry about, one less we have to put in jail and take care of. Send 'em up the river to the big house and fry 'em. We get two for one that way."

It's bad now with kids killing kids. That sort of thing was almost unheard of back in the thirties. Back then, the only killing kids did was make believe with their cap guns. It's a fact there weren't as many guns around then as now, but there were a lot of them around, and most of us boys knew where we could find a gun. My friend, Bud Gillett, and I used to shoot his dad's pistol out the bedroom window when his folks were away. Bud's dad always kept his gun cabinet locked, but Bud knew where he hid the key.

When we outgrew our cap guns, we acquired BB guns. A lot of the back windows of Al Palmer's Pool Hall got shot out. The windows had a lot of small individual panes, thus giving us a lot of targets. The windows were in his storeroom out back making it hard for Al to hear the plinking noise when we shot out a pane. "Besides, Al's a cripple. Hell, he ain't never gonna catch us even if he does see us," we reasoned.

Sometimes we had BB gun battles down by the creek. We chose up sides, half the kids on one side, half on the other side. The rules were you didn't cross the creek and you had to shoot below the belt. When you got hit with a BB, it stung like hell especially if you had the misfortune to get hit in the rear end where your pants were tight against your skin

Fourth of July

When I was young, I never could make up my mind as to which day I liked best, Christmas or the Fourth of July. I think maybe I liked the Fourth the best. I would mow lawns, weed gardens, and do most anything to earn money and save for fireworks before the Fourth arrived. There were cherry bombs, sky rockets, roman candles, and torpedoes to buy, and I wanted them all. I always looked forward to the Fourth of July weeks before it arrived.

I always looked forward to Christmas, too. But there was no use trying to earn money at Christmas time, because you were told you should spend your money on others. Geeze, that was a dumb thing to expect me to do.

Back in the thirties, on the Fourth of July, most folks stayed at home and watched their kids shoot off their fireworks. Sometimes kids would get hurt firing off fireworks, sometimes serious, but most never got hurt, and when they did it wasn't too serious. When most of the states banned fireworks, it took away the most exciting day of the year for young boys, and some not-so-young boys like my father.

Now-days with no excitement at home on the Fourth, people load their kids in their cars, go speeding down the highway and kill themselves running into each other. Better if they could stay home, and take their chances shooting off firecrackers.

"I think maybe I liked the Fourth the best."

The Cannon

KA-BOOM! Dad fired off his homemade cannon to announce the start of Independence Day, July Fourth, Nineteen Thirty-Seven. Windows rattled, dogs barked and eleven year old boys like myself stood in awe with their mouths agape.

I basked in the glory. The kids were saying things like, "Bobby's dad has got a real cannon, an' he made it hisself. Ain't nothin' can make so much noise as Bobby's dad's cannon."

Dad made the cannon while working as a machinist in the Erie Shop's huge railroad round house in Hornell where the Erie repaired and maintained their locomotives.

When someone made something for themselves without the consent or knowledge of the company, it was commonly known as a "Government Job". Government jobs were an industry within an industry. Most people working in shops had a secret government job going at one time or another, be it a poker for their wood stove or maybe a set of hinges and a fancy button for their outhouse door. Sometimes a government job would be a little more sophisticated and ambitious, like maybe making a two and a half foot long, sixty pound cannon.

To fire his cannon, dad would pour a generous amount of black powder in the cannon. Then he wadded up newspaper and rammed it tightly down the muzzle. He attached a string to a triggering device and paid out the string until he was fifty or sixty feet back. Then he would hunch his shoulders, grit his teeth, narrow his eyes until they were nearly shut and give the string a smart jerk. "KA-BOOM!" the cannon would roar and jump about a foot in the air.

Once, he let me pull the string to the envy of all my friends watching. I made a big deal out of the honor. "Everyone back," I ordered, which wasn't necessary, everyone was well back out of danger. Everyone had come to hear the cannon go off, but strangely, they all had their ears covered tightly with their hands and most had their eyes shut.

Some of the young men who hung out in Al's Pool Hall wanted

to borrow the cannon. At first, Dad said no, but after a little coaxing and promising to be very careful, Dad gave in and let them take the cannon. The pool hall gang took the cannon over to the village park and fired it a couple of times without incident, then someone got the bright idea to stick a couple of large ball bearings, no doubt stolen from the Erie Shops, down the barrel. They aimed it at a large maple tree and fired. "KA-BOOM!" One of the ball bearings hit the maple tree a glancing blow, tore off a hunk of bark and whizzed off into oblivion. The other bearing went the whole length of the park and was found days later, embedded in the clap boards of the Kant-U-Come Inn, Almond's only tavern.

Years later, I asked dad whatever happened to that old cannon. He said, "That damn thing was indestructible, so one night, I took it out to the two holer in back of the house and dropped it in. Wonder I didn't blow myself up or kill someone with that damn thing."

Mort

My mother's brother, Howard Pitts, and my grandmother's brother, Uncle Mort Dodge, started a bakery in the mid-twenties in Almond. No bakery made better baked goods, nor did any two bakers work harder at their business than they did. One thing was lacking, most of their customers didn't have much money. My uncles let them run up large bills which most couldn't pay. They had to close down in the early thirties.

My Uncle Mort was a bachelor. He lived in a small apartment over Al Palmer's Pool Hall. There was no bath or shower, just a john. Looking back, I would wager the only time Uncle Mort had a bath was when someone cleaned him up directly after emerging from his mother's womb. His kitchen table and sink were always full of dirty dishes. Uncle Mort only ran a little water over the dishes he was going to use at the moment.

On Sunday mornings, Jim and I had an open invitation for breakfast. Uncle Mort's pancakes and eggs were so good you soon forgot the dirty apartment and the half-washed plate you were eating from. After breakfast Jim would take off to go fishing or something. Then Uncle Mort would want to take his old Model A Ford for a spin.

"Get in Bobby, and we'll go for a ride and get some fresh air."

Cars were foreign to my Uncle Mort, he was brought up in horse and buggy days and didn't acquire a car until he was middle-aged. He was a little afraid of the horseless carriage. None the less he kept up with the times, and learned to drive an automobile. But I don't think he ever got used to it and was always a little scared of driving one. After we got seated, Uncle Mort would light up a fat cigar, puffing hard so he wouldn't have to relight it after we got going.

"Are ya all set? Better crank up yer window, Bobby." Uncle Mort gripped the wheel so hard his knuckles turned white, bit down on his cigar and fired up the old Model A. He ground through some gears, found one that suited him, popped the clutch and we took off with a violent jerk, snapping my head back. We streaked up the Karr

Valley Road, sometimes reaching speeds of up to twenty miles per hour.

Soon the old Ford was blue with cigar smoke, and smoke from the oil smoldering on the hot motor was coming up through the cracks in the wood floor. Both windows were cranked up allowing no way for the smoke to escape.

"Does a man good ta get out and get some fresh air, huh Bobby?" Uncle Mort chirped after our drive. He was still puffing on the stub of his cigar, which by then was wet and pretty well chewed up.

Uncle Howard, leaning against one of the Bakery ovens, Uncle Mort, in baker's hat, my Uncle Alvin Dodge in the background. I don't know who the Gentlemen at the corner is.

***

I used to sit on a flour barrel and watch my Uncle Mort work in his bakery. When Uncle Mort was hand-kneading bread dough, it was well laced with sweat from his brow and cigar ashes falling from the eternal cigar in his mouth. If a fly or two chanced to land in the dough or a spider ventured too close, that was okay, they were mixed in the dough, too. But he drew the line if a dead mouse was in his flour barrel. Once when he found a dead mouse in his flour barrel, he took it by its little tail, gave it a whack against the inside of the flour barrel to knock off the flour sticking to it, then tossed the little critter in the trash. Sweat, flies, spiders, whatever, Uncle Mort's baked goods were delicious, besides the customers never saw what went on in the back. If the breeze was right, the aroma from Uncle Mort's and Howard's bakery carried down the whole block. Mrs. Bensen's flower garden across the street should have smelled as good.

I remember back in the thirties, when they had to close up, my Uncle Mort was dismantling his large bakery ovens and selling the scrap from them to a dealer. At that time, Japan was at war with China, and America was doing a thriving business selling scrap iron to Japan. While watching the dealer load the iron on his truck, Uncle Mort made a profound remark. Taking his cigar from his mouth, and thoughtfully studying it, he said,

"I wonder how many Chinamen my scrap will kill," then he chuckled a little.

I was disappointed in my Uncle Mort. To me, he was acting out of character and he wasn't talking like the kind old Uncle Mort I knew. I had seen pictures of the atrocities the Japanese were inflicting upon the Chinese people and I didn't think Uncle Mort was doing the right thing selling scrap to the Japanese, let alone making a joke about it. One picture foremost in my mind, was of a little abandoned Chinese baby sitting alone, among the rubble of a bombed out street, crying and bleeding.

After the dealer paid Uncle Mort for his scrap, he stuffed the bills in his pocket, sorted through his change, found a dime and tossed it to me.

"Here ya are Bobby, go get yerself some candy," he said talking past the cigar in the corner of his mouth.

The dime fell short, landing at my feet. For a fraction of a second, my conscience told me to leave the dime there, but greed won out. I picked the dime up and headed for the pool room to buy myself an Eskimo Pie. All was forgiven with my Uncle Mort.

A few years hence, the Japanese bombed Pearl Harbor. At the time a young lad by the name of Bob Denene was serving on the battleship Arizona as a fireman in the ship's engine room. We'll never know, but maybe some of the scrap from Uncle Mort's ovens helped make the bomb that went through the decks of the battleship Arizona, killing young Bob Denene from Almond who knew and loved my Uncle Mort and whose remains still lie deep in the bowels of the sunken battleship.

Maybe some of Uncle Mort's scrap iron did indeed kill some Chinamen. It must have taken one hell of a pile of American scrap iron to kill ten million Chinese, and tens of thousands of young Bob Denenes from Almond and thousands of other towns, cities, and farms in America and Uncle Mort's bakery ovens must have been somewhere in that mountain of scrap.

"I wonder how many Chinamen my scrap will kill."

On the far right was my Uncle's Bakery, followed by Knight's Bicycle Shop, a novelty store, Regina's grocery store and Al Palmer's pool hall. I remember Al Palmer was a bachelor and Regina Martin was the lady who ran the grocery store next to his pool hall. It was obvious Al had a thing for Regina, but I don't know if the feeling was mutual or not. I always thought it would have been a pretty good match. Al was a good guy and Miss Martin was a real nice lady. Al was older than Regina, that could have been a barrier to forming a relationship. I never found out if anything came of it.

The Old Stone House

In the early nineteen-twenties, when my father was a young man courting my mother, she was living with her mother, father, and three brothers, Howard, Harold, and Preston. They were living in what was known as the "Old Stone House". She told us a lot of stories about the place. She would say, "It was the first house built in Allegany County, and the man who built the house was a little afraid of the Indians in the area, so he built the walls out of stone. The walls were two feet thick." Grandma Pitts said there was a big flat stone in front of the fireplace that they called the weather stone; when the stone was damp and dark in color it was going to rain, if the stone was dry and lighter color it was going to be nice.

Sometime back in the early fifties, the house caught fire. The fire gutted the inside and burned off the roof. I took this picture in the summer of nineteen ninety-three. I hadn't seen the place in ages, and now I kind of wish I had never gone back there. All that's left of the place is what you see in the picture. It saddened me and made me feel guilty for some reason. Maybe because if I had gone there right after the fire, I could have done something to preserve the house.

When I was laying in bed the night after taking the picture, I thought maybe it was not too late, maybe the house could be restored. If someone cement plastered the existing walls, compacting the joints with a strong mortar mix, and used metal lath for reinforcing, it would seal and strengthen the walls. It should be plastered from the inside, to avoid destroying the original looks of the exterior stone walls. After the existing walls are strengthened the remaining walls could be laid up in the original manner. The floor and inside partitions would lock it all together.

I know I have the savvy to restore the house, but I doubt if I have enough energy anymore. It would be a lot of hard physical work, and I don't have any money to hire help. Best I stay away from the place, best I wipe it out of my mind. For me it's just too sad to think about, I guess I'm the only one who gives a hoot about the old stone house up Karr Valley Road.

A Place of Higher Learning

Looking back on it, failing the third grade didn't matter too much, I got a much better education at Al Palmer's Pool Hall. Al was a crippled man. His right leg was twisted and shrunk from the effects of polio but his upper body was strong and healthy. Al was a good man and he was good to the kids. It was Al Palmer who got the town fathers to make a swimming pool down at the creek. At times Al was a little stingy, though.

"Bobby, will ya sweep off my sidewalk?"
When I finished; "Bobby, would ya burn my papers?"
"Bobby, would ya sweep out the pool room?"
"How 'bout washing my car, Bobby?"

After all this was finished, he would make a big deal out of the dime and Eskimo Pie he gave me. But the best part of my pay was he letting me hang around the pool room.

I had heroes in that pool room with colorful names like Woodchuck, Hammer, and Lightning; just to name a few. Woodchuck had big buck teeth, Hammer had a head shaped like a hammer, Lightning was big and the slowest talking and moving man I ever knew. They all sure could swear good, and could spit Red Man chewing tobacco straight as an arrow. They were, without a doubt, the "best damn shots in New York State." Once Woodchuck killed a deer damn near a quarter mile away with his single shot twelve-gauge; "IN A SNOW STORM, BY GOD."

After eating a quart of raw oysters, Hammer kept a woman happy in bed all night and most of the next day, without even stopping for a beer. I learned a lot. I learned about women, hunting, and fishing. I learned about cars; which ones were the best and which ones weren't worth a good shit. The best ones were ones that they happened to own. A Ford V-Eight was nothing but a "friggin oil burner." I learned about politicians; the ones who were okay, and the ones who oughta have their nuts cut off. I learned if young boys played with themselves they would go crazy or blind, sometimes both. I also learned to smoke cigarettes. One day while burning Al's papers I noticed a Camel cigarette carton in the fire. The fire had burned the end of the carton exposing the cigarettes inside. The carton must have accidentally fallen in the trash bin.

"Holy cow, it's full!" I fished the carton of cigarettes out of the fire, and hid them in the bushes. I'll hide them in the attic when it's dark, I thought. By the time I smoked that carton of cigarettes I felt I was on par with my heroes at the pool room. At least as far as smoking was concerned. Too bad I couldn't brag to them about it. As crude as they were at times I knew they would disapprove of me smoking.

An education like the one I got in Al Palmer's Pool room is priceless. I learned things even a place like Harvard wouldn't teach you, even if they could.

***

I remember sitting in Al Palmer's Pool Hall back in the late thirties, listening to the old men talk about the war in Europe. I must have been about twelve years old or so. One time the front page of the Hornell Newspaper read "Ethiopians Capture Italian Tank." Now the Ethiopians can do something, "They got a tank to fight with," one of the old men remarked. "We oughta go over there and help 'em out," another one cut in. "Yeah," said another. "We could wipe out both the Germans and Italians, in a few weeks." That was their perspective of the war in Europe.

I don't think many Americans realized the reverse was true. If the Axis had decided to invade America, they probably could have wiped us out in a few weeks. America was vulnerable and weak, we weren't ready for any war in the late thirties. We owe a great debt to England, who held the Germans off until we could gear up for war. When the headlines started reading Poland Falls, France Surrenders, German Dreadnought, Bismarck sinks H. M. S. Hood, the old men in Palmer's Pool Hall toned down their nonsense.

Two of the old timers had little to say, they were heroes of mine. They had fought in World War I. I think they knew what was coming, but I don't think even they realized how horrible the war would be, with forty million killed and the agonizing years it would take to bring it to a conclusion. Once Jim told me, "Those old men in the pool hall can talk brave, they know they won't have to go if war breaks out."

***

In the nineteen-thirties, television was only a dream that hadn't materialized into reality, as far as the public was concerned. The kids in Almond didn't need things like television and video games, we had adventure that we found in the woods and hills around Almond. We also had the Canacadea Creek where we could catch nice brown trout and spend hours snatching suckers and mullets with large three-barbed hooks. We had a great place to swim. Every year the town would dig out a hole with a steam shovel, then we would dam the creek below the hole with sandbags. Every spring the high water washed out our dam and the cycle had to be repeated, but it was worth it.

In West Almond, not very far away was a CCC camp. In the afternoon a truck of CCC boys came down to our swimming hole to swim and clean up after a hard day's work. After their swim, the CCC boys would help us work on our dam, and taught us a lot about damming up a creek. When the project was finished, what a good feeling we had. Just about every kid in town big enough to shovel sand in a burlap bag had taken part in building the dam. We all were so proud of our swimming hole, and I think it taught us to work together; it taught us to share. When people from Hornell and Alfred brought their kids up for a swim, we let them even though they didn't help build it. But the main thing I think it taught us was you don't get something for nothing, if you want a nice place to swim you had to work for it.

Can anyone imagine what kind of hell would be raised today if some small town decided to dam up a little creek to build a place for the kids to swim? Today it would require about twenty permits, take two years and cost about a half a million dollars. Even if you got past the bureaucracy you wouldn't be allowed to swim there, too many little wiggly things in the water and someone has a chicken coop only a half mile from the creek. There would be fines because there's no life guard, and the diving board wouldn't meet their requirements.

Well our old swimming hole was there a lot of summers, and to my knowledge, no one drowned, no one got sick because of the little wiggly things and the diving board held up just fine.

This is not to say that there weren't a few close calls. One time I fell off the bridge over the pool. I hit the water flat on my stomach, knocking the wind out of me. I sank to the bottom of the twelve foot deep pool. I laid on the bottom unable to move. Lucky for me, one of the CCC boys saw me fall, dove down and pulled me out. My face, chest, stomach, and legs were beet red from hitting the water flat on.

***

Bud, his kid brother and I were snake hunting along the creek when a real tragedy nearly occurred. My brother, Jim, had won a gun on a punch board at Al Palmer's pool hall, the gun was a big old rifle with an octagon barrel. It was a thirty-two-twenty caliber. I remember it was a single shot. You inserted a shell in the chamber, then cocked it by pulling the hammer back with your thumb. Jim was working, I took the gun without his permission, found the shells in the dresser drawer, took three and headed for the creek. Bud, and his kid brother, were already down there. We started walking up the creek, Bud ahead and to my right and his kid brother on my left. I put a shell in the chamber and pulled the hammer back. Suddenly Bud yelled, "There's one!" It startled me. I squeezed the trigger, the gun went off, the barrel pointed almost directly at Bud's younger brother's head. The bullet must of passed a fraction of an inch from his head. He stood there frozen in his tracks. I can still see the startled expression on his face, his eyes wide and his mouth agape. I never took Jim's gun again. I was content with my Daisy BB gun.

When I was young, Elm trees were growing abundantly in Almond and everywhere else. There were streets, parks and places named after Elm trees. The streets, parks and places are still there with the same name, but no Elm trees. Nearly all the Elms were wiped out by the Dutch Elm disease caused by a little beetle. An Elm as tall and healthy as the one on the picture is a rare sight and this one probably won't make it to maturity. Ironically the Elm is growing about four miles past a little town called Elm Valley, a place without any Elm trees of consequence. My Grandma Pitts told me when she was growing up large Chestnut trees were abundant. We used to gather the nuts from them and roast them in the fireplace. She said nearly everyone had a piece of furniture made from Chestnut. The magnificent Chestnut trees disappeared years ago. They say a fungus in the soil killed them all.

NCAY OUYAY ALKTAY IGGPAY ATINLAY?

    The words above are in pig latin. "Can you talk pig latin?" is what the words say. My friends and I were fluent in pig Latin. I don't think anyone could speak it better than we could. The faster you spoke it the better it worked out, and we spoke it real fast. Our parents and teachers couldn't understand us when we spoke it. This irritated our parents and made our teachers furious, who finally forbid us to speak it in their presence. One time while in class, my friend, Jack Jenkins, whispered to the kid next to him in pig latin,

    "HETAY EACHTAY ASHAY ADBAY EATHBRAY (The Teacher has bad breath). The kid busted out laughing.

    "What's so funny?" the teacher yelled at the kid.

    "Jack made me laugh," the kid tattled.

    "Jack, go to the office," the teacher yelled.

    "What'd I do?" Jack asked with his shoulders hunched, and his eyes wide with surprise and innocence.

    "Just tell the principal you were disturbing the class," she yelled. When Jack got back from the Principal's office, he went to his desk and just stood there.

    "Sit down Jack," the teacher ordered.

    "I can't," Jack answered. He wasn't crying, but I could tell he had been. His lower lip was quivering a little and his nose was in need of a handkerchief. Someone snickered.

    "Quiet," the teacher ordered.

    "It's all right Jack, you can stand if you rather," she spoke softly. There was no sarcasm in her voice now.

    Watching her face I thought she was going to cry. I could see she was very sorry. Her class had never been so quiet.

    As I remember, the principle was a kind and gentle man. But poor Jack had the misfortune of getting sent to the office when the

regular principle was away and someone was standing in for him.

The New Deal

In the late thirties, the great depression was starting to ease throughout the land, except in Almond it seemed. There was, however, hope and excitement; F.D.R.'s new deal was coming to Almond and it was going to help pull Almond out of the muck and misery of the hard times. The news was circulating all through Al Palmer's Pool Hall. The young men who hung out there because they had nothing else to do would have good paying jobs. They could buy cars, maybe even get married and have a kid or two. They were elated.

A large flood control dam was to be constructed in the town of Almond. The project would put a lot of people to work. Even more exciting, a new experimental school was to be built. It was to be called the Alfred-Almond Central School. It was a forerunner of what many schools would be like in the future. The school was scheduled to be finished in nineteen thirty-nine. The dam was to be built later, but was put on the shelf when the war came. The dam wasn't completed until the late forties.

In West Almond, a Civilian Conservation Corps or CCC camp had already been built. The workers there were affectionately called CCC boys. All of them were young and they worked hard for their dollar a day, plus room and board. The CCC boys were "encouraged" to send half their meager pay home to their folks, most did. The boys planted millions of acres of trees, they cleaned creeks and gullies and built fire control lanes through the forest. Many of the seedlings they planted are now tall forest. In Birdsall the CCC boys built a fire tower. From it's perch at the top one could gaze out over the ocean of tall trees the boys had planted over a half century ago.

I remember one time after a flash flood the boys were cleaning out a culvert that ran under the road in front of Uncle Nate's house in Birdsall.:

Duane and I wondered what had come over our older sisters. They were acting so strangely. They were secretive and clannish and wanted even less to do with us than before. *They spoke in soft, excited whispers. They combed their hair 'til it shined, they giggled and primped and they blushed their cheeks with stolen red rouge. They donned their prettiest dresses then they sashayed down to the creek and perched on the creek bank aloof, sophisticated and beautiful, and they didn't even know that there were any CCC boys working around there.*

The CCC boys were so engrossed in their work. They pulled and hauled at broken tree limbs that somehow had grown back in the trees. They lifted fifty-pound stones that magically turned into one hundred-pound boulders as they hoisted them high over their heads, and with loud grunts, they cast them much further from the creek bed than need be! They were shirtless and bronzed, and their muscles rippled and bulged in their exaggerated labors. Their young bodies were shiny with sweat in the warm spring sunshine. They didn't even know that there were three pretty young girls down there.

Alice, Eva's and cousin Regis's mothers were sitting up there on that front porch with cautious, little smiles on their faces and they didn't even know there were any boys and girls down around there.

It was like that on Uncle Nate's farm. It was truly a place of innocence back then.

> *Sing Glorious, Sing Glorious,*
> *One keg of beer for the four of us,*
> *When we're drunk, we're as happy as can be.*
> *For we are the members of the CCC.*
> *Sing Glorious, Sing Glorious.*

Another one of F.D.R.'s new deal schemes was the Workers Project Association or the WPA. The WPA didn't seem to have the respect that the CCC had. Some called them lazy. The newspapers printed cartoons of WPA workers leaning on their shovels and standing around burning barrels. I think a lot of the ridicule was probably political. Even us kids poked fun at them and had a few choice phrases for what WPA stood for.

The Wellsville Post Office was a W.P.A. Project.

Some of my friends and I used to ride our bicycles up to the Alfred-Almond School project and watch the WPA workers who were building the school. As I remember them, I never saw any of them standing around. We got a real kick out of the terrazzo workers. All of them were Italian. They never stopped working, and they never stopped yelling at each other in Italian. We figured most of the yelling were swear words. It was obvious the hand gestures were obscene. Years later, when I was a construction worker myself, the terrazzo workers were still Italian. They still never stopped working and giving each other obscene hand gestures, and they still swore at each other in Italian. This time I knew they were swearing at each other. I had picked up some Italian swear words myself since most of my co-workers were Italian.

When I first passed through the large oak doors of the brand new Alfred-Almond Central School, I was awe struck. I don't recall, but I must have just stood there for a full moment wide eyed, with my mouth agape. I remember thinking, "Gee, I should have cleaned my old sneakers." I didn't want to step foot on those shiny floors in my dirty old worn out sneakers. I thought surely someone would yell at me to take them off.

When I was assigned my homeroom seat, I was once more awe struck. Sitting just a few feet from me was the prettiest girl I had ever laid eyes upon. Her name was Janey. Janey lived in Alfred Station. I lived in my grandmother's house in Almond. You might say the new school brought us together and graciously introduced us to each other. I felt uncomfortable in the new school. I had never been in such a grand building as this. We rode to school in brand new green and cream- colored school buses with shiny chrome bulldogs on the hoods indicating that they were built by the Mack Truck Company, the best money could buy. The school had surgically clean rest rooms and shiny terrazzo floors. The gym had a huge electric folding door so it could be sectioned off, allowing the boys and girls to use it at the same time. The library had beautifully varnished woodwork and sound absorbing cork floors. The library windows faced the east to catch the morning sun. This is how I first saw the room with the sun rays flooding the room with it's light. The sunlight just added to the splendor of it all.

When I came home from school the first day at Alfred -Almond School, I realized just how primitive conditions were at my grandmother's house, with its outdoor toilet, and no running water or electricity, but at least I felt it was where I belonged. I didn't feel intimidated like I did in that palace they called school. After attending the Almond school, and the one room school in Birdsall, the new Alfred-Almond School was overwhelming to say the least. The only thing I liked about the school was seeing Janey every day.

I guess I didn't appreciate that fine school, and all the work and effort that went into building it. The school still stands proud and looks as it did then. If I didn't like the school that was my problem. Every effort was planned to make it a fine place for learning, and it was and is.

Janey and I were in the seventh grade. After seeing Janey, I started to keep myself neat and clean for the first time in my life. I didn't like school, but I never missed a day. I had to let Janey know how I felt about her, so I wrapped a note around a stick of gum and put it back in the pack. I didn't want the other kids catching me passing a love note.

"Psst, Janey, would you like a stick of gum?" I whispered. She nodded yes. I made sure she got the right stick. Janey opened the gum, saw the note and read it, her face flushed and she didn't look at me. When I saw Janey blush I thought, now I've done it. I've embarrassed her, maybe she's mad. She's gonna laugh at me. I shouldn't have given her that note. I wanted to bolt from that room, but all I did was put a book in front of my face, trying to hide, pretending I was reading. After what seemed a long time, Janey got up and walked to the pencil sharpener on the window sill. She sharpened her pencil, then walked back to her desk. As she passed by my desk she dropped a note on it. With dread and trembling hands I started to open the folded note. She's so pretty, how could she like someone like me, I thought. The note's gonna say she doesn't like me. Finally I got up enough courage to read the note.

"Holy cow," I almost yelled out loud - she likes me too! Janey turned and glanced at me for a quick second, then turned away. There was a shy smile on her face when she looked at me. Oh, she's so pretty, I melted like a gob of butter dropped in a hot skillet. Well now, if a young boy could die from shock of too much sudden happiness injected into his heart and soul, I surely would have died right there sitting at my desk in the seventh grade. My heart was pounding so hard I thought the buttons would pop off my shirt. I thought the whole class would hear my heart pound. Who cares, Janey loves me.

One of the last times I was with Janey was in the fall, and I remember Janey, her mother, and I were sitting on their porch steps. When Janey's mother went inside, Janey and I sneaked off and walked to the top of a wooded hill in front of the house. It was a warm sunny October day. Never in my young life was I so aware of how glorious an October day could be in its splendor. I think what made the day so special was sharing it with Janey, otherwise I would have looked upon it as just another pretty October day.

The romance lasted about a year, until Dad got promoted to a supervisor at the Worthington Company. We bought a house and moved to Wellsville. The house was newly remodeled and I had my own bedroom. Best of all we had a real bathroom, and it was all inside. When we left Almond and moved to Wellsville, I was unhappy and lonesome. I had a hard time making new friends. I missed Janey and the kids in Almond. I became pretty much a loner. I spent a lot of time fishing and swimming alone at the river. If I saw some kids swimming or fishing I would go farther up the river until I found a place of my own. The river became my best friend, and I didn't want to share it with anyone

Then early one morning I got on my bike to go to the river. Halfway there I turned around and headed towards Alfred Station, nearly twenty miles away. Quite a chore on the hard peddling bicycles of that era. When I finally got to Janey's house a young boy was playing in the front yard.

"Is Janey home?" I asked.

"No," the boy said, "they moved to Rochester."

To date I have never again heard from Janey. I wonder if on occasion she ever thinks of me or even remembers the skinny young boy who adored her, so long ago. The boy she always saw with a well-scrubbed face and in a clean shirt and pants, his hair slicked down with hair cream. Whenever October comes around Janey comes to mind. Some things a body just doesn't forget.

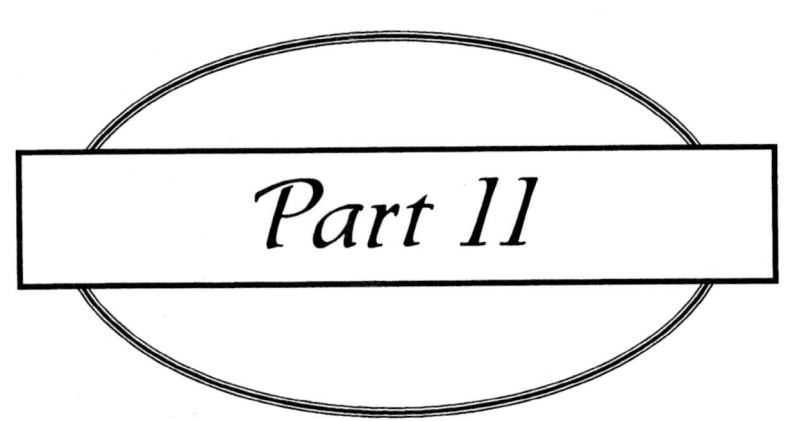

Wellsville 1940

To get to school in the morning I would walk a little way up Brooklyn Avenue to the north end of the Sinclair refinery and turn left down Pig Tail Alley, also known as Dyke Street Extension, to the old B&O railroad trestle. I would stop half way out on the trestle, where I would light up the cigarette butt I usually had in my pocket. It was safe there, no one would catch me smoking. While puffing on the cigarette I would check the water below hoping to catch a glimpse of a trout, or maybe a muskrat swimming across. Then on I would go through Island Park, stopping at the end for a few seconds to admire the old brass Civil War cannon, guarding the entrance to the park, then across the bridge to State Street and the school. It was about twice as far this way, but a much nicer walk.

One morning while walking to school, I came upon the severed head of a dog, halfway out on the trestle. The dog must have gotten trapped and couldn't get out of the way of a train. The rest of the dog must have fallen into the river. When I got to the school grounds, a young boy was telling his wide-eyed friends about the dog on the trestle and was milking the incident for all it was worth.

"An' his head was layin' on the tracks. It's body was down inna river an' there was blood an' guts all over the place, it was awful. When ya go home after school, don't go over the trestle, it'll make ya sick, ya'll haveta puke."

Actually the train had done a rather neat job, leaving only a little hair and blood on the rail of the tracks.

Photo by Bruce Broughton

Photo by the author

Wellsville High School

Signing The Papers

It was November, 1943, I was seventeen. "Dad, I have to talk to you..." He looked a little startled, I think he sensed something was coming that he didn't want to hear. Dad's emotions always showed up in his face. "Dad, I quit school," I blurted out. He was upset.
"You can just go right back and unquit," he yelled.
"I can't, I joined the Navy. I have to have you sign the papers."
The color drained from his face, then in almost a pleading voice, he asked "How can you expect me to do that ? I won't do it." The stress from the last few days had built up to a point where it was difficult for me to handle, my eyes were getting wet.
"Look at you," my father said, "standing there with tears in your eyes, and you think you're man enough to join the Navy. I won't sign any damn papers." There was contempt and disgust in his voice, and it cut deep. On the other hand, I knew why he acted so callous. He would say anything to keep from signing the papers. When I was little, I knew my father thought a lot of me. Little boys just know those things, but later I never knew where I stood with my father. I avoided him as much as I could, but after that day, I knew where I stood with him. I knew my father cared and cared a lot, and the feeling was mutual. I never avoided him again and it was that way until the day he died. Finally Dad sat down at the kitchen table, I sat down with him. We started talking it out. I told Dad that, as far as school was concerned, I was a poor student. I was seventeen and only in the tenth grade, besides the next year I would be eighteen and the Army would draft me.
"I would rather go in the Navy," I told him. I must have had a convincing argument as he reluctantly signed the papers. Up to this point it was the first time we really talked to each other.
Oh, how I remember it all. Dad got up from the kitchen table, walked over to the china cabinet, and got out his big yellow and black Parker fountain pen. Without sitting back down, he leaned over the table and signed the papers. Whenever my father finished using his cherished fountain pen, he always carefully screwed the

cap back on and put it back in it's special place in the china cabinet.

"Jim gave me that pen. It's got a gold tip on it, and you kids are not to touch it," he would scold. But this time as soon as he finished signing his name on the enlistment papers he quickly tossed the pen down without screwing the cap back on. He acted like he couldn't get rid of that pen fast enough; like the pen was at fault for his signature being on the paper. Then he walked over to the kitchen window, and with his hands clasped behind his back, he just stood there looking out the window with his back to me so I couldn't see his face. My mother sat there looking down at her folded hands in her lap. I knew what she was thinking; Jimmy's going to leave and now Bobby is too. She had no say in the matter. The decision was all up to my father as far as the Navy was concerned. There was no laughter coming from the house at twenty-six Whitney Avenue on that day.

I walked out of the house, I knew where I was going. I headed towards the road that went past the oil refinery, a little ways up from our house. Then I just started running as fast as I could. I headed for a place I sometimes went when I wanted to be alone. A place where a half man, half boy could lose his emotions without anyone seeing him. The place was known as the Weidrick Bridge. Sometimes I would fish there trying to catch the elusive brown trout that fed in the shallow rapids under the bridge, but most of the time I went there when I was troubled and wanted to be alone. When I reached the bridge I was exhausted and sweating even though it was cold and spitting snow. I climbed down the steep bank and sat down under the bridge and listened to the water flowing in the shallows. It always worked; sitting a little while alone under the bridge and listening to the water had a tranquil effect on me. I always felt better after a little while under the bridge.

"What a hell of a thing I just asked my father to do," I thought. Signing a paper that gives the government permission to send his son off to war. My father knew the consequences of war even though he never participated in one. He was too young for World War I and too old for World War II. Besides, his expertise in the machine shops and production made him far more valuable in a war plant. Dad's older brother, my Uncle Vern, fought in France in World War I. In a battle charging the German lines, Uncle Vern fell and tore his gas mask causing him to breathe in the devil's delight, mustard gas.

Over the next several years the gas slowly destroyed his lungs and he died a slow agonizing death. I received my middle name from him. Dad's grandfather, Charles Broughton, received a gun shot wound in the Battle of the Wilderness during the Civil War . Dad's great-uncle John, Charlie's brother, was killed in that war as was John's brother-in-law.

I never saw that big ol' fountain pen again after Dad signed those papers. I have a suspicion he may have thrown it away, that's something my dad would do, he was like that.

After an hour or so I was feeling better, I climbed back up the bank and slowly walked back towards the house. With Dad's signature on the paper it looks like I'm in the Navy, I thought. Maybe Mom and Dad will feel better now that it's a done deal and out of their hands. The thought of getting killed or hurt in the war never entered my mind. What worried me most was, if I would be up to doing what was expected of me. I was one worried and unsure-of-himself young man.

Dad's Brother, my Uncle Vernon Broughton. Vern tore his gas mask during a charge on German lines in World War I. Over the course of several years the mustard gas slowly destroyed his lungs.

The Weidrick Bridge

In the early forties, the water under the Weidrick bridge was shallow and flowed fast and noisy over the rocks in the river bed acting as if it was in a hurry to get someplace, somewhat like myself when I was young.

Now the water is quieter, deeper and slowing down, in no hurry to get anywhere. It's like this part of the river has kept pace and changed in tandem with my life, deeper, quieter, slowing down and in no real hurry to get someplace.

Someday this ol' man's gonna spend an hour or two just sitting all alone under the Weidrick bridge. It's been a long, long time since I did that.

'Best shake a leg.

Boot Camp

I got on the train in Wellsville, to go to the induction center in Olean. There we had an eye test and were checked for hemorrhoids. The pharmacist mate told Jimmy, the lad who joined the Navy with me, to drop his pants. "Ah! I don't want to do that," Jimmy said.

"Do what I say," the pharmacist mate screamed, "or I'll kick your little ass all the way to Buffalo."

Jimmy reluctantly did what he was told. I could see the Navy had no room for modesty.

From Olean, we were sent to Buffalo for our real physical. I didn't know there were so many parts to the human body. The old post office was converted into a place for the Navy to give physicals to the new inductees. We were told to strip down to our shoes and socks. For the next ten hours we ran around the two top floors of the post office, naked. There were hundreds of us. We were told to pee in a bottle they gave us. Jimmy was behind me with a worried look on his face.

"What's wrong, Jimmy?" I asked.

"I can't pee." Jimmy complained.

"Don't worry, when no one is looking, pass me your bottle, I've got enough for the both of us."

It was nearly 10 p.m. when the physical was finished. At last they gave us something to eat: an apple, a small bottle of cold milk, and a bologna sandwich. It tasted delicious. After the physical we boarded a train for Geneva, New York where we got on a bus for Sampson Training Center. Jimmy and the rest of the guys were sent to a different unit. Hundreds of guys around, and I felt all alone. I was disappointed, as I wanted to be with the guys I joined up with. When we arrived in Sampson, we had another physical. I heard one fellow complain, "How healthy do you have to be to die for your country?"

After the physical we were given a large cotton bag to put our Navy clothes and gear in. They told us not to carry the bag but to drag it so they could throw our gear in as we went down the supply line. When at last we got to our barracks, we were still dragging our gear in the cotton bag.

"Pick up your gear and carry it!" the C.O. screamed. "Don't you know that's your mattress cover you're dragging in the dirt?"

We had been pushed around, and yelled at, and humiliated without mercy for hours on end, and most of the punishment was coming from people who had little more authority than we had. They were people with no rank and were only a few weeks out of camp themselves. If you gave an enlisted man a little authority he was worse than most of the officers.

One night, a little before lights out, some of the guys came up to me and started talking and asking me questions. They asked about my family, where I was from, things like that. It was nice, someone taking an interest in me. I was starving for a little camaraderie. I wanted to fit in. Being maybe the youngest in the company, I figured most of the guys wouldn't want much to do with me. The guys kept talking to me, some of them grinning a little. Suddenly I felt a sharp pain in the arch of my left foot. I didn't yell out or anything. I did not want the guys to stop talking to me, I just rubbed my shoe against the inside of my right pant leg trying to brush away the pain. Then I smelled the putrid odor of sulfur burning. I knew what they were up to. They had given me a hot foot. I sat down on the deck and took off my shoe and sock. There was a burn the size of a half dollar on the arch of my left foot. They must have used two or three wooden matches instead of the customary one match.

I sat there feeling embarrassed, I had disappointed my mates. I hadn't jumped up and down yelling like an idiot. One of the guys looked at me like maybe he was going to apologize, but he didn't. The rest looked at me like I was a poor sport and walked off. If just one of them had said, "Hey mate, I'm sorry," it would have taken away some of the hurt, but it didn't happen.

"Hit the sack. Lights out," the petty officer yelled.
I was glad it was dark. I laid in my bunk, the burn hurting pretty bad, and I thought about getting up and going to the head and running cold water on it, but I didn't. 'To hell with it. To hell with the guys that did it, too.'

I tried to push the incident from my mind. It wouldn't budge. My thoughts rushed home, I wondered if Mom and Dad were playing their music. The music and verse of the Missouri Waltz started flowing through my mind, washing away the pain of the burn and a bit of the other until I fell asleep.

Navy Boot

I think it was in our third week at Sampson, we had the dreaded Captain's Inspection. There was an old story passed around about the boot who wrote home to his folks about how he was made head guard in his company. And his folks bragged about their son doing so well in Sampson and that they had made him head guard there. Too late, the boot found out "head" was the Navy word for latrine.

Well, much to my chagrin I had the dubious honor of being appointed head guard for the big inspection. The guys kidded the hell out of me, and they called me chief and admiral. Some stood at attention and saluted smartly when I walked by them. There were some however who were disrespectful of my distinguished position. They called me "head turd snapper."

The day of the big inspection had arrived. The windows and decks shined. The mattress covers on the bunks were wrinkle free, the blankets folded perfect, the lockers squared. Each man stood at attention in front of his bunk, shoes so shiny they looked like glass, and their hats squared. They were freshly shaven with nary a hair to be seen on their faces. My mates were ready.

The gold braid walked down one side of the double line checking out each man in turn and then checked the other line in like fashion. They were closing in on me, and I was nervous as hell. When they arrived at the entrance to the head, I saluted smartly and called out, "Head Guard, Co. 358, head ready for inspection, Sir," my voice rising an octave or so, as a male teenager's voice sounds when he's scared or excited and his voice hasn't yet matured.

The captain returned my salute, pulling back just a little like I had something contagious. He gave me a look of woe and proceeded into the head followed by a Lieutenant, our Chief and a yeoman with a clipboard. They were in there a long time, at least it seemed to me they were. Finally, out they came, the Captain, the Lieutenant, and the yeoman who was now writing on the clip board. The inspection was over, but not for me. As soon as the inspection team was out the door our Chief came out of the head, his face was red and his eyes were bulging out of his head. I thought he was about to explode and in a sense he did. He laced me out but good, with words I don't care to print. It seems someone left a bar of soap in the lavatory spoiling an otherwise perfect inspection. It was my job to see that nothing like that happened. I felt bad, like I had let everyone down and I waited in dread as to the punishment I would receive, but the punishment never came despite the bar of soap. We received a well done on our inspection and the soap incident was soon forgotten. I would imagine most boots that went through Sampson thought their company was the best. Company 358 must have been a good one as we won the Rooster, an award for the best company.

We had a real old guy, must have been at least thirty-five, who was our appointed Petty Officer. He had been a sergeant in the Army. He was well-versed in military lore, especially in close order drilling. He had Co.358 looking real sharp in short order. Winning the Rooster meant a ten hour liberty in Geneva. We had heard that the people in Geneva didn't care much for Sailors. We were told there were signs saying things like, "Sailors and dogs keep off the grass". We found this not to be true. The people treated us well, but it must have taxed them all with such a large base so close to a small city like Geneva. With all the Shore Patrol on the streets of Geneva, we must have been about the best behaved sailors on liberty ever.

I got through boot camp with no problems, in fact after the first week, it wasn't as bad as I thought it would be. The thing that was hardest for me was it seemed they never let us get enough sleep. Sampson was cold and windy, and we spent long hours on the drill fields. There were obstacle courses, lectures, and small arms training. I didn't mind any of it. The "abandon ship" drills were right up my alley, as they gave me a chance to show off my swimming skills. The instructor told us to assume the water had burning oil on top. We were instructed to swim under water as far as we could, then surface fanning the water to create a hole in the fire, gulp some air, and repeat the process until we cleared the burning oil. When it came to my turn, I swam the distance of the pool without coming up for air. Back in Almond we used to see who could swim the farthest under water without coming up for air. I always won. The other kids said it was because I was full of hot air. "Do it again, smart ass," the instructor growled. "You didn't fan the water when you surfaced." Some of the guys giggled a little, now I was fitting in.

R.V. Broughton, Seaman Second Class, service number 609-62-19 was home on leave. How sweet it was! No one could do enough for you. You couldn't buy a beer or a cup of coffee. If you ordered something to eat in a restaurant, often a perfect stranger would pick up the tab. All the girls wanted to go out with you, even if you were a scrawny seventeen year old with a few pimples on your face. I loved it.

My big brother, Jim, was a little upset. The town had put up the servicemen's names in front of the library. He had joined the Navy before I did, but they temporarily deferred him because he was a machinist in a defense plant. His name was on the board, but they hadn't gotten around to putting mine there yet.

My brother Jim was the best. He was always good to all his brothers and sisters and was always protecting and helping them. I told him of all the little pit falls to watch out for when he went to camp. I was grateful for a chance to help him for a change. Jim asked a lot of questions. He was a little scared. I told him "Jim, you're smarter than I am, you get along with people better than I do, and you're better looking. You'll do just fine." And he did, too. He came out of the Navy a Second Class Petty Officer.

That's me with the ears in the dead center of the photograph. I don't look like I was enjoying myself.

Songs

Bell Bottom trousers, Coat of Navy Blue
He'll climb the riggin', like his Daddy used to do
Daisy was a bar maid down in lover's lane
She was a kind miss, her Master was the same
Now along came a Sailor, happy as can be
Oh, he was the cause of all her misery
He asked her for a kerchief to tie around his head
He asked her for a candle to light his way to bed
She like a foolish girl seeing it no harm
Jumped into bed just to keep the Sailor warm
Now early in the morning, just at break of day
He handed her a five spot and this is what he say
"Take this, my darling, for all the harm I've done
You may have a Daughter, you may have a Son
If you have a Daughter, bounce her on your knee
If you have a Son, send the bastard out to sea."
The moral of the story is plain as you can see
Never trust a Sailor, an inch above your knee
Singing Bell Bottom Trousers, Coat of Navy Blue
He'll climb the riggin' like his Daddy used to do.

Bless Em all, Bless Em all
The long, the short, and the tall
Bless all the Ensigns that crack the whip
Ninety-day wonders with fuzz on their lip
When they don't know just what they should do
They'll call on a Seaman or two
And as for the Boatswain, well he can go screw
There'll will be no promotions this side of the ocean
So cheer up my lads
Bless Em All.

U.S.S. ARKAB

Boot leave was over. We were in Newport, Rhode Island for gunnery training. Now Wellsville had some big beautiful houses, but the big stone mansions in Newport made the Wellsville homes look like tenant houses. I wondered how one of those mansions would have looked located next to our shack in Canisteo. I thought it might be a good idea to move one down there, so people could see the huge gap between the very rich and the very poor in this country.

***

"Commence firing!" the gunnery officer yelled over the P.A. system. About a dozen twenty millimeter guns opened up all at once. A Navy PBY Catalina was flying over, towing a target sleeve on a long tow rope. I could see why the P.B.Y. had such a long tow rope, tracers were flying all over the place. A few of the tracers were coming close to the sleeve, fewer yet were hitting it.

We also received some training on the three and five-inch guns, and we spent a week on the rifle range. We then boarded the *USS Chilton,* a Navy training vessel. She had a few guns on her, but we never fired them. We cruised along the Atlantic Coast for a few days. Once a destroyer cruised near us and opened up with her five inchers firing at nothing in particular. To this day I don't know what the cruise was all about, but it was a nice ride anyway.

United States Navy Training Vessel U.S.S. Chilton.

"Are you the dirty boy I've been watching walk around here?" an officer asked me. Ship's company was lined up for muster, and the officer was looking us over. We were in Mobile, Alabama. We had been in Mobile only a few hours, and all of us were dirty and tired from the long troop train ride from Newport. We had an overnight layover near the steel mills in Pittsburgh, and the coal dust had laid a fine black film on everyone, not just me. Two hundred and fifty guys lined up, all just as dirty as me, and that S.O.B. decides to lace me out in front of the whole ship's company. As we hadn't been assigned any quarters, there was no way we could get cleaned up. I didn't appreciate being singled out.

"That's about the ugliest f&#$ing ship I ever saw," Reily, our First Class Signalman sighed. They had just trucked us all down to Mobile Bay where the mighty *USS Arkab*, designation AK130 was tied to the dock. We all got to look at our new ship. None of us had seen as many ships as Reily had, but we all agreed with him. With no cargo in her she sat there riding high and light. The rudder and screw were half way out of the water displaying some of her working parts. She was a Liberty Ship, one of thousands that were built during the war to carry supplies to the troops fighting distant battles. There were eight landing craft cradled over her cargo holds, four Landing Craft Mechanized or L.C.M.'s and four Landing Craft Vehicle Personnel or L.C.V.P.'s tucked inside the L.C.M.'s. She was armed with eight, twenty-millimeter cannons, one three-inch fifty on her bow, and a five-inch thirty-eight aft above the fantail.

"Get aboard," Kelly our First Class Bos'n ordered. "And don't forget to salute the Ensign aft before you salute the Officer on the quarter deck...and don't forget to ask permission to board."

"Where's the quarter deck?" I asked Reily.

"You'll know it when you see it," Reily snapped at me.

We were assigned our bunks and lockers. I couldn't believe they were going to cram so many men in such a small space. There were rows of bunks stacked four high. There were aisles between the rows of bunks just wide enough for two men to pass if each turned sideways and sucked in his gut. A modern prison cell on the *Arkab* would have been an absolute luxury. The head consisted of a long trough with rows of seats on each side. At one end was a lever that opened a valve to flush the trough. When a guy was finished, he would tell the guy nearest the valve to "flush." The water would come out like from a fire hose. With the word "flush" everyone would raise up, to avoid getting certain parts of the anatomy wet, when the water and whatever passed under them. The enlisted men's head was a disgusting and degrading place, not much different than the drop in the old cow barn in Birdsall. I wondered if the brass designed it that way so we would know our place. At least the outdoor privies in Almond and Birdsall afforded some privacy. I thought conditions like the head caused low moral on the ship. The Navy could have and should have done a little better by us.

Like Almond, the *Arkab* had some positive things, too. We had good cooks and bakers. The baker on the *Arkab* baked us fresh bread every day and could make the most delicious peach pie from canned peaches you ever ate. All the officers, but two, were fair and respected; even well-liked by their subordinates.

I was lucky. I got a top bunk with an air vent directly over it, and I could reach my locker from my bunk. I wouldn't have traded my bunk for any other in the crew's quarters. This was to be my home for the next thirteen months. There were three hundred and forty-nine other people living in the same home.

"Where is the main mast look-out supposed to be, Sir?" I asked Lt. Roland, our gunnery officer. He rolled his eyes up and focused them on a small cylinder-shaped structure, perched on top of a forty-foot-high pole with a steel ladder welded to it and grinned. "Up there. That's the main mast." It was to be my look-out station. In case of fire, I had to make sure a CO_2 fire extinguisher was at the scene. At my abandon ship station, I was to cut the lashing around a pelican hook. When the lashing was cut, the hook would open and release a life raft into the water. I was told to keep a knife on me at all times. My battle station was gunner on the number four, twenty-millimeter gun on the bridge. We had drill after drill and got all our jobs down pat. We all knew what to do and how to do it.

"Now hear this, starboard liberty party lay to on the quarter deck for liberty inspection," the Bos'n piped. It was good to get off the ship for a few hours. There was a lad on the ship named Johnny Carroll. He was the same age as me, and we always pulled liberty together. We picked up a couple of girls, all we did was talk. I got a kick out of hearing the girls talk. The girl with me said, "Seeing how boys are scarce, I'll just have to settle for a Yankee for the evening." I liked Mobile.

***

"Okay, pull 'em up easy," the Warrant Officer ordered. Johnny and I had just gotten back from liberty. There was a block and tackle rigged up over the 'tween deck next to the crew's quarters. The warrant officer was directing some men pulling on a block and tackle. They were pulling up a man in a wire stretcher who had fallen in the cargo hold under the 'tween deck. Everyone was quiet, all you could hear was a little squeaking noise coming from the block and tackle.

"Who is it?" I whispered.

"It's Tony" a buddy named Merle said in a soft voice. "I saw it happen. Some son-of-a-bitch left a hatch cover off. There was a clothes line strung over the empty space. Tony had just rinsed out his tee shirt and was shaking it out while walking towards the clothes line. He didn't scream or anything. We were talking and he just disappeared." Merle's voice cracked. I was very sorry for Merle. Tony and Merle were good friends. I knew what Merle would be doing after lights out. Tony was a big, handsome, good-natured lad, everyone liked him. He would have made a good shipmate.

"**Look out!**" someone yelled. The long steel cargo boom came down crashing through a life raft secured above the gunwale. The Old Man heard the noise and came running out of his quarters on the bridge.

"**What in the damn hell is going on down there ?**" he bellowed.

Kelly looked worried. He had slipped up. The boom hadn't been rigged up right. Even the best can slip up, and Kelly was one of the best. While trying to get the boom rigged for cargo handling it had gotten away from him. Manion, the second class bos'n said to Kelly, "Tell the Captain something broke in the rigging." With that he climbed up to the top of the mast and yelled down "Looks like a eye pad's missing. I bet it wasn't welded on properly in the ship yard."

The *Arkab* was underway, cruising out of Mobile Bay, headed for the Gulf of Mexico. She must have been a sight to see, riding fat and high. She was on her shakedown cruise which went surprisingly well. Everything was working fine.

"This ship's like my wife back home," Sykes, an old salt from Tennessee drawled. "She's not a very pretty gal, but she's got good stuff in 'er."

When you're young and going to join the Navy, you picture in your mind mighty battleships, sleek fast destroyers, huge aircraft carriers, and other fighting ships, not a wallowing, fat, slow noncombat cargo ship like the *Arkab*. If I could have seen the ship the Navy assigned me to before-hand I would have waited until I was eighteen and old enough to join the Army. But you do what you're ordered to do and the *Arkab* did her job, and did it well.

***

"You don't like your little blue shirt, Broughton?" Kelly asked. One hundred and ten guys lined up with blue shirts on and I had on a black sweater. Jensen, my relief watch, was late, and I didn't have time to put on my blue shirt. I had a choice of two evils; go get my shirt and fall in for morning muster late, or be on time, but out of uniform. I chose the latter, lost my liberty and didn't get to see New Orleans.

We docked a few miles from New Orleans at a munitions depot where we took on our personal ammo for the ship's magazines and then twenty and forty millimeter shells for cargo. Our cargo varied from trucks and jeeps to mail and Coca-Cola, but it was mostly ammunition. Now the *Arkab* sat low in the water. She looked a lot better when you saw less of her. Somewhere along the line, Brooklyn I think, we picked up a huge section of a floating dry dock.

The dry dock cut our speed almost in half. One thing you could say about the *Arkab*, for her size no ship ever delivered a bigger payload.

A few miles out of New York, a sleek destroyer escort came out to meet us. She was to be our escort all the way to Panama, as there were still German subs prowling the Caribbean. When we arrived in Panama, we were told two ships were torpedoed on approximately the same course we took. One ahead of us and one behind us. That beautiful D. E. probably kept us from the same fate.

A Destroyer Escort.

***

"Come on Saila, only two dollas." I kind of wanted to, but did not quite have the nerve. The little Spanish girl was dark and pretty, and I was a little mad at myself for being such a coward. We were in Balboa, Panama in a section called Coconut Grove. One side of the street was lined with gin mills, the other whore houses; a sailors paradise. When we got back to the ship the older guys kidded me to no end. They told me how great the girls were, and went into great detail about all their talents. Hell, I bet it wasn't much better than my experience with the girl down by the creek. Like I said, it only cost me four cents worth of root beer barrels. It cost the guys a whole lot more, two bucks, plus tips and a shot of rum and Coke.

We went through the locks and then picked up a pilot to take us through the cut. The cut was beautiful, with high green cliffs and hills on each side of us. I got a birds-eye view from my lookout station in the crow's nest. We picked up our floating dry dock at the other end of the canal and headed for the Asiatic, Pacific campaign. If the Japs had seen us coming, towing that thing, I bet they would have surrendered and the war in the Pacific would have been over.

We hadn't been out to sea for too long, when one day, eight men's names were called over the PA, "Report to sick bay" the PA ordered. It seems the eight guys had come down with the clapp. For some mysterious reason, no one was kidding me about not going to the whore house in Panama anymore. A series of penicillin shots cured them. They were okay so it was all right if I looked at them, and grinned at them when I saw them.

"Main mast, get your eyes out of your ass, don't you see those ships on the horizon?" the bridge called over the battle phones. I knew the ships were there, but I didn't think I had to notify the bridge, as the previous watch had told me he had reported them. It's a little embarrassing to get chewed out over the battle phones as everyone on watch hears all the reports.

The main mast and fore top lookouts were lonely places as you were all alone. The look-outs in the gun tubs and on the bridge were in groups of three and four, and they could talk when the officers weren't near. No one bothered the main mast and fore top watches as they didn't want to climb up there. You could even sneak a smoke once in a while. Sometimes I would take a can of peanuts with me and toss a few peanuts down onto the guys sleeping on deck. They never got wise as to where the peanuts were coming from. If they looked up I always was busy looking through my binoculars. I missed our friend the D.E. as she had left us in Panama.

"I don't see it yet Sir," the chief pharmacist mate was yelling down to the bridge.

"Keep looking and reporting pollywog," the bridge ordered.

The chief pharmacist mate was up in the rigging looking for the equator line. His pants were off and his binoculars were two Coke bottles. If you had never crossed the equator you were a pollywog, the lowest form of life. You were most unworthy and had to be cleansed by severe punishment. Before you could become a proud shellback you had to be brought before King Neptune and Davy Jones to answer for your crimes. First you were lined up on deck and hosed down. Next you went through a gauntlet of shellbacks swinging paddles. You had to kneel down before King Neptune and the Royal Family. You had to kiss the Royal Baby's diapered behind which was covered with mustard and grease. If you gazed upon the Royal Queen you were immediately executed with an electric prod by the Royal Executioner. It seemed everyone was guilty of looking at the queen. Lastly you reported to the Royal Barber where you sat in a hinged chair and were shaved with rotten eggs for lather. The barber cut off a swath of hair from the back to the front, one eyebrow was shaved off, and you were pushed over backwards into a container of filthy salt water. You were then a shellback and it was so stated in your Navy records.

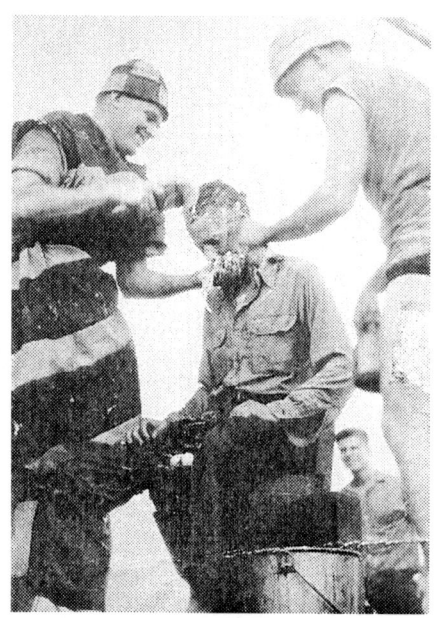

The Royal Barbers gave me a nice shave and haircut - free!

"What's so funny sailor?" the officer of the deck asked. The OD must have caught me smiling to myself.

"I was just thinking Sir. In a few days I'll be eighteen years old, and I don't know how to drive a car yet, and here I am half way around the world learning to steer a ship, sir." I was taking a turn at the wheel as part of the requirement to advance from a Seaman Second Class to First Class Seaman. If I had been asked the question I would have had to stiffen and answer, "Nothing's funny, Sir." You didn't small talk those two.

"You're going to have a lot of catching up to do when you get home," the O. D. said, "like cars and girls." His voice trailed off and he was silent. The young Ensign wasn't a hell of a lot older than myself, and I heard he had a pretty new wife waiting at home. He had a lot of catching up to do himself. We all did.

"Watch the wheel sailor, she's drifting to port."

"Aye Aye Sir," I answered.

Bridge of a Liberty Ship

The dry dock we were towing slowed us down to a crawl. We were lucky when we could make six or seven knots. When we had heavy head winds it looked like we weren't moving at all. It took forty-three days from Panama to Milne Bay, New Guinea where we unshackled our burden. The captain let us have a few hours shore leave in New Guinea. He even let us use one of the landing crafts. We ran the L.C.V.P. up on a sandy beach and went for a swim. There were some Australian soldiers there and I gave them my three cans of three-two beer as I didn't care all that much for beer. One of the Australians asked if we wanted to see some of the area away from the beach. The Australians were very well liked by the Americans and vice-versa. We hopped in back of an open truck and the Aussies took us for a little tour. It was nice. We bounced down some jungle roads and wound up in a real native village. The natives were tall and handsome. It was very enjoyable, especially looking at the native women as they wore very little clothing. For a small town boy like me it was pretty exciting.

"General Quarters - this is not a drill - General Quarters - man your battle stations."

We were a few days out from New Guinea bound for Pearl Harbor. It was nighttime and I was just wiping down from a salt water shower when the alarm sounded. I was so startled I ran for the bridge with only my towel and my belt with the knife on it. I got to my gun first, cocked it, put my helmet and life jacket on and strapped myself in. For about one and a half minutes there was nothing but the thumping sound of running feet, then the sharp clicks of the guns being loaded and cocked, and then absolute silence. No one gave any orders, everyone knew what to do. The bridge started giving the position and range of the target but it was too dark to see. About every half minute each report brought us closer to the target. We were well within range for our three and five inch guns. Then the reports from the bridge indicated the distance was growing. We were running away. A few hours later the order was given to secure from general quarters. The next morning Lt. Roland told us what had happened. We had picked up a Jap sub on the surface with our radar and she didn't answer our challenge. We knew she was Japanese. Our orders were not to engage in any combat if we could avoid it. Our job was to get cargo where it was needed.

After that morale on the *Arkab* kept going down hill.

"We could have had that sub," Reily said. "We had her outgunned and I bet she never saw us. We could have sunk her but we chickened out." Reily hated the *Arkab* and was always knocking her. The O.D. knew this and so did the Lt. They were on him all the time. Reily was a hero to the crew. He had hash marks on his dress blues indicating his years of service. He had several campaign bars and bronze stars indicating battles he was in. Once, when we were in the Admiralty Islands, a ship sent us a message by blinker. Reily received it and reported it. The O.D. ordered Reily to send back his answer. Reily sent the message back so fast the other ship asked for a repeat.

"Slow it down," the O.D. ordered. Reily slowed it down a bit.

"Repeat," the ship requested again.

"Dammit Reily," the O.D. growled. "That's a line ship your embarrassing out there."

"I can't help it if the dumb bastards can't read blinker," Reily snapped. It cost him a stripe. Before I left the *Arkab* Reily had lost all his stripes. Reily was cocky, but he knew his job and he was a proud man. The *Arkab* was beneath him. His resentment of being on a non combat ship like the *Arkab* caused him to lose control thus forcing the O.D. to take his strips. On most ships, slight infractions would get you chewed out; Reily once told us on the *Arkab* you lose your stripes or get ten days in the brig, on piss and punk (bread and water).

"Look at it this way Reily," Brennan, one of the older guys said. "Someday this war will be over. Years from now when we're all grandfathers, this will be something you can tell your grandchildren. You might not have any stripes to show them, but you can show your campaign bars with the bronze stars, and you can tell them you were the best damn signalman in the U.S. Navy as far as the crew on the *Arkab* was concerned."

Subpoena and Summons Extraordinary
The Royal High Court of the Raging Main

Region of the South Seas
Domain of Neptune Rex;

To Whom May Come These Presents
Greetings and Beware

WHEREAS, The good ship U.S.S. ARKAB, bound for the South Seas below the Equator, on a mission of War, is about to enter out domain; and whereas the aforesaid ship carries a large and loathsome cargo of landlubbers, beach-combers, guardorats, sea lawyers, longe-lizards, parlor-dunnigans, plow-deserters, park-bench warmers, chicken chasers, hay-tossers, four-flushers, crossword puzzle bugs, dance hall shieks, drugstore cowboys, asphalt arabs, and all other living creatures of the land, and last but not least, he-vamps, liberty-hounds, Mobile and Norfolk Cabrillo's, masquerading as seamen, of which low scum you are a member, having never appeared before us; and

WHEREAS, THE ROYAL HIGH COURT of the RAGING MAIN will convene on board the good ship U.S.S. ARKAB, on the 8th day of August, 1944, at Longitude -sh-h-h and whereas, an inspection of our Royal Roster shows that it is high time your sad and wandering nautical soul apperas before OUR AUGUST PRESENCE; and

BE IT KNOWN, That we here by summon and command you R.V. Broughton now a Seaman 2nd Class U.S. Navy, to appear before the Royal High Court and our AUGUST PRESENCE on the aforesaid date at such time as may best suit OUR good pleasure.

You will accept most heartily and with good grace the pains and penalties of the awful tortures that will be inflicted on you to determine your fitness to be one of our Trusty Shellbacks and answer the following charges:

CHARGE I: - In that you have hitherto willfully and maliciously failed to show reverence and allegiance to our Royal Person, and are therein and thereby a vile landlubber and pollywog.

CHARGEII: - In that you keep silent about the decks and rob your shipmates of their daily rations.

If you gazed upon the Royal Queen you wre immediately executed with an electric prod by the Royal Executioner.

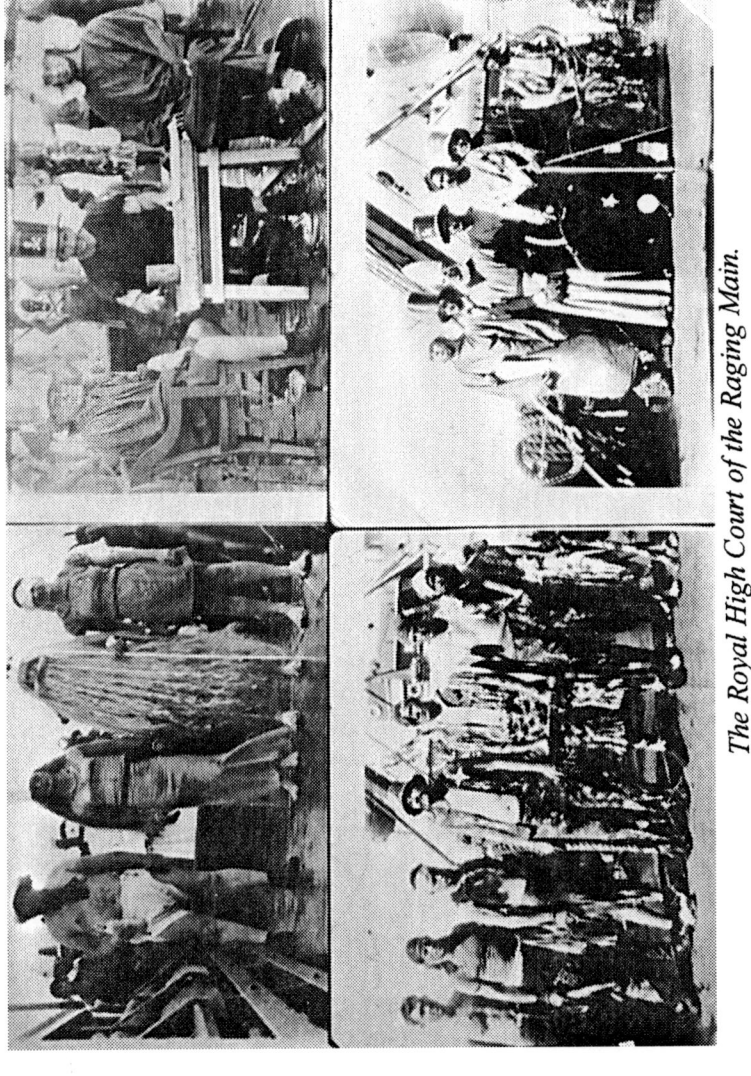

The Royal High Court of the Raging Main.

Praise the Lord!

When a ship is pitching and rolling in stormy weather and the ladder is facing aft, it's best to climb a few rungs of the ladder when the bow is coming up. When the bow starts down you have to stop, press your feet against the ladder rails and hang on until the bow starts back up again. Descending a ladder is done in the same manner.

One night after I had been relieved of my watch up in the crow's nest, I started to climb down the mast. I darn near fell from the mast. It was pitch black, windy and raining. The *Arkab* was pitching and rolling in the heavy weather. I was tired and sleepy after my long watch and I got careless. Instead of waiting for the bow to come up, I started to descend the ladder as the bow was coming down, the force of gravity pulled at me causing my feet to slip off the wet ladder rung. For a few seconds I dangled in space hanging on to the wet ladder with all my might until the bow started back up. The force that had tried to pull me off the mast pushed me back to it. I was shaken and scared as hell. For a long moment I just clung there not moving. The wind and rain pelting my back felt wonderfully reassuring and I praised and thanked God for my life.

Why is it we so-called doubters suddenly become believers when we're miraculously snatched from death? At least we're believers for a little while anyway. When we're confronted with some unknown terrifying thing that we think is about to happen to us we call out to God for help. Then when the threat is over we drift back to being doubters again. If I were God, I would feel betrayed and I would consider sending people like me straight to hell. It is written that god is merciful and forgiving. I sure hope so, it may be my only chance.

In Defense of the Four Letter Word

I know some people will take offense when they come across the four letter word, but had we been forbidden to use it we very well may have lost the war, as we would have had no way of communicating. The word was used as a noun, a pronoun, and adjective - you name it. The ship, the captain, the food, the guns, everything was preceded with the four letter word. It was used in times of happiness, despair, fear, anger and even reverence. If we'd have had a chaplain on our ship I would have given odds he would be using the four letter word by the time he got out of the service, and when he was home sitting at the table with friends and family, he would unconsciously say, "Please pass the f&#$ing salt." We could have won the war without the A bomb, but not without the four letter word, so don't despair when you come across such a useful and versatile word being used.

***

Reily was sitting on his bunk, laughing. He had just gotten off watch on the bridge, and proceeded to tell his shipmates what happened. Some aircraft were flying over in the darkness and the captain ordered the radioman to challenge them. The radioman sent out the proper challenge. There was a long silence; the radioman looked like he was in shock.

"Report to the Captain, sailor," The O.D. demanded. "What's the response?"

"F&#$ you, Sir," the frightened radioman answered. The Old Man's eyes bugged out. The O.D. was outraged. "What did you say sailor?" he asked in a low calculated icy voice.

"F&#$ you, Sir," the radioman repeated, "that's what he said, Sir. That was his response, Sir." The Captain left the bridge in a rage. "When we get to San Francisco there's going to be an investigation about this!" he bellowed.

"I don't know why they were so upset," Reily added. "With an answer like that they just had to be good ol' American boys." Reily's skill at telling the event sent a wave of laughter through the crew's quarters that must have been heard clear up to the bridge.

San Francisco to Pearl Harbor

photo by Bruce Broughton

    The noise from the chipping hammers kept diminishing until no one at all was working. We were passing under the Golden Gate Bridge, headed into San Francisco Bay. Everyone was quiet, the beauty of it all was overwhelming.
    "Now hear this, Mail call; Mail call aft." There was a lot of mail waiting for me, some of it five months old. I climbed up into one of the landing craft where I could be alone to read it. There was a lot of news. Alice and Eva had gotten married, my kid sister Velma was in school, little brother Ronnie was having fun with the bow & arrow and the twenty-two rifle I left for him. Dad was working long hours at the defense plant and teaching machine shop at night. Mom was fine, Maggie had a boyfriend (that didn't surprise me any, she was beautiful) and Jim was a Petty Officer on the Destroyer *U.S.S. Litchfield*. I missed each and everyone of them.

Jim's ship, the Litchfield, was one of the old four stack Destroyers of World War I vintage. She was used to train submarine crews the art of hitting ships with torpedoes. The sub crew would practice by firing dummy torpedoes at the Litchfield.

"Sorry sailor, your I.D. card says your only eighteen, I can't serve you a beer. Come back in three years." I was just as well satisfied, I'd rather have a milkshake anyway. Our stay in San Francisco was far too short. Soon we were passing back under the Golden Gate, bound for the South Pacific, heavy with a load of ammunition. We hit places like the Admiralty Islands, Pago Pago and New Caledonia until we had discharged all our cargo. Scuttlebutt had it we were bound for Pearl Harbor. I was excited. Maybe I'll get to see Jim, if the *Litchfield* was in port.

***

"MY GOD." That's the only way I could describe it. We were in Pearl Harbor. Directly across the channel from us sat the monstrous Battleship, the *U.S.S. Wisconsin*. She was brand new. In the slip on our port side was a huge P.A. with several Jap planes painted on her superstructure indicating aircraft her gunners had shot down. In the slip on our starboard side was a large Submarine Tender. A submarine passed by, her diesels throbbing. She had a broom secured to her couning tower, indicating a kill. Right in the middle of all this sat the *Arkab*, sitting light and high like when I first saw her. Her camouflage paint faded, rust streaks running down her hull from her scuppers, and a wide band of rust running from stem to stern. She looked like she had been working too hard and I kind of felt sorry for her.

"Maybe we could paint a chicken on our superstructure," Reily, our new Seaman First Class, sneered.

The captain wanted to know if any of the crew could play a bugle. Someone told him that 'Chief' could play a bugle. Chief was a full blooded Indian from the state of Washington. We all called him Chief, I never knew his real name. The Captain asked Chief if he knew all the Military Bugle Calls.

"Yes sir," Chief replied.

"Good," the Captain said. "Blow Mess Call." Chief approached the PA system and started. The first few notes were okay, then Chief panicked. The most God awful sounds came out of that bugle you ever heard. A little like Mr. Spratt's chicken when I shot it with my BB gun. All of the crew wanted to find a hole to crawl into.

I bet the crew on the Wisconsin was sure impressed with the bugler on the Arkab.

"Hey Mate," I called to a sailor on the dock. "Do you know where the *Litchfield* docks?"

"Yeah, in that empty slip over there," he pointed. "They must be at sea, I haven't seen her in a few days."

It was a hell of a let down for me. After the war, when I told Jim we were in Pearl Harbor on Thanksgiving Day of 1944, he looked surprised.

"Geeze, I was there too. They needed a machinist at the sub base. I was transferred off the *Litchfield*. I was at the sub base I must have seen your ship, but I didn't know it was yours. I could have hit it with a stone."

That's Jim in the foreground with some of his Mates on the stern of the Litchfield, an old four stack destroyer left over from World War I. The round object the one sailor is leaning on is a depth charge or ash can, a high explosive used to destroy enemy submarines.

Christmas Eve in the Crow's Nest

Sometimes a sailor could be all alone in a space 440 feet long by fifty feet wide, with 349 other people crammed in that same space. The crows nest of the *U.S.S. Arkab* was such a place. Up there in the crows nest at night the only company you had was the stars and the constant wind, whipping the flag just above your head, making it snap and crack until in a matter of a few weeks, the stripes were worn down to it's stars.

I had mixed feelings about my lookout station. There were no officers to chew you out if your shirt was unbuttoned. No petty officer to give you orders. But there was also no one to talk to. Sometime you were so damn lonely and homesick you could hardly stand it!

At times an eighteen year old man could lose his composure just a little, up there all alone on a windy starlit night, especially when that sailor hasn't seen his family in over a year. He's ten thousand miles from home, knowing that each turn of the ship's propeller is taking him even farther away. He's all alone with only the wind and the stars for company and it's Christmas Eve. It would be two more Christmases before I would get to spend one at home.

Well I'm getting old now, but it seems like there has been almost no lapse in time between now and Christmas 1944, when I was serving on that ammunition ship in the South Pacific. Like past Christmases, I'll be spending the day with my wife, kids and grandchildren. When the day is over and the house is quiet and I'm dozing in my chair, my mind will wander back to that Christmas Eve in 1944. I'll be back up in the crow's nest of the *Arkab*, all alone with the stars. The wind will be making the flag snap and crack just above my head. After a short while, I'll awake and realize that I'm home, safe and secure and that I'm not scared or lonely anymore. I'll be at peace with myself knowing that back in the 1940's I did a little to help preserve things, like America's way of celebrating days like Christmas. There will be a little pride in my heart, knowing that I and a few million just like me did our part.

Armed Guard - Treasure Island

"Allenger, Broughton, Hoffman..." and several other names were piped over the PA. "Lay to on the boat deck." We were back in San Francisco. Lt. Roland was waiting for us on the boat deck.

"At ease, grab a smoke, if you like. You men are being transferred."

"Can you tell us where, Sir?" asked Shorty, before Lt. Roland could finish.

"Yes, you're going into the Armed Guard. Pack your gear tonight, there will be a truck on the dock in the morning to take you to the Armed Guard Center on Treasure Island."

"Are we being transferred because we're not wanted on the ship, sir?" asked Hoffman.

"Absolutely not. You're being transferred because you're an experienced gun crew. All of you have had training on the type of guns the Merchant ships are armed with. Good luck to all of you."

"There is one officer I'm going to miss." Hoffman remarked. "Me too," everyone else said in unison. Down in the crew's quarters Reily was getting ready to go ashore.

"Why'd you take off your hash marks and campaign bars, Reily? They can't take them away from you," one of the guys said.

"Those hash marks represent sixteen years in the service. I'm only a damn Seaman First Class. You want everyone to think I'm a dumb bastard?" Reily shot back. Reily was still wearing his white hat cocked over his right eye, in that flippant manner of his.

The next morning I said good-bye to all the rest of my shipmates. We wished each other good luck. None of the officers saw us off or told us we had done a good job. No matter, the *Arkab* was out of my life. I felt neither pride nor shame that I had served on her, just a neutral feeling. As I passed by the boat deck Reily was up there with a paint brush in his hand. He was biting his lower lip and an officer was behind him yelling something about painting over a nameplate.

Davey Jones.

When we entered Treasure Island we were greeted by a large nude statue of the sun goddess. This caused loud whistles and many lewd remarks. It eased the tension a little.

Treasure Island is a man made island, built for the San Francisco World Fair. Most of the original buildings were still standing and they were used as mess halls and barracks. One end was a POW camp. The Oakland Bay Bridge connects Treasure Island to San Francisco on one side and to Oakland on the other, which was handy for pulling liberty.

***

There was silent panic in the barracks. Nearly everyone had gotten a dose of the crabs, but no one would admit it. I felt a little cheated as to the way I caught the pesky critters, off a toilet seat. Everyone was going around scratching himself.

"Fall out," the Petty Officer called. "Fall out for Captain's Inspection." The whole base was lined up on the parade grounds in the hot California sun. We had to stand at attention in our heavy Dress Blues. The crabs attacked. they never bit so hard or so often. They must have known there was nothing I could do. They were even biting in my arm pits. The sweat was running down my face. It was a long inspection. When we got back to the barracks, Shorty had had enough. He stood up on a table and bravely confessed, "I've got the crabs and so has all the rest of you bastards. We're going down to Sick Bay and get rid of them."

At Sick Bay the Pharmacist's Mate gave us a tube of blue ointment, the Navy's old stand-by for killing crabs. It worked.

The Day Our Leader Died

In the early spring of nineteen forty-five the *Liberty Ship U.S.S. Arkab* slipped quietly into San Francisco Bay for voyage repairs after over a year of shuttling troops and cargo to faraway places like New Guinea, Saipan and New Caledonia in the South Pacific.

Shortly after our arrival, several of my shipmates and I were transferred off the *Arkab* and into the Armed Guard stationed on Treasure Island in San Francisco Bay. We were granted a seventeen-day leave and told that when we got back we would be assigned to a Merchant Ship as a Navy gun crew.

Most of us lived on the east coast, so we were to have a long train ride home. All the trains were running at full capacity with passenger trains being the lowest priority. We would sit for hours at siding so the troop trains and trains loaded with war goods wouldn't be slowed down and could get their cargo to the coastal cities. The goods were shipped to the war zones after being loaded on the merchant ships whose sailors took great risks with little recognition for their courage and valor. A great many sailed away from their country never to return, especially in the North Atlantic, where they were sitting ducks for the German U-boats.

We were on the trestle spanning the Great Salt Lake in Utah. The train was moving very slowly along the rickety old wooden structure. Most of the passengers were soldiers and many had to stand in the aisles. No one complained, we were going home. There was a lot of good natured kidding and some bottles were passed around. The car was noisy and full of laughter and blue smoke. In those days most everyone smoked.

We had traveled a mile or two out onto the Great Salt Lake when the conductor entered the car.

"Attention Please," he pleaded. The somber look on his face told us he had something important to say.

"I have some sad news for all of you...I just got word, President Roosevelt is.....," his voice cracked. He started again, "The President is dead."

We all sat in stunned disbelief. The only sound in the packed car was the rhythmic clack, clack coming from the wheels of the slowly moving train running over the joints in the rails.

I was eighteen, and the only President I could remember was Roosevelt, now he's gone and this guy Truman is going to take over. I worried. I had seen pictures of Truman, to me he didn't look like he knew enough to pour water out of a boot, but I guess we would just have to wait and see, I thought. Everyone in the packed car must have been thinking along the same lines. For a while it was quiet and still in the packed car but after a spell some started talking in low and soft tones.

It was sad that President Roosevelt never saw the fruits of his labors. He never lived to see the end of World War II.

Somehow it seemed appropriate that the train was moving so slowly across the lake, kind of like showing respect for our lost Commander-in-Chief, who we all loved or at least respected and had taken us so far in our struggle. The whole nation and half the world went into mourning.

The only President I could remember was Roosevelt, now he's gone and this guy, Truman is going to take over.

A Hug and a Kiss

I think the most important thing in my father's life was his family. I'm sure he loved us all, though he never was one to show affection through hugs and kisses. He was standoffish, and I guess I was, too.

The one time I can remember him giving me a hug and kiss was during the war. I had come home on a short leave from the war in the Pacific. I had been overseas for more than a year and had been granted a seventeen-day leave. The leave was much too short. Ten days were used up by traveling back and forth across the country on a train. And now it was time for me to go back to my ship in San Francisco. My father thought it best I say good-bye to my mother at home. I gave my mother a hug and a kiss and told her I loved her. It was a rare thing for me to do, and she started to cry. Then Dad and I left the house and started walking uptown headed for the Erie depot, maybe a mile or so from our house.

At first we walked along the darkening streets mostly in silence, not saying much; "Be sure to write when you can," things like that, the usual stuff. After a bit we both loosened up and started to talk freely.

"When do you think the war will be over, Bobby?" he asked. It made me feel good my father valued my opinion on such an unknown thing. "I have no idea, Dad," I told him.

"The Japs are tough and fanatic. They won't surrender to the Marines, even when there's no chance of them winning a battle, so the Marines just have to kill them all. Maybe we'll have to wipe out the whole race, I don't know Dad. I don't see how they can hold on much longer. Dad, you ought to see the stuff we have to throw at them, you wouldn't believe it."

My remarks seemed to please my father.

"Good." he said. "Maybe we should kill them all, maybe we shouldn't let them surrender even if they want to."

We were halfway to the depot and had lots of time. We stopped part way out on the tired old State Street bridge and leaned on the rail, looking down at the dark water.

"Ya know Bobby, your Uncle Rob, says if you have rattlesnakes in your garden, you have to kill all of them, you can't let any of them get away. If you do they'll be back and sooner or later they'll nail you."

I knew what my father was saying was mostly just talk. Hell, he couldn't kill anything, not even a chicken. My thoughts reflected back to Almond. A neighbor had given him a chicken.

"George," my mother said, "kill that chicken and I'll dress it out. We'll have it for Sunday dinner. Well, Dad couldn't kill that "damn chicken" as he called it. So he talked my brother and I into doing the job. Jim got out the ax and I found a block of wood to lay the chicken's head on. I was to hold the chicken, Jim was to do the dastardly deed of chopping the chicken's head off. When Jim raised the ax, it frightened the chicken. It was flapping it's wings in my face and squawking. I held on gamely until something soft and runny flew in my face, then I let go of the chicken. The chicken scampered across the road just a-clucking. It made a bee line towards Al Palmer's pool hall storeroom. It ran under the crawl space and wedged itself between the floor and the ground. We had lost Dad's chicken.

"Geeze, we lost Dad's chicken dinner," I told Jim.

"He's gonna be mad as hell, you know how much he likes chicken."

"It's your fault, you let it go" Jim yelled at me.

You scared it!" I yelled back.

When we told Dad, he summed up his feeling with just one drawn out word - ssshit.

Now we were walking up Pearl Street and almost to the station. We turned silent. We entered the depot and found a seat on the oak benches built like church pews with arms on them. The arms were there mostly to keep bums and undesirables from sleeping on them. The depot was crowded with young men and their families. The young men were dressed in khaki, olive green or navy blue as I was. All of us were wearing hats, ties, or kerchiefs. We were clean shaven, our hair short and our shoes shining. Many of us proudly wore colorful ribbons on our chest, some with tiny bronze stars fastened to them, a few of the ribbons were purple. We young men sat there with people we loved waiting for the train, waiting for the Erie to take us back to the ships, the tanks, the airplanes and fox holes. Most of us would be lucky and someday the Erie would bring us back home, changed but triumphant and hopeful. Some would come back home with parts of their bodies missing and they won't be as hopeful as the others. And the Erie will bring some home silent and broken, lying in flag-draped boxes. They wouldn't be called soldiers, sailors or Marines anymore, they'll be referred to as "remains". Still, the mothers, fathers, and wives will want the Erie to bring them back to Wellsville.

Then over the murmur of the people talking softly the wail of the west-bound train drifted ever so faintly through the station. Most didn't hear it. The old gent sitting next to my father, who I thought was asleep, tugged at a gold chain dangling from his vest pocket. A big shiny railroad watch popped out.

"She's a passin' Elm Valley, she's a runnin' late," he said talking to no one in particular. A few moments passed and the whistle blew for the Proctor District crossing. That time everyone heard the whistle and a hush fell over the station.

A young mother holding her sleeping baby started to cry softly. Her husband, dressed in an Army uniform put his arm around her. She looked at his face and tried to smile. My father and I just sat there watching the people. I watched with envy as a marine about my age kissed a pretty girl wearing brown and white saddle shoes and ankle socks. I was told those girls were called bobbysoxers. I wished I had a girl I could kiss good-bye. The train's whistle blew even louder for the State Street crossing and the station started to tremble. Now the station buzzed with noise and the people were scurrying about. The train passed Fassett Street moving slowly, her bell clanging loudly. It coasted to a smooth stop at the station. The conductor climbed down from the train and carefully placed his boarding steps on the platform. The passengers came pouring out. They were anxious and in a hurry. They were mostly young warriors coming home for a little while. Most hadn't been home for months, some for years. They let out joyful shouts when they spotted a loved one, anxiously waiting at the back of the platform. They ran up to them and hugged and kissed them. Some were picked up and spun around like rag dolls, others had unabashed tears running down their faces. Then they quickly melted away and the platform was void of people for a short while, with only the sounds of hissing steam and the heavy panting of the big steam engine sounding as if it were a live thing, catching it's breath until the next hard run would start.

Inside the station the young men shouldered their bags and embraced their loved ones with their free arms as they walked to the platform, hanging on as long as they could. They smiled and acted brave, but their emotions were running amuck and silent tears escaped from their eyes and wet their brave smiles.

"All 'board," the conductor called. I reached for my bag and started to say good-bye to my father.

"Bobby, I'm going to kiss you good-bye," he blurted out. His voice tense, he said it as if he wanted me to be prepared for what he was about to do. And I wasn't prepared. He gave me a quick peck on the cheek, hugged me and patted my back a couple of times. My feeble response was, "I gotta go, Dad."

I turned and hurried for the train. I was lucky and found a seat by a window. I wanted to have one last look at my father. I saw the loved ones standing on the platform silent and sad, some still waving good-bye. My father wasn't among them. I wanted to go back in time a few moments. I wanted to go back and say good-bye to my father the way a son should say good-bye to a good father, with a hug and kiss and and "I love you Dad."

"Jesus Christ," I said out loud. I felt like crying. The conductor signaled the engineer, swinging his lantern in a wide arc. The engineer answered with a blast of the whistle. He eased ahead on the throttle and the slack in the couplings was taken up causing the cars to jerk a couple of times. The engineers hand was light on the throttle. The power of the steam was hard to control. The big driving wheels slipped and raced a little. Then the train started picking up speed in rapid powerful surges.

The conductor walked through the swaying cars staggering a little like a man who had a bit too much to drink.

"Olean, Olean, next stop, Olean, twenty-five minutes," he called out. I thought about my father walking down the partially blacked out streets alone with his thoughts. He'll be okay when he gets home. Mom will have a beer and a cheese sandwich waiting for him, or something else he likes. She knows what to do when he gets feeling down. The whistle blew for the crossing between Scio and Belmont. Dad must be home by now. I felt a little better.

***

The Erie's powerful west-bound engine number seven wasn't just a huffin' and a puffin' along them rails anymore. She was a highballin' down them rails just a smokin' and a steamin'. Her fireman pourin' the coal right to her, the engineer leanin' out that open cab window looking down the rails, his hand heavy on the throttle. He's runnin' three minutes late. He's got some time to make up. He laid on that whistle at the crossings and scolded the people who stopped their cars too close to the rails.

"Back off, keep out of the way, don't ya know there's a war going on," he yelled at the people as his big locomotive thundered past the crossing. The people couldn't hear what he was a yellin', they just smiled and waved.

That's about the way that old retired brakeman with the big shiny, railroad watch in his vest pocket would have told it if you had asked him. He probably would have told you even if you hadn't asked him, given the opportunity.

The Erie train number seven was highballin' me west and she wasn't about to bring me back home to Wellsville for at least another year, you coulda bet on that. From Wellsville to San Francisco, I witnessed the same drama at every train station along the way. There was great joy and deep sadness all happening at the same time in those stations. It must have happened in just about every railroad station in America. The drama took place night and day seven days a week until the great war ended.

The Erie Depot, Wellsville, New York

My leave was over. I was back in San Francisco after five days on the trains.

138

"Would you like to come up to my house and have a drink or something? I couldn't believe what I was hearing. Shorty and I had practically given up trying to pick up some girls. We were in golden Gate park, bored and about ready to go back to the base a day early, when this pretty woman and her mother came up to us and asked us up to their house. Shorty was about ten years my senior, so he started talking to the mother, who must have been twenty years older than Shorty. No matter to shorty. Sandy, the daughter, must have been in her early thirties.

Shorty bought a bottle and I bought some barbecue and we headed for Sandy's house. Sandy paid the babysitter to take the kids, she had two boys, about three and four years old. I was admiring a model of a submarine on a shelf.

"It belongs to my husband. He's out in the Pacific on a submarine," Sandy confessed.

We each had a barbecue, then we had a couple of drinks. They went down hard for me, even with the Coke chaser. It was only the second time I ever drank whiskey.

"What's the matter Bob? You don't talk much; don't you like me?"

"Yeah, I like you. I like you a lot, Sandy, it's just I haven't had any experience with women, just a few girls is all."

"Don't worry," Sandy said with a little laugh.

It wasn't right, but it was a long war. Everyone was lonely, and tired of the war and we were getting to the point where we thought it would never end. After a couple more weekends at Sandy's house, Shorty decided we had better not go there anymore.

"We're pushing our luck," Shorty said. I reluctantly agreed with him.

I was outside the barracks on Treasure Island washing my clothes when whistles started blowing, car horns started honking, bells ringing, anything and everything that could make a noise was doing so. No one had to tell me what had happened, the war was over! I put on my dress blues and headed for San Francisco.

Market Street was a sea of people. Sailors were grabbing the girls and kissing them. They didn't fight back. Someone took my white hat. A girl came up to me and gave me a hug. then she pulled off my kerchief and ran off with it. Who cares? The war is over!

Harry

Well, Harry got us through the war in the Pacific, and he did it in damn short order, but it was done with one of history's most precise and brutal acts. I'm glad he had to make the decision to drop the atomic bombs on Hiroshima and Nagasaki and not me. I never really could make up my mind if dropping those bombs was the right thing to do. Killing all these people bothered me, especially killing little children.

If it were the other way around and the Japanese had the bomb they wouldn't have hesitated to drop it on our cities. The attack on Pearl Harbor and their fanatical resistance proved that. I know if the bombs had not been dropped I would have been in the invasion of the Japanese homeland as part of an Armed Guard gun crew on a merchant ship. Not having to invade Japan probably did save many thousands, if not millions of lives, both Japanese and American. Given that scenario, I guess it was the right thing to do. Maybe dropping the bomb even saved my life. Who knows?

I wonder how old Harry would have felt, if he would have had a ring side seat to the bombings and saw with his own eyes the horror of it all.

Apparently, making these horrendous decisions didn't bother old Harry too much. He ran for and won a second term and decided to stop the Communists in Korea. He called it a police action, but in reality, it was one damn nasty war that killed some fifty thousand American kids and two million other people. The war ended up in a draw and proved nothing. It was never declared officially started or ended, only a truce was called.

I hated that war and hated Harry for getting America in it. Many a night I had bad dreams of being back in the Navy and going to Korea. They call the Korean War the "forgotten war" and it's true. Most people except the one's who were in it have forgotten it.

This memorial rests in front of the Wellsville American Legion. While in high school, young Calvin's greatest desire was to join the Army. He wrote an essay about why he wanted to join the Army and he received an A-plus on it. Young Calvin had two brothers, George and Bill, both now residing in Wellsville. Bill told me his brother had premonitions, he pretty much knew he wasn't coming back from Korea. You could tell when you read his letters.

I also had a friend I went to high school with who was reported missing in action and to this day nothing has been heard of my friend, Billy Saddlewasser.

Welcome Home ?

"The war is over! In a few weeks I'll be home," I thought. How wrong I was. I didn't get my discharge until almost nine months later. The great masterminds decided it would be a bad thing if all of us got home too quickly. What their reasoning was, I don't know. They came out with a point system, the older you were the more points you got. You received points if you had a wife, more if you had dependents and points for the length of service you had. The more points you had, the sooner you were let out. A nineteen year old with no wife or kids and two years of service didn't get a hell of a lot of points.

The last nine months were wasted time. We were at Camp Shoemaker, California. The base did have good recreational facilities. There was a pool, a bowling alley and a movie house. Some of the ship's company had their wives near the base. They were allowed to take their wives to the movie theater. After the show they would announce, "Enlisted men and their wives remain seated until officers and their ladies clear the building." Must be the enlisted men's wives weren't considered ladies.

R. V. Broughton ex-seaman first class was back in Wellsville. No one was patting him on the back or paying for his beer or coffee anymore. No one wanted to hire him. He didn't have a high school education. Without a high school education he wasn't able to sweep floors in a factory or clean the johns. I finally got a job in the oil fields digging ditch for eighty-five cents an hour. After a few weeks of digging ditch, I asked the straw boss, "How long do I have to dig ditch before I get a better job, like pulling wells or something?"

"Stick with 'er sonny, in three or four years we'll get you something better." When I got my pay that afternoon I knew I wouldn't be back.

When I was going to school I had a job in a grocery store, working in the produce department. I asked my old boss, Tom, if he had anything for me. He said yes, but the pay wasn't much, eighteen dollars for a forty-hour week. Back in the forties, a law was enacted requiring employers to give returning vets their job back that they held before they went into the service. Tom must have thought I would use the law to force him to hire me back. After I went in the Navy, he had hired a replacement to fill my job managing the produce department in the store.

The new lad, Larry, was a son of one of his good friends. Tom never told me how he felt. If I had known, I never would have asked for my old job back. I was hired and they kept Larry on also. No one spoke to me much. the girls at the registers would yell, "Carry out, Bob," never asking Larry to help carry out groceries.

Tom would ask Larry to make out the produce orders which used to be my job. "Sweep the floor or go clean the cellar," he would tell me while Larry made out the produce orders. Fred and Jim who worked in the meat department never spoke to me either unless it was something nasty or sarcastic.

"The produce truck is here Bob, you go out and unload, Larry, you wait on the customers."

When it came time for coffee break, Tom would ask Larry to go back to the meat department, and they would have a nice long coffee break together, leaving me to wait on the customers and have my coffee break on the fly.

I didn't understand. Before I went in the Navy and I was working in the store, we were all good friends and got along very well. It finally dawned on me, Bob Broughton just wasn't welcome in the old grocery store anymore. "The hell with them, I'll stick it out until I can find another job," I told myself. I didn't complain and I did my work. I would always try and keep one jump ahead of them. I would shovel the snow off the walk as soon as the store was open, before Tom could tell me to. I kept the produce rack neat and full. I would watch the girls at the registers and grab the carry-outs before they could yell for me. I never gave anyone much chance to give me any orders. I think this kind of irritated them all a little.

Well, they're all gone now. Tom was replaced as manager, when the owners built a new store. Shortly after that he died from diabetes. Fred, the meat department manager, died from a heart attack at not too old an age. Jim, the meat cutter, was killed in an auto wreck. The head cashier also died from a heart attack, and Larry - well I never knew what happened to him. Old Bob, the ex-produce man is still going strong for his age. Funny, I never did find time to go to any of their funerals.

None of them ever served in the Armed Forces. Maybe my being the only one working in the store who did, gave them a guilty feeling or something. My presence was annoying to them somehow. I don't know for sure what the deal was, but before I went into the service I know they liked me and we were all good friends, except Larry who didn't work there then. All I know was my feelings were hurt pretty bad at the time. The fact that none of them were in the service made no difference to me. The war was over and we had won it, that was all that mattered. To this day I never made a big deal out of being in the service, hell, I came out unscathed. I never felt my country owed me much, all I wanted was to have a job and be able to take care of myself. Besides I figured that everyone back home was doing their part anyway. It wasn't easy for them either, what with government mandated rationing on meat, butter, sugar, tires and gasoline to name just a few things they did without.

The government would give you books of stamps, and each stamp would allow you to buy a designated amount of rationed product. You couldn't buy tires for your car period. There was some grumbling about the rationing, but most didn't complain. The people on the home front were almost fanatic in their patriotism. They did a lot more than just wave the flag. They worked seven days a week in the defense plants which ran twenty-four hours a day. They invented car pools and used their cars very little for pleasure.

Iron fences in front of their homes were torn down and people scrounged for scrap metal to help the war effort. Kids in school spent their money on war stamps. Before the war, women mostly stayed home. Now they were running huge lathes and milling machines, they were welding and learning to fly airplanes, doing all the jobs that they weren't supposed to be able to do, and doing as good a job as any man.

I doubt America will ever again be so united as we were then, and their perseverance prevailed. They did it all with style and class and they hung tough, even when the dreaded knock came at the door and a telegram was handed to them. They didn't have to open it, they already knew what the message was. A half-million of them sadly hung gold stars in their windows, then went back to work in the defense plants even more resolved to make machines and munitions to kill the hated Germans, Japanese, and Italians. In the war years, the American people were magnificent, they were at their zenith. Unpatriotic people were few and far between, and there wasn't enough of them to do much harm to America. I think my mother and father's generation of Americans were the greatest of all the generations of Americans.

In their lifetime it must have felt to them that God went away on vacation and left Satan to mind the store. But they stood up to every horrendous challenge that was thrown at them. They fought and died in World War I, the first war to end all wars and they struggled through and beat the most brutal and cruel depression over. Then a mad man named Hitler came along and teamed up with two other evil bastards, Tojo and Mussolini, and they had to do it all over again. They showed kindness and compassion to their defeated enemies and helped rebuild their bombed out countries. Even when they started dying off in the sixties and seventies they were still standing tall against the communists who were ruling half the world and wanted to rule the other half. They did beat them by standing firm and insisting America stay strong. I think my generation who are now starting to die off pretty fast did a good job too, but maybe not as good as our predecessors did.

When I came home from the Navy, the first thing I wanted was a car. Cars were scarce and a good one was hard to find. The first car I bought was a nineteen-thirty-six Pontiac. Glen, the guy who sold me the car, assured me it was a darn good car. We drove it around the block and it seemed to run fine. Glen told me he wanted two hundred dollars for the car. I had set aside most of my mustering out pay to buy a car. Glen said he had to have cash and wanted it up front. Well, the dumbest kid in the third grade was ten years older, but hadn't gotten much smarter. I gave Glen the two hundred and Glen gave me a receipt paid in full for one nineteen thirty-six Pontiac, four door sadan. Glen said he wanted to "do a few things" on the car and would deliver it the next day. Sure enough Glen delivered the car as promised, he was a man of his word.

I drove Glen home and dropped him off at his house. I was nearly back home when all hell broke loose. The car started to lose power, then a cloud of steam and water started shooting out from under the hood. I got the car home, let it cool down and filled it with water. The car started and ran fine for a while, then the same thing started all over again.

I called Glen and told him what happened. He said he did not know what was wrong with the car, and I must have "done something to it." I told him I wanted my money back, but he said, "a deal is a deal," and he wouldn't give me my money back.

I had a friend who knew all about cars, his name was Howard Bergerson. Howard found the trouble, the car had a cracked block. The engine was worthless. Howard and I found another motor for the car in a junk yard. After a lot of trial and error, Howard got the car running, but that motor wasn't much good either. The car never did run very well.

Some good came out of it all, however. Howard learned a lot about cars while working on my nineteen-thirty-six Pontiac and in later years became one of the best mechanics in Wellsville. In fact Howard made a good living fixing cars and had his own garage.

I went to work at the worthington and was able to get a better car. A neat little forty-one Mercury coupe. It was a good car and I enjoyed it a lot, maybe too much at times, especially with the motor shut off, the radio playing some Glen Miller songs and the car parked in some secluded place.

I was on my knees sorting apples, when this beautiful set of legs walked by me at eye level. They belonged to a girl, named Ester. Ester had gotten a part-time job in the store. She was a sexy, attractive girl with a nice little figure. About the third day she was at the store, I asked if she wanted to go down to Cretekos's ice cream parlor and have a sandwich and coke after work. She said, "Sure." We hit it off very well at first, but she drove me up a wall. She would go out with other guys, but I always would want her back.

I don't think Ester liked me very much, but I was handy until she could find someone more to her liking. Falling in love with Ester was not as intense a feeling as it was with Janie, but I was pretty well hooked, and I thought a lot of her. Almost from the start I knew I couldn't keep her. I would tell myself, I'm not going to see her anymore, but I just couldn't do it. I knew she was going to hurt me, but it wasn't her fault. I don't see how she put with my sulky moods, and I was constantly jealous. I would find out she was dating other guys and I wanted her for myself. I didn't want her going out with other guys, which wasn't fair to her as she was only sixteen. She was smart and ambitious, she knew what she wanted and went for it. Me, I didn't know what I wanted out of life, hell, I didn't even know who I was really.

One thing I found out back then, in nineteen-forty-nine, you can't lose something you never had, but I sure was one lonesome and unhappy man when Ester left Wellsville and went to Buffalo to be a nurse and found a new guy more to her liking. I bet she made a real good nurse. I carried a torch for her for a very long time.

"Bob, I think I can get you a job at the plant," Dad said. "they need someone in the stock room, I told them you worked in a store and you would fit right in working in the stock room."

They hired me the next week. The job paid over a dollar an hour. I was able to buy a nice little forty-one Mercury. I left home and got a sleeping room for five bucks a week. I had a lot of girl friends, but I would have swapped them all for Ester.

I worked at the plant for awhile then took on a part-time job in the diner, where I made life-long friends. Woody Davis, the man who owned the diner and the manager, Don Marsh, became my best friends. I also met some other great people who worked at the Diner, Jeff Thompson and Neil Mott.

Don, Jeff, Neil and I worked nights in the diner, and we raised a lot of hell. People would come in every night just to watch the antics. I would walk up to a table scratching my rear with one hand and pretending to pick my nose with the other. "What'll ya have?" I would ask with a flick of my finger.

Don would drop a hamburger on the floor. "Good thing that paper was there," he would say, as he slapped the burger on a bun and served it. By inserting his thumbs and eight fingers deep into the glasses of water, Neil could serve up ten glasses at one time, taking care of two tables in one trip!

Jeff was always spilling things, then he would ask, "Did ya get any on ya?" The customers loved it and business was good.

One night while working in the diner, a friend of mine by the name of Billy Saddlewasser, came in with a nice looking blond girl.

"I want you to meet my girl, Bob. Her name is Myrtle"

"What a name for a girl as nice looking as her," I thought. Business was slow so I sat down in the booth with them and we talked over a cup of coffee. Billy was home on leave, he told me he was going to Korea. Well, young Billy did go to Korea, and a short while after he got there, he came up missing in action. To this day nothing has ever been heard of him.

A few weeks after Billy came up missing, Myrtle came in the diner. I served her coffee and we talked about Billy for a little while. Myrtle asked me if we could do something after I got out of work.

"It's after one now, I told her. The bars are closed, we can't get a drink or anything. Besides I don't get out of work until four in the morning." I started getting a little desperate, I wanted to take her out.

"How about I sneak out of here and we go up the river for a swim. Can you swim, Myrtle?" I asked.

"Sure," she said, "but I don't have a swim suit."

"That's okay, Myrtle, don't worry about it. I don't have one either," I lied. "We can swim under the bridge at York's corners, it'll be dark and no one will see us. If a car comes, we'll be under the bridge out of sight."

When we got to the bridge, we climbed down the bank and walked out on the concrete base at the bottom of the bridge. The air was cool and fog was rising off the river. We turned our backs to each other, undressed and dove in. The water was nice and warm. After a lot of giggling, laughing and fooling around in the water, I got out and ran up to the car and got a blanket. I spread the blanket on the concrete. The air was cool, but the concrete had retained some of the day's hot August heat. Myrtle pulled herself up on the ledge and laid down beside me on the warm blanket.

And poor Billy was in far-off Korea, missing in action, either killed or captured by his enemies. For the moment we gave Billy no thought, we had buried him in our sub-conscious for now. The guilt would come later.

Can you swim, Myrtle?"

Last Hunt

    I needed something to take my mind off losing Ester. "Maybe I should take up hunting," I thought. I loved the outdoors and hunting sounded like something I would like to do. It was deer season, so I bought a deer hunting license, a new twenty gauge shotgun, a box of deer slugs, a pair of boots and headed for the great outdoors.

    The first few days, I tramped for miles and never saw one damn deer, but I enjoyed walking around the hills and woods, and there was always a chance I would shoot me a "big buck" with a "huge rack," and when I did I'll have him mounted, I thought.

    There were only a couple days of deer season left. Maybe if the deer won't let me come to them, I should fool them and let them come to me. I chose a spot halfway up a hill under a large pine tree. The spot overlooked a long narrow field with a little half frozen stream running through it. I leaned up against the tree and waited.

    Bang, Bang, Bang. My heart started beating fast, someone has flushed some deer. Maybe one will come this way, I reasoned. Sure enough, a nice big buck was running my way. I raised my shotgun - too far away. He's coming this way, I'll let him get closer. Suddenly the big buck fell down but quickly got back up, leaving a spot of red in the snow where he had fallen. I could see it all from where I was standing under the tree. The hunter was tracking the deer. The deer ran a little farther and fell once again. Each time he got up and ran, the distance was shorter. The last time he got up he just took a few staggering steps and when he fell he was only a few yards from where I was standing. He couldn't get back up again. He was pawing at the snow with his front legs trying to keep going. He kept turning his head looking back. He knew his tormentor was coming. When the hunter reached the deer, the buck followed his every move with his head. The deer was looking wild eyed at the hunter and making a little bleating noise, not unlike what a sheep would make. I wondered if the bleating was caused by the pain of the wound, or his great fear of the hunter, or maybe both, I thought.

    One thing I did know. I never saw such a valiant act as what that big buck had done trying to save himself. Even up to the very end, he used every fiber within him to save his life, even when he was down and couldn't get back up, he tried to lurch his body forward, away from the hunter. The hunter took aim, fired one last shot, the deer stiffened, then lay still. Without hesitation, almost in one motion, the hunter unsheathed his knife, thrust the blade into the side of the deer's neck and worked the blade across the deer's throat. As if planned to enhance the drama, and on some mysterious cue, the sun broke out from behind the clouds, causing the snow to become a blinding white. Like magic the snow around the deer's neck turned brilliant red, to me it seemed the reddest red I ever saw.

I was shocked by it all. I noticed my hands were shaking when I lit a cigarette. "It's only a damn deer," I told myself, "why the hell can't I be more of a man?" I felt less a man for getting so worked up. "It's only a damn deer," I kept telling myself. I don't know, maybe if I'd been the one who had shot the deer, it might not have been so upsetting for me. Maybe, the excitement of the hunt would have overcome my compassion for the big buck, but to have such a graphic view of the whole incident was very upsetting for me.

I started walking back to the road where I had parked my car. On the way, I saw three deer in the distance, they were standing there like three statues, looking at me.

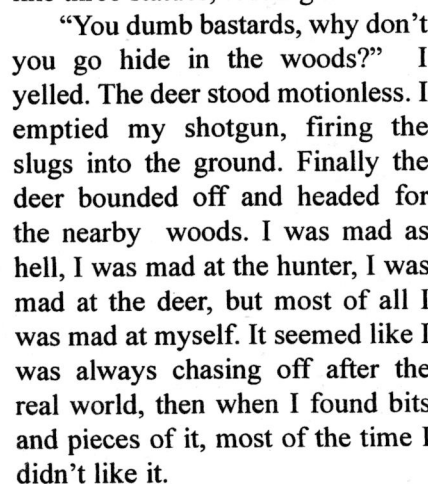

"You dumb bastards, why don't you go hide in the woods?" I yelled. The deer stood motionless. I emptied my shotgun, firing the slugs into the ground. Finally the deer bounded off and headed for the nearby woods. I was mad as hell, I was mad at the hunter, I was mad at the deer, but most of all I was mad at myself. It seemed like I was always chasing off after the real world, then when I found bits and pieces of it, most of the time I didn't like it.

I drove back to town and stopped at the diner for a hot cup of coffee. Woody was working.

"Did you get your deer, Bob?" my friend asked as he served me coffee.

"Naw, Woody, there ain't no deer out there. How about one of those good looking doughnuts," I asked, quickly changing the subject. I never went deer hunting again.

Religion

When it comes to religion, I don't know what to think. I'm not sure if there is a heaven or a hell. I do know there's a lot of people a lot smarter than I am that think there is. My friend, Don, said there was. I noticed that when Don was dying he took a lot of comfort and solace in religion and his pastor, in his last days.

I sometimes wish I had a strong belief in something that would help me get through bad times, like when my little Grandson died while undergoing heart surgery. Without strong religion there was no one or anything to ease the hurt, even my family couldn't help.

I've noticed that people who have religion seem to get through the sad times better than people like myself, who don't know what to believe. I think people who have religion are fortunate, indeed. If there is a heaven it sure would be preferable to going to hell.

If the scenario is reincarnation and you have to come back after death as either an animal, vegetable, or mineral, I think I would like to come back as a mineral. I'd like to come back as a stone, but with my luck if there is reincarnation I'd probably come back as a frog. One cool August night I'd be skinny dipping thinking I was all alone in a place like York's Corners bridge, and I'd look up and there would be a pretty girl frog sitting on top of a rock protruding from the water.

She must have been skinny dipping too 'cause like me she's all nice and naked. She's sitting there on the rock shrouded in the light of a moon beam that's shining through an opening in the golden rod growing on the nearby bank, her spots highlighted by the moon light, her beautiful green skin shining in the night. Oh, I am attracted to her, she's absolutely irresistible. I climb up on the rock and position myself next to this gorgeous creature.

We frogs waste no time when it comes to making love. I'm about to demonstrate my macho froghood, about to start the most exciting experience of my young froghood. Our naked bodies touch and the desire and lust flows through my whole body causing me to tremble from my bulging eyeballs down through my muscular frog legs to the very soles of my web feet.

Alas and alack, just as I'm about to couple with this gorgeous jade goddess, a large snake slithers up behind me, grabs me in his huge open mouth and eats me alive.

Then the reincarnation cycle has to start all over again.

A Bad Fire

"How would you like to join the Fire Department?" my friend Jeff asked me. "We need two new guys. You had fire fighting training when you were in the Navy. I bet the members would like to have you."

"It sounds like something I'd like Jeff, I'll give it a try if the members will accept me." On Jeff's recommendation I was accepted in his hose Co., the McEwens.

The Fire Department was a good outlet for some of my frustrations. I spent a lot of time in the old fire station and made a lot of new friends, and I found myself wishing the fire siren on the top of the old three-story building on Main Street would go off. I liked the excitement of hearing the siren go off telling us there was a fire someplace. When the siren sounded I would drop whatever I was doing and take off on a dead run for the fire station. My sleeping room was only a block away from the fire station and most of the time I was the first firemen to arrive at the station and therefore rode the fire truck to the fire instead of driving my car.

We would take off in the old open truck, siren screaming, and bell clanking. Most times it wasn't much of a fire, none the less it was very exciting and made the adrenaline flow.

Then early one cold winter morning about daybreak, the siren sounded. This time it was going to be different. When I got to the fire station, only Bob Prescott, our Captain and Jeff were there. We took off anyway, knowing the rest of the firemen would drive their cars to the fire.

The fire was at the top of Madison Hill, a very long and steep hill that went through and past the village. The old truck was slow and under-powered. Prescott kept going through the gears getting the most he could out of the old truck. Jeff and I were hanging on the back, ducking down to keep out of the bitter cold wind. The old truck took too long getting us to the fire. When we got there the house was entirely enveloped in flames. The fire was feeding off a strong north wind. We knew the house was beyond saving, none the less, we hooked our hoses up to a nearby oil field pump station hydrant and put out the fire. Very little was left of the house.

Whenever a house completely burned down, we had a crude pun, "we saved the cellar." But this time it was no joke. A young girl and her baby had burned up in the fire. Mr. Hadley, the girl's father, tried to get them out.

"I just couldn't get them out," he kept repeating. After awhile he slowly walked to the back of the old Buffalo truck, sat down and cupped his face with his blackened hands and wept. Escaping the fire and not being able to get his daughter and grandchild out must have caused horrendous guilt, compounding his grief and misery.

When we found Mr. Hadley's daughter and grandchild, they were huddled in a little ball not three feet from where an outside door use to be. Their bodies were charred black and still smoldering.

"Jeff, you and Bob wet them down with the booster hose, use a fine spray." Prescott ordered.

"Could you do it Jeff?" I kind of pleaded. "I'll borrow someone's car and go down to the diner and get some hot coffee for the guys." After that, it wasn't a game anymore. The fire department was serious stuff. Once more I found a fragment of the real world out there, and once more I didn't like it.

"I just couldn't get them out," he kept repeating.

"Lay five shots of two and half and break it!" Prescott yelled. We had a working fire on Main Street in a old three story building over a drug store. Jeff and I put two turns of fire hose around the hydrant and Prescott took off in the Buffalo truck. Like a long snake uncoiling, the hose slithered off the back of the old truck picture perfect. Jeff disconnected and yelled for me to hook up, while he ran back to the truck to get a nozzle for his end.

"Something's wrong!" I yelled to Jeff. "I can't get hooked up." Just about then our assistant Captain, Ray Smeltzer arrived.

"You dumb shit," he yelled at me. "Ya got the wrong God damn end. Run up and drag the other end back and take this end with you." By this time a large group of people had gathered to watch the excitement.

Jeff and I were highly embarrassed and knew we would hear about our blunder for the rest of our lives. A few days before that we had a fire drill down in the park. We tested all the two and a half inch hoses for leaks. After the test Jeff and I loaded the hose back on the truck. We were very careful, laying the hose back and forth in an accordion shape, so it would pay out smoothly and not tangle when needed. This was all well and good, but we had loaded the hose on backwards.

I understand now they use adapters at the hydrant and have eliminated the chance of making this mistake. After we finally got the hose hooked up to the hydrant and the nozzle connected, Prescott, Ray, Jeff and myself hauled the hose up to the third floor where the fire was.

"Charge the hose." Prescott yelled down.
The hose became a live thing, about all Jeff and I could handle as the pressure at the main street hydrants in Wellsville was very high. Prescott ran through the hallways, opening doors and kicking in the ones that were locked yelling "Fire in the building, everyone out."

"I think most of the fire is on this side," Ray yelled.
A lot of smoke was coming out from under the doors, one in particular.

"Kick it in, Ray" Prescott ordered, "and stand back as soon as you do, it's hot."

Ray was a big man about fifty years old, tall and strong and a very enthusiastic fireman. About the third kick the old door flew off its hinges. Smoke and heat came belching out. It was like kicking in the door to hell itself. The heat was unbearable, Ray got his lungs full of smoke and heat. He staggered down the hall over to the outside window, broke it out and stuck his head out to get some air. Jeff and I played the hose in the fire, Prescott telling us where to aim it.

Prescott saw that the smoke was getting to me. He wet his handkerchief and held it over my mouth and nose for a few seconds. It did the job. Prescott told me to keep as low as I could.

"If it gets to you too much go back and send someone else up. If you do, be sure to follow the hose back." he ordered. It would have been easy to get lost in all the smoke. I stuck it out.

"What the hell is the matter with Ray" Jeff asked. Ray was yelling and screaming out the broken window.

"He got sick and heaved his false teeth out the window. He's yelling at the people below not to step on them" Prescott chuckled.

The Emerald Hook and Ladder was having a little problem. Their ladder was jammed and they couldn't extend it to the top of the roof. But not to despair, Homer the village drunk, was staggering around yelling orders as to how to get the ladder unstuck. One big Irishman had had enough. He grabbed Homer by the back of his collar and the seat of his pants and ushered Homer off. At times little Homer's feet cleared the ground by six inches.

The Wellsville Emerald Hook and Ladder Co., was made up of mostly Irish Lads, who knew their jobs and had a fierce pride in their company. Their white, green, and gold truck was the envy of every volunteer fire department for miles around. Their beautiful truck was a standout in the parades and even strutted her stuff in the St. Patrick's day parades in New York City and Buffalo. It must have been very humiliating for them when their ladder jammed in front of all those people.

Yeah, we had some snafus at that fire, but all and all we were pretty pleased with the job we did. The fire had gotten a good start in a tinder dry building. If it had gotten away from us half of the town could have burned down.

I should mention that Wellsville also had three other companies, The Genesee, The Dukes and The Dyke Street Companies, all as good as the McEwens and Emeralds. Having five companies all striving to outdo each other, makes for a very sharp department and Wellsville's fire department stacked up to any around.

***

Whenever Ray drove the old Buffalo truck to a fire, and I happened to be on the truck with him, I wished to hell I would have driven my car to the fire. Ray would take off full bore out of the fire hall, and head down Main Street full gate, weaving in and out of traffic, like A.J. Foyt at the Indianapolis five-hundred. Ray drove like a man possessed, never letting up on the gas, even when he approached the traffic lights and intersections.

Once, while getting close enough to see the smoke and flames coming from a large barn fire, Ray got so excited while driving the old Buffalo truck that he kept letting go of the wheel. He would raise his arms up in the air and rub the palms off his hands together, while looking down at the floor boards of the old truck.

"Look at 'er burn," he howled in glee. Once Prescott laced him out telling him he had to calm down while driving the truck or he was going to kill someone. It must have hurt Ray's feelings, as I never saw Ray drive the truck very much after that

Ironically, on April Fools Day, nineteen fifty-four, the old city hall that housed the village jail and the McEwen, Genesee and the Emeralds fire companies burned to the ground.

The fire was believed have been started by a drunk housed in the jail. The fire companies managed to get all their trucks out and fought the fire that was consuming their own station. They were unable to save the building, but did a good job containing the fire, thus little damage was done to the surrounding buildings.

I was out of town when the old city hall burned down, and was kind of glad I was. When I was an active member I practically lived in the old building. I slept many a night on the couch in the McEwen hose room. I would have felt bad to see the old building burn down, the fire station was like a second home for me.

I was dropped as an active member when I left Wellsville and took a job working on the lake freighters out of Buffalo. I don't think I would want to be a volunteer fireman in this day and age even if I was young and healthy. It seems everybody and their brother wants to run the fire department. Years ago we knew how to run a fire company safely and efficiently without any "help". Older guys like Bob Prescott, Ray Smeltzer, and other experienced firemen taught us younger guys. We learned from their experience and it was an ongoing process. All the years I was in the fire department,

I can't think of any serious injuriues other than smoke sickness and some minor cuts and bruises. We never had a major fire get away from us due to lack of skill or knowledge as to how to fight it. Sometimes when we got an alarm too late, we would lose a house or building because the fire got too much of a head start before we arrived.

Most of us were in the fire department because we figured we were just doing a good thing for Wellsville and because we liked the excitement. We liked riding on the back of an old fire truck, we liked a little danger and risk. Today, some people think they can create absolutely safe fire departments with mountains of rules and regulations. Would anyone still want to be in a volunteeer fire department if fire fighting was absolutely safe?

Wellsville's fire departments stacked up to any around.

Ironically on April Fools Day, nineteen fifty-four, the old city hall that housed the village jail and the McEwen, Genesee and the Emeralds fire companies burned to the ground.

Maria

One night I stopped at the Drug Store on Main Street, for a cup of coffee. I sat down at the counter. Maria, the waitress came over and took my order. After she brought my coffee, she asked, "Bob, would you take me home after work? I don't have a car."

"Sure," I told her. I only had a speaking acquaintance with Maria. I had never dated her or anything.

"All the lights are out, Bob, my folks are in bed. We can sit in the car for awhile, if you want to," she said after we got to her house. Well, she was a hot blooded sexy, little Italian girl and I was a healthy, easily aroused young man. It was a warm summer night, and we were all alone in my neat little forty-one mercury coupe. Why not?

"I'm pregnant, and you did it," Maria yelled at me.

It was a few weeks after my one night stand with Maria, and now she was saying I was the father of the baby she was going to have. She kept at me until I was half convinced I should marry her. I didn't know what the hell to do. I felt guilty and ashamed. I was very sorry for her, but I just wasn't ready to marry anyone. Hell, I could hardly take care of myself, say nothing of taking care of a wife and kid. The thought of being a father scared the hell right out of me. "I should have thought about all this before I got in this fix," I said to myself.

Finally I told my best friends, Don and Woody about my dilemma.

"Do you love her?" Don asked.

"No." I said. "If I married her it wouldn't last."

"You know," Don said, "she has a lot of boy friends. Be me I don't think I would marry her until I knew for sure."

Wellsville is a small town. Everyone knew of my predicament and I over-reacted. I walked away from my good job at the Worthington, sold my neat little forty-one Mercury coupe and then telling no one, I silently slipped out of Wellsville, catching the train bound for New York City via Jersey City.

My plan was to see if I could get a job in the Merchant Marine. I felt like a coward, and maybe I was. I tried to solve my problems by running away, or block them out of my mind. There weren't many passengers on the train, so I took a seat by myself and put my legs across the rest of the seat next to me.

I was lonely and scared, but I didn't want to talk to anyone. I bet no one will ever miss me. The hell with them, who cares about any of those sons-of-bitches out there anyway. Who needs them I was telling myself, if Ester hadn't dumped me, I wouldn't be in this fix, to hell with her too. I was feeling sorry for myself, but maybe I had a right to, even though I had made my own bed so to speak. It was one of the lowest times of my life. I felt drained and bone tired. I shut my eyes, but sleep wouldn't come.

When I talked to the people at the shipping hall at the Battery in New York, they told me I had little chance of shipping out.

"We have a lot of men on the beach and you don't have your papers yet." I got back on the Erie at Jersey City, and came back to Wellsville. I stopped at the diner and saw Neil. I told him I was going to Buffalo, to see if I could get a job on one of those "lake boats" I had heard about, but never seen.

"Can I come with you, Bob?" Neil asked.

"Sure, glad to have you, Neil."

The next morning Neil and I hitchhiked to Buffalo. My money was nearly gone and Neil was broke. At the Lake Carriers Association, they told us we could get a job as ordinary seaman, but we had to go to the Coast Guard to get fingerprinted and an ID card. The Coast Guard was located at the Post Office. It brought back memories, none of them good.

Back at the Lake Carriers, they told Neil and I to go to Ganson Street, where we would see a boat called the *Cuyler Adams*, tied up near a grain elevator.

"Go aboard and give these papers to the Captain, or one of the mates."

The cab let us out at the Ganson Street bridge. There she was, tied up near the elevator. The ship was like no vessel I had ever seen. It was longer and had a narrower beam than the *Arkab*. The stack and engine were aft and the pilot house was forward. There were no cargo booms and almost no rigging, just a spar forward and spar aft on the boat deck. The only purpose for the spars were to carry her running lights. She was old, but very neat and had an uncluttered look about her. "Not too bad for an old gal," I thought. The boat belonged to the Tomlinson Fleet and was to be my home for the next three years.

On the Great Lakes, a ship is called a boat, a porthole was a deadlight, a captain was called Cap and a helmsman was called a wheelsman. Everything else was about the same lore as salt water. The *Cuyler Adams* had a crew of thirty men. You stood watches, four hours on and eight off. Twelve to four, four to eight, and eight to twelve. I liked the four to eight watch. You worked seven days a week and about nine months a year. There were three men to a room. We had adequate toilets and showers, and the food was excellent. Not much to complain about, but there was always some who did.

From the west end of Superior, to the east end of Lake Ontario is fifteen hundred miles. The Great Lakes are immense. They have been called fresh water seas. They also can be mean and nasty when they so desire.

The Cuyler Adams

On the Great Lakes

"Are you the Bos'n?"

"This Boat don't have a Bos'n," the man answered.

"Could you please tell me if the Captain or one of the mates is around, we're the new deck hands."

"No," he answered without looking up. He was checking out the gear in a life raft on top of the pilot house. It was plain he wanted nothing to do with us. His name was Ed Miller. He was a wheelsman. I took immediate dislike to this man, and Neil did too.

"You the two new deck hands? I'm Mickey, the second mate," another man said with a smile on his weathered face. Mickey was pushing fifty. He was the complete opposite of the man we first met. He took our papers.

"Your timing is pretty good. It's coffee break."
In the crew's mess Neil and I had our first cup of steamboat coffee, a little strong but very good. The second cook brought in some freshly made doughnuts.

"Bet you're the new deck hands. My name's Tommy. If you want more doughnuts, holler. Coffee's on the galley range in the big granite pot. Help yourself."

"I think I'm going to like this job," Neil said.

It was March, fit-out time. As soon as the powerful ice-breaker *Mackinaw* broke the ice in the channels the shipping season would start. If the boat wasn't ready by then, there would be hell to pay from the owners in Cleveland.

"Make sure there's a life jacket in all quarters, there should be a jacket for every bunk." Louie, the first mate, was putting us to work. Neil and I were now ordinary seamen, deck hands on the Great Lakes. Louie was a short stocky man with a quick temper. Sometimes when he got angry, he would throw his hat down on the deck and stomp on it, much to the delight of Neil and I, as long as he wasn't mad at us. His temper would vanish about as quick as it would flair up.

We cast off the tugboat's towline. We were on our own, heading out of Buffalo Harbor into Lake Erie bound for Toledo, Ohio to pick up a load of coal destined for Superior, Wisconsin, nine-hundred and thirty-six miles away.

***

"Hang on," Tom, the third mate said. "And make sure your well over the dock before you try getting out of the Bos'n's chair." It was always a tense time getting the deck hands down on the dock to handle the mooring lines. It was a scary and dangerous job. The Bos'n's chair was attached to a boom about twenty foot long. The boom was swung out from the ship's side and the deck hand was lowered down to the dock. This was done on the fly, as the boat came along side of the dock. If you missed you could be crushed between the boat and the dock.

"Bob, you're the most experienced, you go first" Tom ordered. Tom and the watchman, Dan, lowered me down smooth as silk.

"Come on Neil, piece of cake," I yelled up as I trotted off to catch the stern line. I was shaking like a leaf.

The coal dock in Toledo had a rig that would lift an entire railroad car, turn it upside down and empty it's contents into the cargo hold. At Toledo they could load a coal car every minute. After about ninety minutes, the *Cuyler Adams* was full to the top of her hatches and we headed for the Detroit River.

The weather was cold and damp, but not much wind for the last of March. After leaving the coal dock the boat had to be hosed down and the white paint on the pilot house had to be scrubbed. A cold wet job. It was always good to get a break and go to the crew's mess, where it was warm and Tommy always had hot coffee and something fresh out of the oven. If we had the right watchman, our ten minute coffee break would last about twenty minutes. Coffee break was the best part of the day for me. The older guys always had stories to tell. Sometimes I thought their adventures were a little exaggerated, maybe the waves were a little higher and the winds a little stronger then they actually were, but they were good stories and they didn't hurt anyone. I liked the camaraderie at coffee time. It was as warm as the crew's mess itself. Your shipmates were your brothers, you trusted and depended on each other like no other people I ever worked with.

"What in the Hell's going on?" I turned on my bunk light; Neil was sitting upright in his bunk. It was after midnight when three short blasts from the boat's whistle woke us up. I looked out the deadlight and saw nothing. We were socked in with fog. The boats on the lakes are required to sound three short blasts at regular intervals while navigating in fog. I shut off my bunk light. In the distance I could hear other boats signaling. One of the whistles was getting louder and louder until it seemed she was right on top of us. I lay in the dark with my eyes wide open. I could picture a monstrous ship's bow crashing through our hull, heading straight for my bunk. Then the blasts got quieter as we safely passed each other and the distance between us grew. It was a routine happening on the lakes, but I did not know this and it was a little scary the first time.

The trip up-bound to Superior, Wisconsin was cold with a combination of rain, sleet, and snow. The rivers and cuts had a lot of ice in them. Sometimes we were barely able to make forward progress. The Coast Guard ice-breakers never let us down. The Coast Guard people were great and always around when you needed them. They kept the channel markers and lights in good working order, and you knew if you needed them, they would be right there to help you, sometimes at risk to themselves.

The coal dock at Superior was as primitive as Toledo's was modern. I don't recall how long it took to unload, but Neil and I had plenty of time to go to a surplus store and get some much-needed warmer clothing for working out on deck. We had a couple of beers at a sailor's hangout on main street. I think the town had a lot of their men working the lakes. Everyone treated us good, and we sensed we were welcome there.

When we got back to the boat the clam bucket rigs hadn't made much progress at unloading the boat. The ore docks outside Duluth were high, trestle-like structures constructed of large, wood timbers. They reminded me of the bridges and trestles you sometimes saw in movies about the Old West. The trains would haul their string of ore-laden cars onto the top of the trestle. The ore cars were constructed with a trap door in their bottoms. When the trap door was opened the ore would come roaring out into a large chute, whose end was centered over the hatch of the boat. There were several of these chutes. The boat would strain at her mooring cables from the force of the sudden weight thundering into her cargo holds. At the ore docks a boat could be loaded as fast as her hull could take the sudden weight. The mate, directing the loading by hand signals, would be busy and tense trying to keep the boat trim and loaded in a manner as to get maximum cargo, without going past the maximum draft the Coast Guard said she could carry.

We left Duluth with eight thousand, five hundred tons of Taconite pellets in our holds. The four hundred seventy-four foot *Cuyler Adams* was drawing twenty foot of water, and was on an even keel, everything was just the way it should be. You could see the Bullmate was proud of the job he did and he didn't even have to stomp on his hat to do it. We headed down-bound for Buffalo and the steel mills at Lackawanna.

The Lackawanna steel mills were a huge complex. The boat wasn't there long enough to allow a sailor time to go ashore for a haircut or to take in a movie. At Lackawanna, small boats would tie up along our outboard side and sell us everything from radios to girlie magazines. They were stocked with jeans, cigarettes, watches, candy, anything a sailor might want. We called them bum boats and they were always welcome.

When you were off watch there wasn't much to do on a steamboat. I read a lot and had a radio on a shelf over my bunk. When navigating the rivers on a hot summer day, it was nice to watch the girls sunbathing with a pair of binoculars. Sometimes we would pass only a few yards from the docks of the cottages, and we wouldn't need binoculars. A sailor could yell out, "Hi There" or maybe whistle at them. Most of the times the girls didn't take offense, and they gave you a smile and a friendly wave. I used to wonder if they were teasing us a little, or maybe they just understood and knew we were lonely, and sure would like to be there on the dock with them. I like to think the latter was the case. The trouble with watching the girls was it made you aware of what you were missing on a steamboat, working seven days a week.

Playing poker was another pastime I enjoyed. At first I lost pretty bad. I would see a big pot on the table and stay in the hand until the last card was dealt, even though my hand didn't stand much chance of winning. After a while I learned to fold my hand when it wasn't too good and did pretty well after that. If you get greedy and try to win all the hands dealt you, you're gonna lose. I think getting greedy is the downfall of a lot of people, be it a poker game or anything in life. If you get dealt a bad hand, get the hell out, no matter how big the pot is. I say this, but I don't follow my own advice. If life is like a poker game, I've spent most of mine drawing to inside straights, and I haven't hit one yet. If I'm gonna connect with one, it better be pretty soon. I'm no spring chicken anymore.

The steel mills had rigs called ukes. The operator sat above a large, hinged bucket that they rode right down into the cargo hold, where they took out boxcar-size bites of ore at one time and deposited it in huge piles on the dock.. When the boat was nearly empty, they would lower small bulldozers into the holds to pile up the remaining ore. Neil and I took care of the very last operation. We were sent down into the holds to sweep up the last bits of ore with heavy stiff push brooms, and shovel it into the uke buckets. Then we hosed the cargo hold with a high pressure fire hose, as we headed up-bound for Port Arthur and Fort William, Canada on the northwest end of Lake Superior, for a load of wheat, destined for Oswego, New York.

When we tied up at Oswego, Neil told me he wanted to quit. He liked the job, but he didn't like being separated from his wife. I told him I would miss him, but I understood how he felt and didn't blame him. I didn't even have a girlfriend anymore. I guess I was lonely and feeling a little sorry for myself. Hell, seems like I'd felt lonely most of my life. I thought I best learn to live with it.

All the boats picked up their mail while passing Detroit. The fast, open mail boat would come dashing out to meet you and the watchman would lower a bucket to the mail boat running along side us. The mail was put in the bucket and the watchman hauled it up. By lowering a ladder down into the mail boat a sailor could climb aboard the boat or get off. We lowered our ladder and Slim, our new deck hand, climbed aboard.

Photo courtesy of U.S. Coast Guard

The Ice Breaker Mackinaw.

"I did a lot of serious reading in my off hours."

I was walking up the deck eating a banana, when Neil came at me making like a monkey, which wasn't hard for him to do. One of the deck hands took the picture. It's good to have someone around like Neil to make you laugh, especially on a job like steamboating. The monotony could really get to you sometimes and people like Neil helped to break it up. Neil was a good shipmate, he was easy-going and good-natured and always did his fair share of work. But he wasn't really cut out to be a sailor, he missed his wife and did not like the confinement of living on a boat.

Slim

Our new deckhand was a tall, gawky lad and a real character. When one heard him speak you knew he hailed from the deep South. Getting aboard must have been a harrowing experience for him, climbing a ladder resting on the deck of a bobbing mail boat, with the top of the long ladder held by two men he never saw before. Luckily for him the pilot of the mail boat was skilled. He kept the boat close to the hull of the *Cuyler Adams* and maintained a like speed in the turbulent water. When he reached the top of the ladder the new deckhand quickly scrambled aboard, his eyes were wide and his mouth open. He must have been thinking to himself, "I wonder what they all are gonna make me do next."

Dan, the watchman tossed a line down to the mail boat pilot and the pilot tied on the deckhand's tattered old suitcase, then sped off leaving a white wake behind him. Dan hauled up the old suitcase, untied it and handed it to the new man.

"Come on Slim, follow me, I'll show ya to the deckhand's room," Dan said. The name Slim stuck, that's the only name most of us ever knew him by. Right from the start Slim proved to be a real character, although he didn't intend to be. It was just his nature. At his first meal in the crew's mess, Tommy set a large bowl of beef stew down next to Slim's plate. Before anyone could say anything Slim started digging in with his spoon. We all just sat there watching him. The bowl of stew was meant to be passed around. One of the firemen, Goldie, a character in his own right, grumbled, "That boy must be damn awful hungry." We all had a good laugh. Tommy mumbled something about it being a good thing he had some beef stew left in the pot. He went to the galley, filled another bowl, and set it in front of Dan, the watchman. Dan rubbed his hands together; looked lovingly at the stew and reached for a spoon pretending he was going to eat from the bowl. Everyone started yelling in jest at Dan until he placed some stew on his plate and passed the bowl. Slim was oblivious to his surroundings, he just kept shoveling down his stew.

When Slim placed food on his plate, he piled it on altogether. If Tommy brought in ice cream or pie, that was piled on top of whatever else was on his plate and he wolfed it down. There wasn't anything he didn't like, he ate anything placed on the table.

One time the deckhands were painting the deck and the watchman in charge said something about Slim leaving too many holidays or bare spots. It hurt Slim's feelings and when it came time to knock off Slim wouldn't quit working.

"Come on Slim, time to go clean up," the other two deckhands urged. Despite all their coaxing he just kept on working; he kept working until it was too dark to see. Finally he cleaned out his brush, placed the cover on the five gallon can of red lead paint, went to the galley, made a huge sandwich and drank about a quart of milk. Then he went to the deckhands' room and took off his coveralls and shoes. Leaving the rest of his clothes on, he crawled into his bunk and for the first time went to sleep, without saying, "Goodnight ya'll," to his mates. His mates felt bad about that.

The *Cuyler Adams* eased into the slip at the coal dock in Superior, Wisconsin. The deck hands slipped the eyes of the mooring cables over the bollards, one at the stern and one at the bow. The watchman up on deck tightened the cables with their clattering steam winches. The *Cuyler Adams* was safe and snug tied up at the coal dock after her rough trip up-bound on temperamental Lake Superior. She was loaded to the top of her twenty-eight hatches with ninety carloads of Pennsylvania coal.

No sooner had the boat tied up when a gal in a short skirt and tight blouse came out from behind a coal pile. She sashayed over to a bollard, sat down and lit up a smoke. Most of my mates knew her and the ones who didn't, knew of her. She was known as coal pile Annie.

The coal dock was Annie's turf. If one of the other local working gals ventured on the dock she told them to get the hell out and most did. Coal pile Annie would sit there on a bollard smoking a cigarette until a sailor approached her, then she would lead the sailor around the back of a huge coal pile where there was a small tool shed. She had converted the shed over to her workshop. It was here she performed her versatile and numerous tricks. All her many customers agreed coal pile Annie was one talented gal indeed.

Slim was looking her over pretty good, but made no move to approach her. The other two deckhands started in on him.

"She's pretty nice, ain't she Slim?"

"Why don't ya go down and talk to 'er, Slim?" They kept it up until one of them asked "What's the matter, Slim, scared of girls?"

That did it.

"I ain't scared of no darn girls, I'll show ya all." With that he climbed down the ladder to the dock and ambled over to where coal pile Annie was perched on the bollard. Annie got up and took Slim by the hand and led him to the back of the coal pile.

Later one of the deckhands asked coal pile Annie how it went with Slim.

"He's different," Annie answered. "When we got to the shed Slim just stood there so I told him to take off his coveralls. Would you believe under his coveralls he had on a sweater, a shirt, two pairs of pants and long legged underwear. I thought we would never get at it. When he peeled off enough clothes so we could get started, I asked Slim how he wanted it. He just shrugged his shoulders, so I told him I'd give him a half and half. Well we didn't get through the first half, when Slim let out a groan. He was all done. The groan was the only sound that came out of him all the time we were together. I never saw anyone so bashful. You know, Slim is pretty young, I asked him if it was his first time, he didn't answer. If I'd been sure I was his first I wouldn't have charged him," coal pile Annie said with a wicked little grin.

***

"Bob, Cap wants to see you. He's in the pilot house," Mickey informed me. Cap Hanson was Swedish.

"Bob, ve gonna make you a deck vatch. Get your tings and move to da deck vatch room. You gonna have da four ta eight vatch."

And so it went seven days a week, four hours on, eight hours off. Duluth, Chicago, Cleveland, Detroit, Buffalo, Erie, Gary and a host of other cities and towns I can't recall. All hungry for ore, coal, or grain. It got pretty monotonous.

At last we were in Duluth getting our last load for the season. A load of storage wheat for Buffalo. The temperature was below zero, when we were tarping down the last of the Cuyler Adams twenty-eight hatches. A miserable job, even in good weather, but when we got to Buffalo it would be lay-up time, some time off.

The trip down Superior was rough. We would slam into a wave, spray would fly and freeze wherever it landed. When we arrived at the Soo locks we were covered with ice from stem to stern. When we arrived at Buffalo however the weather was balmy for the last of November. We buttoned up the boat for the winter. Cap Hanson gave me my pay and bonus money. He shook my hand and told me to come back at fit-out time in the spring.

I was very pleased with myself. I had over three-thousand dollars in the bank and a pocketful more, a tidy sum in nineteen fifty-one. I also had three months to blow it in, and I did. No matter, Florida was kind of nice and I missed a cold New York winter. It was worth it, I hate the cold.

View from the stern of the Cuyler Adams looking forward. Those are my pants flying in the breeze.

Coal Pile Annie.

"She's pretty nice, ain't she Slim?"

Before I went back to Buffalo, to sign on the *Cuyler Adams*, I chanced upon Sharlett, a girl I use to date. Sharlett was a good kid, we did a lot of things together; swimming, roller skating, things like that. We weren't serious over each other, just very good friends. She and I had a nice long talk. "You know, Bob, that baby Maria had and said you were the father of ? She lied, you weren't the father. She told her friends who the real father was and one of them told me. In fact they got married and she had a little girl that looks just like the guy she married."

When Sharlett told me I wasn't the father of Maria's baby a flood of relief flowed over me. For a long time thoughts had been gnawing away at my mind: "Did Maria have the baby, was it a boy or girl, will I ever see it?" Then I would push the thoughts out of my mind for awhile, but they always came back. Now it was resolved and I felt a wave of relief. I look back at events like my experience with Maria and I'm absolutely astounded at how such a trivial little act like stopping at a drug store for a cup of coffee can have such a profound effect on one's life and cause such a radical change as to what course of events will take place. Looking back, I'm glad I made out with Maria that warm summer night in my little forty-one Mercury. I'm thinking she set me up but good that night, but I have no regrets. I wouldn't change a thing. A lot of good things happened to me in my life after I left Wellsville.

When I was nearly broke and wanted to take Sharlett skating, she would get some guy to take her up to the rink and buy her ticket, then Sharlett and I would skate together most of the time, leaving the poor guy sitting on the side lines. Sharlett was a good skater, she knew all the dance steps and was especially good when it came time for the waltzes. She was pert and graceful and danced the waltz flawlessly. She made me look good, and we always got compliments after a waltz. Just before the last skate of he evening, Sharlett and I would sneak out of the rink and I would take her home. What a rotten thing to pull on the poor guy who bought her ticket.

Sharlett was much different than Ester. She was carefree, and cheerful. Her main goal in life was to have a good time, and to hell with the serious stuff. She was a lot of fun to be with, and no matter what we did together, we always had a good time.

I used to tell myself, why the hell couldn't I have fallen for Sharlett like I did for Ester. Sharlett and I were very compatible and probably could have spent our lives together relatively happy. Whereas with Ester, for me, the flame was there, but if we would have tried to spend a lifetime together one of us would probably have killed the other.

Photo by Dick Neal

One Bad Apple

It was early spring nineteen-fifty-two, I was back on the *Cuyler Adams*. Sad to say, one of my old shipmates, Ed Miller, was back too. The weather was warm for that time of year, so the mate thought it would be a good time to paint the forward spar.

"Will you go up, Bob? You're light and easy to pull up."

I didn't like the job, but I told him I would do it. When I had painted my way about a quarter of the way down, Tom, the third mate told Ed to watch my line so he could take a break and get a cup of coffee in the Galley. I think this ticked Ed off. He didn't like taking orders. A short while later I hollered down to Ed, "Lower me down about four feet, Ed." This really must have ticked him off. "Now a damn deck watch was telling him what to do," he probably said to himself. He must have taken off all the turns on the cleat that was holding my line but one. Without warning, he let the Bo'sun's chair I was in free fall the four feet, before he snubbed the line to stop my fall with a violent jerk, shaking the whole spar.

"Oh, I'm sorry," he lied. It scared the hell out of me and paint slopped out of the bucket and ran down my leg. After I was back down I told Tom that was the last time I would paint the spar if Ed was going to watch my line.

"When we get to Duluth, Bob, why don't you go to the Coast Guard station and take the test to get your Able Seaman papers?" Tom asked me. I didn't think too much of the idea, but I told him I would. The tests weren't bad, mostly basic questions about seamanship, about the same as the test I had taken in the Navy for Seaman First Class. A short time after I got my Able Seamen papers, Cap Hanson approached me.

"Bob, ve gonna teach you to veel. Ve gonna make a Veelsman out of you."

"I kind of like the job I got Cap."

"Get your tings and move into da Veelsman's room."

Now I would be close to my buddy Ed. We would share the same room. I wasn't too happy about it. Ed wasn't much of a problem however, he stuck to himself, and when he was off watch, he slept most of the time. He never had much to do with anyone. He never went to the crew's mess to have coffee or play poker. He had a passion for working crossword puzzles. I guess that way he didn't have to talk to anyone. When he did talk it was when he wanted to bitch about something. On the Fourth of July, the cook and Tommy went all out fixing the crew thick steaks, mashed potatoes, salads, the works. Ed complained because we didn't have cheese to go with the apple pie.

Once, when we were loading grain at Fort William, Ed got drinking a little more than he usually did. Maybe it was the good Canadian whiskey, anyway, he was downing it pretty good when I hit the sack. A few hours later something warm and wet woke me up. Ed was taking a leak on the deck, and some of it was running into my bunk.

"What the hell are you doing ?" I never, never, was so mad in my life. I grabbed Ed by the shirt.

"Oh, I thought I was in the john," Ed muttered. I shoved him across his bunk. He hit his head on a book shelf and passed out, half sitting and half laying on his bunk. If I'd had a club, or a knife, or a gun in my hand, Ed would have been a dead man. I threw my bedding on Ed's bunk, took a shower, and spent the rest of the night in the Windlass room. Granted, Ed was drunk, but I think he half knew what he was doing. I didn't confront Ed about the incident. Some day my chance will come and I'll get him, I thought. I never did get even. Ed is probably gone now, or at least he's a very old man. But to this day I'm mad at myself for letting him get away with what he did. It kind of makes me feel less a man. At the very least I should have hit him. When I look back and think about all the people I have known in my life, Ed Miller is the only one I have any real animosity towards. I would even give the third grade teacher a big hug if I could see her. I might speak to the Lt. if I saw him, but I wouldn't shake his hand. I don't dwell too much on things that happened in the past, but sometimes I have strong feelings about them when they come to mind. The bad apples don't count, all you can to do is sort them out, and throw them away. Then enjoy all the good ones that are left.

"Will you go up Bob?"

One of my favorite story tellers was a tough old timer we called Goldie. Goldie was one of our stokers and hailed from Toledo. He had done time for armed robbery. Goldie told us about the time he and his partner held up a jewelry store in Chicago.

"I went inside to pull the heist, while my partner waited outside in the getaway car with the motor running. I took too long in the store," Goldie went on. "I guess I got too excited when I saw all them jewels, I wanted 'em all. Someone in the back of the store must have seen me and called the cops. When I got outside the getaway car was gone. The son-of-a bitch took off when he heard the sirens. If he'd waited a few more seconds we woulda got away with it. I started running," Goldie said, "but I didn't get much more 'n a block away and the bastards nailed me."

"Let me give ya some advice," Goldie added, "if yer gonna pull a heist, ya better make damn sure yer the one doing the driving." Then Goldie said with a far away look in his tired old blue eyes, "If I coulda got away with that one I'd been set for life and I wouldn't be feedin' coal to a hungry old scow like this one, I'd be shacked up with some ol' haybag and drinkin' the best darn booze money can buy."

There was a catwalk above the stokehold where on occasion I would go and watch the stokers stoke the furnace down below and I would wonder how anyone could stand such a place. When a stoker was down in the stoke hold of the *Cuyler Adams*, he was about as close to hell as a man could be without actually being there.

***

The coal bunker bulkhead was only a few feet from the furnaces. The stoker opened the stoke hole door using his shovel to raise the hot lever and open the door. In the same motion he quickly pivoted turning his back to the brutal heat, took a few long strides towards the coal bunker, filled his shovel, turned and took a long step back towards the stoke hole. At the same time, with a long swing of his arms, he sent the shovel full of coal flying through the air into the stoke hole, not dropping one lump of coal on the deck. It was all done quickly and in a rhythmic and graceful motion until an even blanket of black coal covered the hot, bright fire bed.

The stoker used his shovel to slam the stoke hole door shut and stepped back from the furnace as far as he could to catch his breath. No sooner had the stoker shoveled in the coal when he noted the blue flames breaking through the black blanket indicating the heat was causing the gases in the coal to release and ignite in bright blue hungry flames. He knew soon the cycle would start all over again. He knew, too, that he had a hot fire - maybe too hot, he thought, as he watched the steam pressure gauge slowly but surely rise.

Damn, she's gonna pop off, and the chief is gonna give me hell. Ya just can't win with a job like this.

For awhile he thought about quitting and getting off on the mail boat when they reached Detroit. In his heart he knew he wouldn't quit. He'd tough it out. His wife and kids back in Green Bay needed the money.

"Damn it, ya popped 'er off again! Coal's money! When ya burn too much coal it's the same's burnin' money," the chief yelled down the stoke hold. The stoker loosened a large, dirty bandanna from his neck and mopped his brow and face.

"You can just kiss my sweaty ass chief," he muttered to himself.

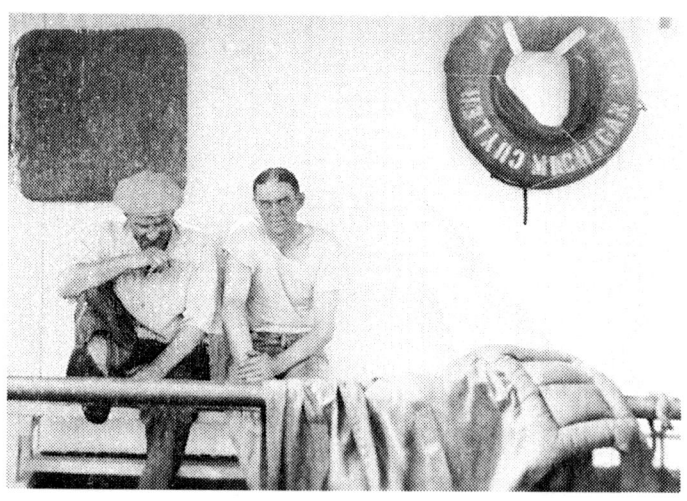

No one had a tougher job than the stokers on the Cuyler Adams.

Ve Gonna Make You a Veelsman

After a few weeks at my new job, I started to really enjoy it. But sometimes while steering at night in the rivers I would get pretty tense. Especially when the fog would sock us in, and we had to navigate by radar. The mate would be glued to the radar, picking out channel markers, and giving headings to the wheelsman.

A gyro-compass makes two clicking noises for every degree the boat's heading moves. If the wheelsman is wandering a little the gyro-compass always tells the mate about it, with its little clicking noise, then the mate would grumble, "keep her steady."

Steering in the Welland Canal is a challenge to any wheelsman. Sometimes you pass other boats so close you could jump from one to the other if you had a mind to. Of course the Captain always told you where he wanted you to steer. How it was done was pretty much up to the wheelsman. I think it takes a lot more skill to be a Great Lakes mariner than salt water. So much of your time is in rivers and channels, you're in close contact with other boats in heavy traffic. On salt water they think in terms of miles, on the lakes, it's yards.

The first time I had to steer in the Welland Canal, Cap Hanson saw I was apprehensive.

"Don't vorry Bob, dars a bank on both sides, ve can't get out," then he chuckled at his little joke. But a little while later, he wasn't laughing. I got too close to the right bank, and suddenly the boat's bow started going left at an alarming rate.

"**Hard right,**" Cap Hanson quickly ordered in a loud, but calm voice. Getting the boat too close to the bank caused a suction action from the screw turning in the shallow water close to the bank. The *Cuyler Adams* was going down the channel at a forty-five degree angle. Her bow passed the center of the channel, her stern nearly in the right bank. If you stopped the engine the stern would crash into the concrete bank. All you could do is keep the wheel hard right. After what seemed an eternity, the bow started right.

"**Take off two turns,**" Cap ordered. The bow stopped swinging right, then the bow started left again.

"**Hard right,**" Cap ordered. When the bow started right the next time, Cap told me to take off only one turn. Gradually we worked our way to the middle of the channel.

"Would you take the wheel Tom? I have to go to the head, if it ain't to late."

***

Another boat is approaching us. We're in the St. Mary's River on a foggy night. The radar tells the mate or captain we are closing fast and the captain gives a long blast on the ship's whistle telling the oncoming boat we are navigating to the starboard. A short silent pause, then one long blast from their whistle. They are navigating to their right. The decision has been made as to how we are going to pass. The captain, mate and the wheelsman are all equally tense and the mood in the pilot house is total concentration. The watchman on the bow is staring ahead but sees nothing in the thick fog. We know the same scenario is taking place on the boat ahead. Suddenly, an eerie white glow appears in the fog; it's their masthead light. The watchman yells up to the pilot house, "light off the port bow," but we have already seen it, all four of us saw it at the same time. A few seconds pass then the massive bow looms into view through the fog. The quickness of it startles the watchman, who takes a few quick steps backward and grasps the rail.

The steamboat men in the pilot house of the Cuyler Adams slowly exhale the breath they have been holding back. The gigantic ship is right where she should be. Her bright red and green running lights glowing in the fog tells us so. Our own lights tell them we are where we should be and that all's well.

We glide past each other, red light to red light, with a little, but not much, room to spare. As we pass, we give them a little half wave, half salute. Even though we can't see the steamboat men in their darkened pilot house, we are sure they are giving us a little salute towards our darkened pilot house. I'm amazed at how two such long, massive structures can pass each other so quietly with only some soft whispering sounds coming from the wakes of the bows as they push the water aside.

Finally it's four a.m., time for the next watch to take over. We're still in the Saint Mary's River, and it's still foggy. I go below to the wheelsman's room in the bow. I undress and crawl into my bunk. I hear a long blast from our whistle aft, a pause, then a long blast from the boat ahead of us. I'm not concerned about it. I hope I have some mail waiting for me at the Soo Locks. I turn off my bunk light, close my eyes and go to sleep. Just before I go to sleep I hear a little swishing noise coming through the open dead light near my bunk. We must have passed, I say to myself. To my way of thinking, it all boils down to respect and trust. We place our trust in the boat ahead of us, and the boat ahead of us places their trust in us. It's a good feeling especially when you think about the fact that all of us are strangers to each other. Without each other's trust we would have to lay at anchor in a safe place, waiting the night out until the morning sun burned off the thick fog.

Sometimes you pass other boats so close you could jump from one to the other if you had a mind to.

"Bartender, We'll Have Another

At the coal dock in Erie, Pennsylvania, it took a long time to load a boat. I was off watch, so I decided to go uptown just to get off the boat for awhile. I ran across some of the crew walking down the street.

"Come on Bob, we're gonna go have a few beers, you can come with us if you think you can keep up," Roger, the first cook kidded me. We went into a nice little tavern on the main drag. After a couple of beers I got feeling pretty confident.

"Bartender, we'll have another round of beer, with a whiskey this time, if these guys can handle it." I started talking to some dolly sitting at the bar. Roger ordered another round.

"We'd better get back to the boat after this one," he wisely proclaimed.

"You guys go ahead, I'll be there in a little while." I don't remember much after that. I woke up on the coal dock a little after daybreak. I didn't even know how I got there. The boat was gone. The loading crew had gone home. I was sick, my white tee shirt was black from sleeping on the coal dock. I reached in my pocket. Thank God, my wallet was there. But when I looked inside all of my money was gone. I went through my pants pockets - not a penny.

I splashed some cold lake water on my face, turned my tee shirt inside out to hide some of the dirt, and staggered uptown. I sat down on a bench in the park to ponder my situation. I didn't know anyone in Erie, I was sick and filthy dirty, I didn't have a dime to make a phone call. I took a drink of water out of the fountain in the park, and promptly threw it up.

There was an old gent there in the park watching me. After awhile he walked over to me.

"Do you have any money, Sonny?"

"No, I'm broke," I told him.

"Here's fifty cents, why don't you get something to eat? If you can keep it down, you'll feel better."

"Boy, I must look in sad shape," I thought. That fifty-cent piece looked like a million dollars to me. I thanked the old gent warmly, and told him to give me his address so I could pay him back.

"Forget it," he said, and walked off. I bought a cup of coffee, drank it and held it down. Then I got Woody out of bed with a phone call.

"Woody, I'm here in Erie, broke; could you send me twenty-five bucks, Western Union?"

"Sure Bob, right away." After picking up the money at Western Union, I bought a work shirt and a pair of pants at a surplus store. Then I went to the bus station, cleaned up, changed my clothes and bought a bus ticket for Buffalo to catch the boat.

It was hot as hell on the bus, which didn't help my hangover very much. I kept forcing back the dry heaves, but these funny little noises would come out of me every time I tried to hold them back. The little old lady sitting next to me kept giving me dirty looks. I think she was as worried about me getting sick as I was. It sure was a long ride to Buffalo, but when I got there the *Cuyler Adams* was patiently waiting for me.

Funny how a little act of kindness will stick in your mind a lifetime. I will never forget that old gent in the park in Erie, Pennsylvania.

The Little Pilot

As near as I can gather from listening to Captain Hanson, he must have immigrated from Sweden to America when he was in his early twenties. His English was broken, but he always got his message across especially when he was angry. If he took a likening to you, you could do no wrong, but if he didn't like you, you couldn't do anything right.

I thank my lucky stars he took a likening to me. I went from ordinary seaman, to deckwatch, to able seaman deckwatch and by the end of the season was watchman. At the start of my second season he made me a wheelsman.

Cap Hanson would show me all the little tricks of wheeling and point out tricky spots in the rivers and showed me how to overcome them.

"Ve gonna make you da best damn veelsman on da Great Lakes," he once told me. "Den ve gonna send you to mate's school in Cleveland and get your license, so you can be my terd mate."

Well, I never did go to mate's school in Cleveland to get my mate's license, but through Cap Hanson's efforts I turned out to be a very good wheelsman. Cap Hanson had a license for all five Great Lakes and all the channels and rivers that connected them except one, the upper Niagara River, like most wise old steamboat captains. He was more than happy to let a pilot take his boat down the Niagara.

The *Cuyler Adams* made several trips down the Niagara a year, to a coal dock owned by the Wickwire Company. If a boat any larger than the *Cuyler Adams* made the run they would be asking for disaster, it was the last dock a boat the size of the *Cuyler Adams* could navigate to on the upper Niagara so the *Cuyler Adams* supplied Wickwire with much of their coal.

When the *Cuyler Adams* made a run to the Wickwire Plant we picked up a pilot at a lock a little way down from the mouth of the Niagara River in Buffalo. The pilot we most often got was a little German guy, who spoke broken English and was hard for me to understand. He knew his job and sure knew the river, but sometimes he would stand directly in the line of sight of the wheelsman. Despite his small stature he was tall enough to block the wheelsman's view and force the wheelsman to stand to one side or the other of the wheel, thus causing the wheelsman to steer in an erratic fashion. Then the little pilot would bitch, "Vot's da madder wid you Sonny, can't you keep 'er steady?" You wanted to tell him to get his skinny little ass out of the line of sight but you didn't. A wheelsman doesn't criticize God and the pilot on a steamboat is God.

In one particularly difficult spot to navigate, the Coast Guard had erected a set of range markers. The markers were two signs with white lights mounted on the riverbank. The wheelsman would line up the steering pole on the bow with the range markers. When all three lined up he was said to have made the range. At that instant he took a compass reading.

"Vot's da compass heading Sonny?" God asked me.
When I told him the heading, he was angry and started chewing me out.

"Vell you missed da range lights didn't you, Sonny? Come right five degrees" he snapped.

About then, Cap Hanson spoke up, "God or no God, maybe if you get out of da vay a little, da veelsman could see and do better."

After that he wasn't God anymore, he was back to being the little pilot, he kept out of the line of sight and everything went a little better.

When the *Cuyler Adams* was about one hundred and fifty yards or so from the Wickwire dock, the little pilot would let out a flurry of orders.

"Start her right, Sonny, put da veel hard right," he ordered. Then he set the dial on the telegraph to full astern and the water beneath the fantail started churning and boiling and the whole boat was shaking. He snapped, "Put da veel midship." I breathed a sigh of relief. All I had to do then was stand by and watch. When the *Cuyler Adams* was making almost no forward progress, he rang stop engine on the telegraph, then leaned out the pilot house window and yelled down to the watchman on the bow

"Let loose da starboard hook, Sonny, and let out da chain 'til I tell ya to stop."

Dan released the brake band on the anchor windlass and the chain came roaring out from the chain locker down below until the little pilot yelled, "Stop da chain, Sonny, hang on to 'er." The anchor got a good grip on the river bottom and the slack in the chain came out. The *Cuyler Adams* pivoted on it's tether and swung one hundred eighty degrees, her bow facing up stream, her port side parallel with the dock. Heaving lines were hurled to the line handlers on the dock who caught them, hauled in the cables and dropped the eyes over the bollards. The watchmen tightened up the cables with their steam winches fore and aft. Dan hauled in the anchor with the powerful anchor windlass and the *Cuyler Adams* gently snuggled up to the dock.

We didn't care too much for the little pilot, but despite his unorthodox manner of giving orders, he sure knew how to navigate the river and dock a boat at the Wickwire dock. When you consider all the facts, such as a four or five mile-an-hour current that took a lot of steerage away, a boat that was a little too big to be there in the first place, and a channel so narrow that the only way to turn a boat around was by utilizing the anchor, it was about as tough a dock to make, anywhere.

The coal had been loaded at Erie, Pennsylvania, it had been processed down to a consistency of silt and coated everything with a gritty black soot. The coal was unloaded on to a large conveyor belt, one of the largest of it's kind, I was told. It was good when we got back on Lake Erie, where the air was fresh and the boat was clean after the deckhands hosed it down and Cap Hanson was once more master of the *Cuyler Adams* and the little pilot was back there on the river bitching at some other poor wheelsrnan.

I wondered about the little pilot. I wondered what he got out of life besides piloting steam boats up and down the river. I wondered if he had a wife and kids, and I was thinking if he did I bet she had to kowtow to him, and if he had kids, I bet they were scared of him. On the other hand, maybe there was a good side of him when he was off the river. Maybe I was judging him too harshly.

I Youst Touched Da Piers

I was walking aft to the Galley to get a cup of coffee and a sandwich before I relieved the watch, when I heard a high pitched yell coming from the bow. It was Corkey, the watchman yelling up to the pilot house.

"We're gonna hit Cap, you want an' anchor, or something?"

Then I felt the deck tremor from the engine being slammed into full astern. Too late - a loud bang, and I was neatly deposited on my posterior. Mickey came running out of his room.

"Follow me, Bob!" he yelled. We climbed down the ladder to the chain locker and forepeak.

"Go back and get a light, Bob," Mickey ordered. I could hear water gushing in the forepeak like a broken water main. In the little time it took to get the light, the forepeak was half full of water. "Even if it filled we would be in no danger of sinking, but the collision with the concrete pier must have done considerable damage," I thought. At first I was astonished at Mickey's reaction, he was ecstatic. He danced a little jig, and started to sing "Clancey Lowered the Boom." Then it dawned on me, Cap Hanson was in big trouble. Mickey knew his tormentor would be no more. Cap Hanson, Master of the *Cuyler Adams*, would surely be busted down to a mate at very least. I liked both of these men, especially that hard ass old man up in the pilot House. I was ticked off at Mickey for being so jubilant about Cap Hanson's misfortune, but I understood. Cap Hanson was down right mean to Mickey. He never had a good word for Mickey. I never knew why Cap felt that way.

We proceeded to the coal dock and Cap Hanson went ashore to call Cleveland and tell them what happened. I was told it went like this:

"I youst touched da piers."

"How much damage?" Cleveland asked.

"Da forepeak is full of vater, da stem is smashed in, I tink maybe some plates are buckled."

"Were you drunk?"

"I had nothing to drink, I vas sober."

"Maybe you should have been drunk, then you probably would have missed hitting the pier."

When the old man hung up there were tears running down his cheeks. He knew he never again would be called Cap Alf Hanson, Master of the *Cuyler Adams*, or any other Lake Boat. I think steamboat captains are the proudest men on earth, and rightly so. It takes most of a lifetime of dedication to get there, and once you're Captain, you're in absolute control, but your responsibilities and accountability are absolute too.

The captain is held accountable for every thing that happens on his vessel. In this case I don't think it was Cap Hanson's fault. No matter, he still had to take the blame. John was a wheelsman for a long time. He could handle a boat like no other seaman I ever knew, he knew exactly how much wheel to apply, or take off while navigating in the rivers and channels. It was effortless for him. When steering by compass, his wake was as straight as an arrow, while my wake would have a turn in it here and there. John could bring a boat into a dock so gently, you never knew when the boat and the dock were one. Sometimes when I was at the wheel making a dock, I would rattle the dishes in the Galley, and sometimes cause the coffee to spill from my mates' cups. They would mutter, "Bob's at the wheel," Tommy once told me. But in my humble opinion, John was a no good son of a bitch, the worst kind of shipmate. He surely knew we were going to hit that pier.

I wasn't at the investigation, but naturally John was; as he was the wheelsman on watch when we hit. I bet he told them, "I was steering the course they gave me," which was probably true. I think Cap Hanson and the mate were talking, not paying much attention to John, as it was such a routine thing, going through the breakwall at Superior. The most basic and easiest to remember rule of the road was broken. R.R.R. meaning Red, Right, Returning. The red light or marker should be on your right side while returning or entering a port. The red light was a hundred feet off our left side when we hit. John had to know we were too far to the right at least a mile before we got to the breakwall, but he kept to the compass heading they gave him, kept his mouth shut and simply let the boat smash into the pier. He was that kind of man. Naturally I can't prove this, but in my mind I know this is what he did.

At the hearing when they questioned Al all he had to say was "I was steering the last course the mate gave me," and he was off the hook. In fact, Al should have been steering by sight and not the compass as it was not needed on that calm moonlit night. It was bright enough where you could see the harbor markers for miles.

"I youst touched da piers."

After unloading our cargo of coal, we headed for the shipyards in Superior. At the shipyards they told us it would take about three weeks to install a new stem and replace a number of bent and buckled plates in the bow.

The shipyards were within walking distance of the Saint Paul Rooms and Hill Rooms, two very fine houses of ill repute. There were some taverns nearby and a coffee shop, the latter of which was lowest on our list of priorities. We all enjoyed our stay in the shipyards, but after the third week our wallets were getting a little thin. I noted some of my shipmates were getting a little thin too. It was time to leave and load our storage grain for Buffalo.

Cap Hanson was still Master of the *Cuyler Adams*. He told me his hearing wouldn't come up until March.

"After da hearing I von't be Captain anymore, I tink."

He kept pretty much to himself, in his quarters. When he went to the dining room he waited until the officers and wheelsmen were nearly through eating. Then he didn't eat much, Tommy told me.

I don't think hitting the pier was Cap Hanson's fault, but he never tried to blame anyone else. It didn't seem fair to me. Alf Hanson was a damn good captain; year after year he took boats safely up and down the lakes. Three times I personally saw him save the *Cuyler Adams* from serious damage, once when I was at the wheel. By putting his trust in the wrong man, for one moment, a goal that took Alf Hanson most of his life to reach went down the drain.

Maybe Captain Hazelwood of the *Exxon Valdez* got a bum rap too. After all, he had a third mate and helmsman on watch who should have been competent enough to navigate Prince Albert Sound, with all the room there. The captain can't be on the bridge twenty- four hours a day.

A little 'Rest and Relaxation' at the Shipyards.

Part III

Beulah

When we got to Buffalo for lay up, Chief Swartout asked me if I would work for him in the engine room for a couple of weeks. I didn't think I would like a steady job in the engine room, even though I kind of liked the jobs the Chief gave me.

Chief Swartout taught me how to cut and thread pipe. I did a lot of painting and cleaning. The only distasteful job was crawling inside the boiler and knocking off the build-up on the boiler tubes with a chipping hammer.

We finished about a week before Christmas, and I hopped the bus for Wellsville. This time I had nearly four thousand in the bank and a pocketful more. "Must be I was a little smarter poker player this season," I thought.

"Phyllis, I got a nice Mercury in the lot, and I don't want to smash it up. I'm going to get drunk and when I do, take me home, wherever the hell home is."

"Sure," Phyllis said with a laugh. I tossed the keys down in front of her and ordered a round for the bar.

"I'll take those keys," this very pretty girl said, with much authority in her voice. She reached over, took the keys and stuck them in her pocket. Her name was Beulah.

Earlier I had met Beulah and her friend, Betty, in a tavern on main street and asked them up to the Vet's Club for a drink.

"I'll meet you up there," I told them. After I got up there I spotted Phyllis alone at the bar. I didn't think Beulah and Betty would take me up on my invitation, so I made a play for Phyllis.

I had known Beulah for a long time, but only to speak to. I never tried to date her for fear of rejection. Getting someone to go out with her was no problem for Beulah. I never thought I would stand much of a chance getting a date with her. But after that night at the Vet's Club, Beulah was my girl. Three months later, I asked her to marry me and lucky for me she said "Yes."

"I'll take those keys!"

Beulah was the best thing that ever happened to me. I wasn't lonely anymore, I didn't have time to be. Beulah had more energy than ten people. When she wasn't working at the phone company, we were out on the town. I swear, I didn't think I could ever keep up with her.

When I told Don I was going to marry Beulah, he was pleased. "You two will hit it off good. When you going to tie the knot?"

"In July," Beulah says. "On the Fourth of July."

"On Independence Day?" Don snickered.

Before I started going with Beulah I was lonely, moody, and I didn't give a damn about anyone or anything. Beulah changed all that. Beulah was so full of life and a joy to be around, I just could not help being happy when she was with me. I was very proud that she was my girl, and I still am. I wasn't the only one who loved Beulah, she had friends everywhere. And she still does. What a lucky man I was. What a lucky man I still am.

Spring went by. I was back on the boat and everything was going routinely. The weather was good and the boats were setting new records for hauling iron ore. There were new boats on the drawing boards that were over a thousand feet long with one hundred-foot beams. A few years later they became a reality. I sure missed Beulah, but soon I would be getting off the boat to get married. Captain Jappman assured me my job would be waiting when I got back.

Al wanted some time off, but he would have to stand my watches while I was gone. I was to pay him back by standing his when I got back. I think Al knew I had had enough of his nonsense. In fact, we got into a verbal fight as to who's turn it was to clean our room, and I invited Al down to the dock as you could lose your papers for fighting on the boat. He declined my offer.

Beulah and I got married as planned. The wedding went just the way she wanted it to. It was about as nice a wedding as anyone could ask for. I think Beulah was happy, I know I was. We didn't have a lot of time together, as I had to get back to the boat when the boat docked in Coneaut, Ohio.

My sister, Alice, and her husband, Don McGillivray, drove Beulah and I out to Coneaut in my car. It wouldn't have taken much to talk me out of going aboard that boat.

It was about as nice a wedding as anyone could ask for.

July 4th, 1953. Beulah gets lucky.

A Real Steamboat Man

The Captains, Engineers, Mates, Oilers, and Able Seamen were called Steamboat men. Anyone less was not considered a *real* steamboat man unless he distinguished himself in some way to deserve the title. If you did a good job when you were a deckhand, the mate would sometimes say, "now you're steamboatin', " but to be called a *real* steamboat man you had to do something out of the ordinary. If you were a lowly deckhand, there was little chance of having that honor bestowed on you.

March, nineteen fifty-three was mild, the warm weather allowed for an early shipping season. Back on the *Cuyler Adams* we had two new deckhands. One was Leo, a lad from Wellsville, the other my kid brother, Ronnie, all five foot, five inch, one hundred - twenty pounds of him.

When Ralph Olson, the new Bullmate first laid eyes on Ronnie, he was a little dismayed. He must have thought Ronnie had lied about his age and that Ronnie was about thirteen years old.

"Can't you go find a place to hide?" he growled at Ronnie.
I felt sorry for Ronnie, but I didn't say anything to Ralph. "You'll see," I thought to myself. I think Ronnie and Dad had a little falling out. Ron had quit school and told Dad he was going to join the Army. Mom and Dad were beside themselves. There was a compromise, I was to try and get Ronnie a job on the boats. The situation was kind of like mine back in November nineteen forty-three. This time it was a hard time for Dad, Ronnie and my Mother.

Ronnie had no trouble fitting in. He did his work as well or better than any of the deck crew. I could see Ralph, the first mate, was taking a liking to Ronnie and was gaining a lot of confidence in him.

***

"**Son of a bitch, damn it to hell.**" Ralph was scared and frustrated. We had a man in the water and we were helpless to save him. If we didn't get Leo out of the icy water quickly the frigid water would kill him.

We were tying to get the *Cuyler Adams* into the coal dock so we could fill our coal bunkers. The boat was light, the wind was blowing the wrong way, and it was the first time Leo and Ronnie handled the mooring lines. We managed to lower Ronnie and Leo safely down on the dock, but the wind was fast blowing the boat away from the coal dock. We got a heaving line to them and they started pulling in the wire cable. Ralph was frantically signaling me to let out the cable faster. I opened the winch wide open. Leo and Ronnie managed to get the cable onto the dock and nearly had it on the spiel, when suddenly the cable started taking in instead of paying out. The cable had become wedged on the drum of the winch. I was watching Ralph's hand signals and didn't catch it in time. Ronnie and Leo hung on to the cable desperately. When the cable was near the edge of the dock, Ronnie wisely let go, but Leo panicked and held on until it pulled him into the icy water.

Ronnie acted like this was something that happened every day. One hundred-twenty pound Ronnie picked up the heaving line, threw it to Leo and managed to haul the soaking wet, Leo up onto the dock. The water must have been five or six feet below the dock and Ronnie had to stand on the very edge of the dock to get Leo out. This put him in danger of going in himself. If Ronnie went in they both would be in big trouble. There was no one on the coal dock and neither one would have been able to get out by themselves.

No one said so at the time, but everyone knew, Ronnie the deckhand was a *real* steamboat man.

It wasn't my fault, but I felt like it was. For a fraction of a second I saw a little boy named Clayton Henry with muddy brown water pouring from his heavy overcoat.

Shortly after his little bath, Leo packed up and went back to Wellsville.

No one said so at the time, but everyone knew, Ronnie the deckhand was a real steamboat man.

Lake Superior's Wrath

I left the crew's mess room after dropping a few bucks at the nightly poker game and headed up the deck for my bunk. I noticed the wind was picking up but didn't think too much about it until hours later. I was awakened by a lot of banging in the windlass room next to the wheelsman's room. Loose gear was flying all over the place. The boat was pitching and rolling so hard that I couldn't believe I had slept so long without waking up or falling out of my bunk. It was nearly time to relieve the twelve to four watch, so I got up and put on my foul weather gear. I knew the short trip up to the Pilot House would be windy and wet. When I opened the companion way door to the deck, I was nearly knocked over by the wind. I knew I would be in for a long watch, and that this would be the roughest weather I was ever in.

When I got in the pilot house, no one even looked up. Cap Jappman was hanging onto the binnacle, staring out the front windows. The mate was hanging onto the chart desk looking aft. Ed was standing at the wheel with his legs spread wide apart, trying to keep his balance. When I took the wheel Ed told me how the boat was responding.

"She wants all right wheel. All you can do is put the wheel hard right 'til she starts to go too far then take one or two turns off. As soon as you take a little right wheel off, she wants it right back, for Christ sake, don't let her get away from you. If we get in the trough of these waves we've had it."

I looked at Cap Jappman. He just nodded his head. Spittle was running down the corners of Ed's mouth. He was seasick, but not to the point of throwing up. I was already nearing that point. "I'll use that wastepaper basket," I thought.

The ship to shore had constant chatter on it. Everyone wanted to know what conditions were at different areas. The Coast Guard weather station reported winds of seventy miles an hour. The freighter Maryland's skipper was frantic.

"For Christ sake we need help, we're gonna go aground!" I don't know what he thought any one could do. Shortly after her call for help she did go aground and took her bottom out. The *Henry Steinbrenner* sent out a distress call. The seas were taking off her hatch covers. Later she went down, taking seventeen sailors with her. The *Cuyler Adams* was also in trouble. Around daybreak I sensed something was wrong. The third mate kept looking aft. When I saw what he was looking at I yelled, "Jesus, that's land off our stern!"

"Yeah, that's Isle Royal" the third mate calmly stated. Its been there all night."

We had been going backwards all night.

"Take the wheel a second, I'm sick as hell, I've got to throw up."

"Cap! Cap! The wheel won't go left! I'm hard right and I can't put on left wheel!"

Cap Jappman's jaw dropped, and his eyes grew wide, but he kept his cool, and quickly called the engine room and told them to check out the steering cable. The third assistant and the oiler quickly found the trouble. The cable had come off its guide, a large crescent shaped shive the cable rides on to make the rudder turn.

"Cap, she's swinging too far right, we have to have left wheel!"

"Maybe if you check the engine to half speed, Cap, she will stop going right," the mate calmly suggested. Cap Jappman quickly rang half ahead on the telegraph. It worked. By checking the engine to half speed, the screw was pushing less water against the jammed rudder. We quit going right. Somehow the oiler and the third assistant got the heavy cable back on the shive. How they did it I'll never know. They were seasick and had to work in a space so confined they almost had to lay down. Before it was over, they had to repeat the process two more times.

Usually when a boat gets through a bad blow, the people in the pilot House get the credit for getting the boat through. In this storm the oiler and third assistant were the ones who deserved the credit.

When the eight to twelve watch came on the *Cuyler Adams* was holding her own. After my relief took the wheel I picked up the wastepaper basket so the wheelsman wouldn't have to look at it.

"Could you clean it and bring it back, Bob?" he asked.

"Ain't steamboating fun, Bob?" The third mate jeered as we were getting ready to make our dash below. He was a cool one, that third mate, but just about then I felt like kicking him overboard. Through sheer perseverance the *Cuyler Adams* fought her way out of her peril and crawled her way to Duluth. We had taken on some water and popped some rivets, but all in all we came out of it pretty good; much better than the *Henry Steinbrenner* I was sad to say. I felt guilty we fared so well and the *Steinbrenner* lost so many men. They weren't that far away from us when she sank, but we couldn't help them. We were lucky we didn't meet the same fate.

The Shipkeeper

"Maybe you do outrank Bob, but I outrank you. Bob gets the job." The second mate off another Tomlinson Boat wanted the Shipkeeper's job on the *Cuyler Adams*. He told Cap Jappman he should get the job as he was a second mate and I was only a wheelsman. Cap Jappman stuck to his guns, and I got the job.

Beulah quit her job at the telephone company and set up housekeeping in her new four hundred-seventy-four foot long home on the water front. The *Cuyler Adams* was buttoned up for the winter. Only the cook's room, galley and mess were heated by the big galley stove. The rooms were warm, except for the steel decks, which were ice cold.

We were tied up at the old D&L railroad station, at the foot of main street in Buffalo, the toughest part of town at the time. Once we saw a body floating down the channel, face down. Beulah had a hard time learning to cook. The galley range was as big as a Sherman tank. The pots and pans were huge. The cook had left us a winter's supply of food. The canned food came in one size - one-gallon cans.

"I think you may have killed a lot of sea gulls," I once told Beulah, as whenever she cooked or baked something that didn't come out right she simply flung it overboard and the poor dumb sea gulls ate it. Our boat had a lot more sea gulls hanging around than the other boats had, "and some of them don't fly too good," I told her.

Shipkeeping was a good job, you got paid a monthly wage just for staying on the boat. The shipkeepers all had a job working with the winter gang, that paid by the hour. The company furnished all your needs. Life was good.

"How are you Cap? It's good to see you again."

"I'm not Cap anymore, I'm terd mate on da Ranny."

"In my book your still Cap," I told him.

Alf Hanson was no longer Captain, but he was in charge of the winter gang, and everyone still called him Cap.

The Winter Gang

"Bob, ve gonna shift da *Davidson* to da elevators. Go up ta Handanari's and see if ya can get a crew."

Handanari's was kind of like a sailor's home. Some of the old salts would send part of their pay to Handanari's during the shipping season, and Handanari would let them stay the winter months in a couple big rooms over his bar. The rooms weren't furnished, just some mattresses on the floor. He fed them, and when the money they had sent him ran out he would let them have a bar tab. His establishment was appropriately called the Two Bit Club.

I would go in the bar of the Two Bit Club and announce, "We're shifting a boat, anyone want to make some easy bucks?" Most weren't interested.

If we needed ten I would try to get twelve, as some would change their mind during the four block walk down Lower Main Street to the boats.

It must have been a most impressive sight to see indeed, rendezvousing at the Two Bit Club, then me at the head of my troops marching down Main Street, leaning into the strong, cold, Buffalo winter winds. Most of my troops were hatless and without gloves. They wore half-buttoned overcoats that flapped in the brisk winds blowing off Lake Erie. Well, maybe they weren't much to look at and they were heavy drinkers and a little obnoxious to be around at times, but that doesn't mean they weren't men; and men are human. Humans have feelings. I noticed that Cap Hanson treated them with respect. I did, too.

I think bad things must have happened to some of these men. They had to be very lonely. Maybe if I had not met Beulah, I would be sleeping on a mattress over the bar in the Two Bit Club. I was fast going down that road before I met her.

By prying a crow bar in the teeth of the gears of the deck winches, we could rotate the drum of the winch and tighten the bow cable. The boat would very slowly move down to the grain elevator. Once there, the boat was unloaded with a large conveyor. Everything was done without steam to run the mooring winches and the smaller winches to open and close the heavy hatch covers. It took the better part of a week to move and unload a boat; sometimes longer. At the elevators in the winter, everything seemed to go in slow motion.

They were called grain scoopers. Their work was hard and dangerous. Grain dust was like a cloud around them. When one looked down into the cargo hold where they were working, they looked like ghosts moving about in the dust. Most of them are gone now. Buffalo still has a few working the grain elevators there.

The Shipkeeper's Wife

When it was the *Cuyler Adam's* turn to unload, word must have gotten out about the shipkeeper's wife on the *Cuyler Adams* that always fed the crew who worked on her husband's boat. We never seemed to have any difficulty getting a crew out of the Two Bit Club. The other shipkeepers always had hot coffee for their gang, but they never fed them.

Beulah's specialty was Hungarian Goulash. It really was very good. Beulah would set the crew's mess table just like a family meal at home. She would cook a huge pot of Goulash and set it in the middle of the table, steaming hot, with lots of bread, butter and hot coffee. Then Beulah and I would sit down and eat with them.

Beulah would sit at the table watching them eat, savoring the many compliments the men gave her about her good cooking. She was radiant, and very, very pretty. Why the hell didn't I tell her then how proud I was of her?

You never saw such a transformation as there was in these usually uncouth men. They were using words like "please" and "excuse me." Not one wore a hat or used a cuss word at Beulah's table. I bet that night when they laid down on their mattresses over the bar in the Two Bit Club they were thinking "that shipkeeper on the *Cuyler Adams* sure is one lucky steamboat man."

Where Did All The Boats Go?

The winter went by very fast. Soon it was May, and still no sign of fit out. Things must be slowing down, I thought. Must be the Laker's carried so much ore and coal last season the steel mills had a large supply left. That was some of the problem, but imports were starting to take their toll too.

I think the mid-fifties were the beginning of the end of the glory days for the North American Lake boats. In the early fifties there were nearly five hundred boats on the Great Lakes but a rather nasty combination of events was occurring. Steel mills didn't modernize their plants, unions got too greedy, the regulators invaded the plants like Christ coming to cleanse the temple and the government agencies wanted too much too fast. All the politicians wanted feathers in their caps and shutting down polluters was one way to get them. The Japanese were soon able to make and sell good steel cheaper than America.

There wasn't a need for as many Lakers plying the Great Lakes. Now I hear there are less than forty American boats. Well, now the regulators, good union people, and politicians don't have so much to worry about anymore. Most of the steel mills are long gone and they can say they did their part, and as a bonus, got rid of most of those smelly old boats too.

Anna III

"Why don't we look into this, Jack?" Jack was a shipkeeper on another Tomlinson boat, the James E. Davidson. Jack was a Third Mate. He had a wife and two kids. I was reading the classified ads in the Courier Express, the Buffalo paper;

"Sightseeing boat and business for sale."

It gave an address in Youngstown, New York. Jack was interested.

"Why don't we go down to Youngstown and see what there is to it."

Dick and Susan Taylor, the owners of the sightseeing boat, were a middle-aged roly-poly, but not jolly, couple. They had little sense of humor and were strictly out for the buck. They were hard people for me to like.

"We want ten thousand for the business with twenty-five hundred down. We'll take a note for the balance and work out a payment plan. Get in my station wagon, and I'll take you down and show you the boat."

Dick drove us down to the dock. The boat's name was Anna III. It was a converted salt water fishing boat. Dick had sailed her up the inland water way from Florida.

The Anna III was just under fifty feet long and was powered with a one hundred-horse Gray Marine engine. She was old, but strong, and almost unsinkable. Jack and I both liked what we saw.

Dick was in the process of painting it and getting it ready for the tourist season. When Dick was out of earshot I suggested to Jack, "Why don't we offer to help? That way we can check the boat out real good for dry rot."

"Mr. Taylor, Bob and I don't have anything to do today, we could help you with the boat if you like."

Dick looked surprised. "Okay," he said.
At the end of the day the boat was bright and clean and freshly painted red, white, and blue.

"Always paint a boat red, white, and blue and you can't go wrong," Dick said. Dick was happy with the day's progress.

Susan came down to the boat and showed us the books. The books showed the business was making a profit, and each year the business was getting better.

"We'll get back to you," Jack told them. Driving back to Buffalo, Jack was excited.

"Running a business like that wouldn't be work, it would be fun." I agreed with him.

We talked it over with Rose, Jack's wife, and Beulah. The girls thought it was a good idea, too. We had a slight problem, no money for a down payment. With the help of Ronnie and Betty, who were now married, Beulah's folks, and my folks, we raised enough for the down payment. Jack and Rose said they couldn't raise any money as they had just bought a new car and they were making payments on a house trailer.

Since Jack had a mate's license, he would run the boat most of the time. Jack was adept at giving the lecture, as sometimes he gave the sermons at his church, and didn't mind talking to a crowd of people; something very hard for me to do.

Beulah would run the ticket stand in front of the post office on Falls Street in Niagara Falls, and Rose would run the stand in Youngstown. It would be my job to get the people from Niagara Falls to Old Fort Niagara, from Fort Niagara to the boat, then back to Niagara Falls. It was hectic, and everything had to go like clockwork as there were three trips daily.

I enjoyed the people. They were just out for a good time, and usually they gave me good tips. I always told the people I only worked for the business. We had little books of snapshots of the boat and sights along the Niagara River. We had them made up for a dime each and sold them for sixty cents. I told the people the proceeds went to the people who worked for the business. They sold like hotcakes. I could still con a little.

I don't think Bill and Jean approved of Beulah and I. We both smoked, and on occasion, liked to go and have a drink or two. Except for the four letter word, Beulah could swear as good as I could.

A two-hour cruise.

The Anna III, Lower Niagara River Cruise.

Scenic Beauty AND Historical Lore

COMBINED TO MAKE A
GRAND BOAT CRUISE

Your Boat trip starts from the quaint old fishing village of Youngstown. As you cruise north towards Lake Ontario, beauty is on every side. To your left is the Dominion of Canada and to your right is the United States of America.

As you near Lake Ontario, you pass the old Lighthouse and United States Coast Guard Station. Here you will see the boats and equipment used by the Country's oldest military service.

From your comfortable seat, as the Guide aboard the boat narrates the story, you will see Fort Niagara which was built by the French 226 years ago. At the conclusion of this trip those who wish will have an opportunity to go through these old buildings.

Your boat now forms a circle in Lake Ontario that brings you in close to the Canadian Shore Line. For the next 30 minutes you will be cruising in Canadian waters to see such points of interest as Fort George, Niagara-on-the-Lake, Fort Mississauga, Queenston Heights and Brock's Monument all of which will be explained by your Guide.

As you approach the mouth of the Great Gorge of the Niagara, words cannot describe the wonders of the sheer rock walls and the rushing torrents of water, which you will view from a safe distance, then turn and follow the American Shore Line back to the dock at Youngstown.

We feel sure that you will agree that nowhere else in the world can there be found such a concentration of natural beauty and historical lore and that this exhilarating 2 hour cruise will be one of the highlights of your memorable trip to Niagara Falls.

HOW TO GET TO THE YOUNGSTOWN BOAT DOCK
11 MILES NORTH OF NIAGARA FALLS, N. Y., ON ROUTE 18F

From Downtown Niagara Falls—Go North on Main St. (Route 18) to Lewiston, N. Y. Then take Route 18F to Youngstown.
From Niagara Falls Boulevard (Route 18)—Follow Route 18 to Route 265 North to Lewiston, N. Y., then follow Route 18F to Youngstown.
From Route 104—Follow Route 104 to Lewiston, N. Y., then follow Route 18F to Youngstown.
From Buffalo, N. Y.—Follow any Route to Niagara Falls, then take Route 18 North to Lewiston, N. Y., then Route 18F to Youngstown.
From Grand Island—Follow Route 324 to Route 265 North, then Route 18 North to Lewiston, N. Y., then Route 18F to Youngstown.

RESERVATIONS AND TICKETS are available at your Hotel, Cabin, Tourist Home, Travel Agent or Call Us.

MAIN TICKET OFFICE   22 Falls St., Niagara Falls, N. Y., Phone 4-8000
YOUNGSTOWN TICKET OFFICE   Phone Youngstown 7-2779
ADDRESS ALL MAIL TO: ANNA III CRUISE, YOUNGSTOWN, N. Y.

A Champion Falls

"My name's Vic Christie. I would like to talk to you about chartering your boat." Vic Christie was a pro wrestler on TV. He was also the trainer and manager of a very famous long distant swimmer, Florence Chadwick.

Miss Chadwick had swum the English Channel and was considered one of the best women long distance swimmers in the world. It was to be the grand opening of the Canadian Exposition. A very big event. If Miss Chadwick chartered our boat, we would get a lot of publicity and we would be part of the event. The Expo publicity promoters wanted Miss Chadwick to make a swim from Old Fort Niagara to Toronto, Canada, a distance of forty miles. One hell of a swim. The event was to take place on Labor Day.

"Labor Day weekend should be the best weekend of the year for business," I reminded Jack. "We should have a full boat every trip."

"Okay," Jack reasoned, "why don't we go by that; six trips at one hundred twenty dollars a trip. Seven hundred and twenty bucks."

"Okay," Vic Christie said, "but we will have to make a trial run out three or four miles, before the weekend."

"Fine with us," Jack and I agreed.

Miss Chadwick was one very pleasant lady. We all liked her from the start. She was very friendly and nice.

"You'd never know she was famous," Beulah remarked.

When we left the mouth of the Niagara River on the trial swim it was very rough out on Lake Ontario. Anna III was pitching violently in heavy green swells. Miss Chadwick had a big grin on her handsome face. She loved it. She dove in and started her swim. I never saw anyone move so effortlessly in the water. The power she had in her strokes was unbelievable. Two reporters along with Rose, Beulah and one not too well-hidden stowaway had come with us. The lady reporter got terribly seasick. Rose also got sick as well as the other reporter, but like an old salt he hid it pretty well. Jack was a little sick, so was I. The only ones who didn't get sick were Beulah and the stowaway. At least I don't think the stowaway got seasick. Vic Christie was a little green around the gills.

When we got back to the dock in Youngstown, Miss Chadwick was happy and excited. The trial swim went very well. "I can do it," I heard her tell Vic Christie.

"And I was worried about you, Beulah!" Miss Chadwick said with a little smile. I think she was picking on the rest of us just a bit.

It was nearing midnight. Soon it would be Labor Day, nineteen fifty-two. Anna III was tied up at the dock at Old Fort Niagara. It was Anna's most glorious moment, her red, white and blue paint shining in the glare of the television lights. She had a string of blue lights along her sides so Miss Chadwick could distinguish her from all the other boats that had gathered to witness the great swim. Our biggest fear was losing Miss Chadwick in the dark vastness of choppy Lake Ontario.

We had a problem. Miss Chadwick had gotten a virus. She had a fever, and an upset stomach. Vic Christie wanted to call off the swim but Miss Chadwick insisted she would go and she won out. She dove off the dock and the swim was on.

"Maybe if you sent out a Coke, it would settle my stomach," Miss Chadwick called out from the darkness. She could see our blue lights, but we couldn't see her.

"Get the life boat," Vic ordered.

When I went to get the life boat. It was gone. I cursed Jack under my breath. "A third mate and he don't know shit. I should have tied the life boat on myself."

Jack eased the Anna III close to Miss Chadwick and we managed to get the Coke to her with the aid of a pole we were allowed to use. If Miss Chadwick touched the boat, she would be disqualified.

"I think we should call it quits," Vic Christie said. Miss Chadwick drank some of the Coke and continued her swim but she was slowing down. We were going so slow the generator couldn't keep the blue lights burning. Every so often we had to put the engine in neutral and rev up the engine to keep them going. Now Miss Chadwick was really sick. We could hear her vomiting.

"That's it," Vic Christie said. "Shine a light on her. We're pulling her in, like it or not." When we pulled Miss Chadwick into the boat she was sobbing so hard her chest was heaving up and down. Vic put a blanket around her and took her below where it was warm, and we had a bunk she could rest in. It was very quiet in the little pilot house of Anna III. No one felt like talking the whole twenty-three miles to the Yacht Club in Toronto. About all you could hear was the slapping of the waves of choppy Lake Ontario against the bow, and the throaty sound of the Anna's exhaust.

Miss Chadwick swam a little more than seventeen miles. When we got to Toronto there were no reporters, no crowds of people, just a caretaker who took our lines as we eased into a slip at the Yacht Club.

Vic Christie thanked Jack, and I and shook hands good-bye. Miss Chadwick didn't say a word. She just looked down like a little girl who had done something wrong. Little did she know how proud we were just to know such a fine, gallant lady as her.

Jack was exhausted. I told him to go below and get some rest, I would take Anna back to Youngstown. Alone in the pilot house I had time to reflect back on the last twenty-four hours. "By the time we pay for our expenses and for the lost rented life boat, we won't make any money," I thought. But just having the honor of knowing Miss Chadwick and Vic Christie and the experience of it was pay enough for me. When I was halfway across the lake I thought about the forty-mile swim. It seemed like an impossible feat for a human being to do. How wrong I was.

We didn't know it at the time, but shortly after Anna III left Old Fort Niagara with Miss Chadwick swimming alongside, a young sixteen year-old girl dove off the same spot Miss Chadwick had. Her name was Marilyn Bell. She was a Canadian girl. Marilyn Bell wasn't as strong and as fast a swimmer as Miss Chadwick. It took her a long time to make the swim, but she went the distance, and that's what counted. Miss Bell made the headlines and Canada had a new hero. One of their own had beaten the best from the great colossus to her south.

Bob Broughton Will Accompany Chadwick In Lake Ontario Try

A Wellsville sailor will be in the swim of things when Miss Florence Chadwick attempts to conquer Lake Ontario on Labor Day Night.

Miss Chadwick, Holder of the women's time record for swimming the English Channel will try to master Lake Ontario in an estimated 18 hour swim which will start at Fort Niagara and end in Toronto. Lake Ontario is one of the hardest places for distance swimmers to conquer because of the changing tided and currents.

Bob Broughton, a Wellsville native who now owns a sight seeing cruiser named Anna III will accompany the swimmer. His wife, the former Miss Beulah Sick, may also make the trip.

Mr. Broughton and his partner took Miss Chadwick's trainer out on Monday for a survey of the Lake.

If Miss Chadwick manages to swim the treacherous Great Lake she will be the first to have done so.

(From the Wellsville Daily Reporter)

Beulah, Bonnie, and Bob

"If your father was here, he'd do something." Beulah was in labor and in a lot of pain. She was mad as hell at me. I was to blame and I should be doing something.

"If your father was here he would make the doctors and nurses do something. He wouldn't let me just lie here in all this pain," she cried. It took over twenty-four hours, but at last it was over. We had a gorgeous baby girl and Beulah wasn't mad at me anymore.

That's who the stowaway was on Florence Chadwick's trial swim. We named her Bonnie. When someone says "there goes the proud Daddy," that's one hell of an understatement.

Now that I was a Daddy and the tourist season was over, I was desperate for a job. Just previous to the big swim, Rose's brother Walt had come up from New Orleans to stay with Rose and Jack. Walt was a construction worker, a metal lather.

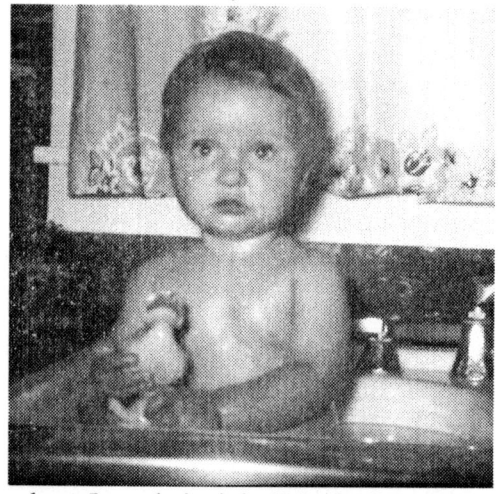

Walt found out I needed a job. "Maybe I can get ya'll a job as a Lather," Walt said.

"That would be great Walt. What the hell is a Lather?"

"It's kind of hard to explain. I guess it's a little like Carpenter work, but ya'll work in metal instead of wood. Ya'll build partitions and ceilings out of metal channels and studs. Then ya'll tie on the metal lath. It takes a long time to learn. Ya'll have to start out as an apprentice and ya have to join the union. The apprenticeship rule is ya'll can't be over twenty-one and ya'll all supposed to have a high school education. That part ya'll will have to work out somehow. I'll talk to the Lather's business agent, the B.A. that is."

Carmen Bonjouinne was the Lather's B.A. He was in his late forties, bald and powerfully built.

"How old are you?" he asked.

"I'll be twenty-one in a few weeks," I lied. I was twenty-seven.

"Did you finish high school?"

"Yes Sir, I did," I lied.

"Get a pair of wire nippers, a rule, and a pair of tin snips. Have Walt show you what to get. We'll give you a try. Go to the new school being built on Pine Ave. Be there on Monday morning by eight."

It was as easy as that. All you had to do is lie a little. Why the hell didn't I do that when I first got out of the Navy?

Carmen taught me a lot. He taught me to lath houses, how to suspend channel iron ceilings and tie on the metal lath. He taught me how to make jigs and bend channel iron to form graceful curves and make Gothic Arches like you see in some churches. He taught me the art of running metal beads that act as a guide for the plasterers to follow. Later I became very good at that. When I got to be a journeyman lather I was known as a good bead man. This skill most always insured me a job if there was one to be had.

There was an older man, Carmen, teamed me up with. His name was Gene. Gene was good to me, and I learned a lot from him. He was knowledgeable about everything under the sun. I sometimes wondered why he was a lather instead of a doctor or a scientist or something of that nature. He told me his brother was a corporate lawyer for Bell Aircraft, a very big outfit in Niagara Falls. Gene would say his brother was brilliant, but I don't think Gene was very far behind. For some reason Gene and his brother would have nothing to do with each other.

The other guys I worked with were mostly in their early twenties. I was pushing thirty but they all called me the kid.

"Hey kid, give me a hand here."

"Hey kid, go get a bundle of lath."

"Send the kid out for coffee."

I got a kick out of it. It was hard work and I was always tired at the end of the day, but it was a good tired. The kind of tired that was worthwhile. Carmen was a working B.A. He was always a foreman and I was Carmen's apprentice. He took me on every job he went on. No one ever misused the new apprentices, I wonder why that was.

Lathers hanging channel Iron.
The man standing furthest back is Gene Conners.

Beulah, Bonnie, Barbie and Bob

"You weren't man enough to make a boy the first time, were you?" Beulah was mad as hell once again. She was having a very long and painful delivery, and this time she stayed mad even after the baby came. I thought it best that I get out of sight for a while.

When I went to the delivery room to see my new daughter, I was kind of shocked. She had large red marks on her head and her whole face was very red. Was she ever objecting to being brought into the world! Her little fists were doubled up and she was kicking and crying so hard it drowned out the sound of all the other babies.

"Is she okay?" I asked the nurse.

"With a cry like that she has to be," the nurse assured me. We named her Barbara. What an absolute joy she turned out to be. I did not go back to say good-bye to Beulah. I just walked out of the Wellsville hospital, got in our old Ford and headed for Niagara Falls, one hundred miles away, but more like a thousand in that old Ford.

Bang! Oh boy! That's all I need. A blow out ! The wind was blowing, it was snowing and bitter cold. When I got out the spare tire, it was flat also. I knew there was a gas station about a mile and a half up the road, but I didn't know what time it closed. It was nearing ten at night. When I got to the station, the owner said he was closing and couldn't fix my tire.

"Put some air in it," he said. "Maybe it has a slow leak."

I filled the tire and it held. The station attendant didn't offer to drive me back to my car. He sure wasn't as generous as that old gent in Erie, I thought. By the time I walked back to the car and got the spare on, I was half frozen. The heater in the old Ford barely put out enough heat to keep the ice off the windshield. 'Hope I got enough gas to make it,' I worried. 'I wished I had said good-bye to Beulah, but she was so mad at me! Best I get back to the Falls so I can get a little sleep before it's time to go to work. I sure can't take any time off, we need the money so badly.'

It was a long, cold, lonely drive back to the Falls.

Spring of nineteen fifty-four was near and we didn't have the three hundred dollars to get the Anna III out of hock at the boatyard. They wouldn't put the boat back into the water until we paid up.

"I'll give ya seven-fifty, not a penny more," the dealer said.

"But it's worth a hell of a lot more," I complained.

I was in Wellsville trying to sell my car so we could get the Anna in the water. It broke my heart, but I sold my neat little fifty-two Mercury and bought an old nineteen forty-one Chrysler. I paid four hundred for the old Chrysler, which left three hundred fifty to get the boat into the water.

I told Jack I was going to keep my job lathing. As I was putting up all the money I would only work on the boat weekends and nights. This arrangement put too much strain on Beulah, so we got my kid sister, Velma, to help out at the ticket stand.

The old Chrysler was an undertaker's limousine. It could carry nine people comfortably but Beulah would manage to pack in about twelve. The Chrysler was ideal for the boat business, but it also had to be my personal car. I felt a little strange driving it, it was damn near as long as the *Cuyler Adams*, it seemed.

***

It was getting near the end of the season. The Anna III seemed to be carrying lots of passengers on the weekends, but we weren't covering our expenses. We had a big gas bill, the dock rent wasn't paid and we were starting to owe a lot of people money.

"Why don't you come down and see our new trailer?" Rose asked. Rose and Jack had traded their modest trailer for a big beautiful new mobile home - a Spartan, the Cadillac of mobile homes at the time.

The Anna III wasn't any fun anymore and Beulah and I wanted out. It was agreed if Jack and Rose paid the bills we had acquired, Beulah and I would just walk away from the business, forfeiting the money we put up initially.

Beulah and I never contacted Rose and Jack again. I later heard they lasted about half the next season, then they bellied up.

Beulah, Bonnie, Barbie, Bruce and Bob

We were living in Jack and Rose's old trailer all the time I was an apprentice. When Jack and Rose traded it for their new trailer we bought it off the dealer he traded with. The trailer was small, eight feet wide and thirty feet long. Beulah, Bonnie, Barbie, and Bob were packed in pretty tight.

Gene bought a tiny old trailer and moved it next to ours at the trailer park we were living in just outside Niagara Falls. I don't know if Gene adopted us, or we adopted him. Anyway he became one of the family.

My three year apprenticeship was over. I had my book. I was a Journeyman Lather. I was free to work wherever I wanted to. Beulah and I decided to move to Wanita Lake. I would transfer to

Elmira, where there was a small Lather's Local of about fifteen lathers.

Wanita Lake was a very pretty little lake located between Seneca and Keuka Lake, two of the Finger Lakes. I bought a small lot there with lake frontage and hauled our trailer there with my old nineteen-fifty Buick. Before we got there the rear end of the old car developed a howl that sounded like a fire engine every time you slowed down. I drove it that way for two more years.

Sometime in the late nineteen-forties the great politicians of New York State decided they wanted to show their gratitude to their World War II veterans. They decided to give all the vets that served overseas a two hundred fifty dollar cash bonus. I used this money to buy the lot at Wanita. The bonus was to be paid for by levying a four cent tax on cigarettes and a three cent tax on gasoline. The tax is still there today. After buying about 40,000 gallons of gasoline over forty some years, and probably 30,000 packs of cigarettes between Beulah and I, that bonus cost me about two thousand, five hundred dollars. Please politicians, don't give me any more 'bonuses.'

"Well you did it. You got your son this time." Beulah wasn't mad at me. It was a tough delivery, but I had a fine handsome son. We named him Bruce. I'm very proud of my son, he's a fine man.

Well, with Beulah, Bonnie, Barbie, Bruce and Bob, the old trailer was busting at the seams. Work was good so Beulah and I traded our trailer in for a new one that was ten foot wide by fifty foot long. It was very nice and we enjoyed it a great deal.

"Bob, Gene called. He wants to come to Wanita. He wants to bring his old trailer," Beulah said.

"The neighbors aren't going to like it, and the lot is really too small for two trailers. But okay, if that's what he wants," I said.

Sure enough, Gene moved his old trailer down from Niagara Falls and parked it next to ours at the lake, and sure enough the neighbors didn't like it one bit.

I told them, "I owned property on the lake long before they did, and if they didn't like it they could move."

One of the neighbors called me an arrogant son-of-a-bitch, but they shut up and left us alone.

Gene had been a lather most of his life, and wanted to quit.

"Why don't we build houses?" he asked me one day.

"I don't know anything about building houses," I told him. "And I don't have any money to start one."

"You can read a blue print, can't you? You know how to read a level, plumb-bob and square, don't you? You're an expert at lathing houses, and you can learn to plaster. Plastering shouldn't be much harder than spreading soft butter on bread and there's good books on plumbing and wiring I'll get you. I never saw a new house that did not sell," he added. "I'll put up all the money, you do the work, and we'll sell the house when it's finished, and split the profit." Then Gene looked me in the eye as if defying me to give him a negative answer, and I couldn't.

"Okay," I said, "why not? But I can't quit my job lathing." "I've already found some land outside Elmira and Horseheads. It's got a partially built house on it." This time he had a kind of a smug look on his face. Well, to make a long story short, Gene bought the property. The half-built house was crooked as hell. It was out of square, out of plumb, and the whole back wall had to be dug out and replaced. It was poorly designed and it would have been much easier to have started from scratch, building from our own plan.

I did most of the work like we agreed, and the house turned out to be quite nice. One thing I learned while working on the house, plastering was a hell of a lot harder than spreading soft butter on bread.

This time I think I got conned a little. We hit a snag. The property only had a dug road up to the house. When Gene bought the property, the seller told him the town had a deed to the road. The town had to improve and maintain the road.

"Not so," said the town supervisor, "we don't have a deed to the road, and we won't improve or maintain it."

Well, here we were with a house without a maintained road to it. When it rained, it was too muddy, and in the winter it was blocked with snow. The bank wanted no part of it. We had a nice, almost new house that wouldn't sell.

Beulah, Bonnie, Barbie, Bruce, Billy and Bob

"I have to go now!" Beulah cried.

"But you always take at least twenty-four hours to have a baby after you get to the hospital, what's the big rush?" I asked.

"I have to go NOW!" Beulah yelled. The tears started running down her cheeks.

I quickly got the kids dressed and in the car, and took Beulah to the hospital. While they were taking Beulah to her room, I told her I would take the kids to her mother's in Wellsville, and get back as soon as I could.

When I got back from Wellsville, I dreaded going to her room. I didn't like seeing my wife in a lot of pain, and I just knew she was going to be mad as hell at me again. When I went in the room, Beulah was sitting up in bed. A sister was combing her hair and she had a little make up on. Beulah was never more beautiful. I was confused. This wasn't what I expected.

"What's the matter, your pains stop?" I asked.

"Yeah, they stopped. You have another son," she said, still wearing that beautiful smile. Beulah wasn't a bit mad at me. I loved her, but I knew I wouldn't tell her sometimes having a baby isn't a bit hard on Dads. Matter of fact, sometimes it's very, very, nice.

We named our new son Billy. Everyone says Billy looks and acts just like his old man. I don't know if this is good or not, but I know I like it. One thing I know for sure is I have four good kids I'm very proud of and I think the world of them. I'm not going to write too much about my kids. It would be another whole book, if I did. I want them to write their own stories and when they do I want to read them. I'll find out things I never knew about them, like they're finding out about me.

Well now, with Beulah, Bonnie, Barbie, Bruce, Billy, and Bob Broughton, even a ten by fifty trailer was pretty small.

Gene suggested I buy the house from him for what he had into it. "You can pay me what you can. Besides, I eat my meals with you, that can count as some of the payments."

The deal worked out well for both of us.

The little house in Horseheads.

Bonnie, Barbara, Bruce & Billy.

The Machine Shop

In the early sixties things were going along pretty well and lathing was good. Gene and I bought an ancient old 'Cleat-Track' bulldozer. I taught myself how to run it, built a pond, and a dug road to the top of our hill. I also built a fireplace in the house.

Beulah talked the town supervisor into building a road up to the house. The town told us they would build and maintain a good gravel road, if we would pay for all the gravel. Then Beulah talked the other three land owners who would benefit by the road into helping pay for it. Some gal, that Beulah.

I told Gene, now that we had a good road, the house would sell, but I think he liked it the way things were. He didn't want to sell. Something's up, I thought. I was getting suspicious. He's got another damn brainstorm smoldering away in the back of his head, I told myself.

"Why don't we build a small machine shop, Bob?" Gene asked out of the blue one day.

"I don't know a damn thing about running machines," I told Gene.

"I know, but your Dad does, there isn't a machine your Dad can't run, he can teach us how to run them."

Oh boy, here we go again. I knew Gene was going to talk me into building a machine shop.

"Where in hell are you going to get the machines? Do you know what just one lathe would cost?"

Once more, Gene had that familiar smug look on his face.

"At Shulman's Scrap Yard, they buy up these old machines the factories replace and resell them for about twice the scrap value. You can buy them dirt cheap. Most need work on them, but your Dad knows how to fix them up, he can get them running, if he'll help us."

"Okay, okay , where do you think a good spot to build the shop would be?" I asked.

"Just above the house, I've already got it staked off. Oh, by the way, I bought a lathe, and a small milling machine yesterday.

They're going to truck them up next week. I'll have to buy a tarp to cover them if we don't get the building up by then."

"Good Lord," I muttered to myself as I cranked up the old bulldozer.

Dad was retired from the Worthington and was restless and bored. When Gene and I told him about our plans he was excited.

"All my life I've wanted a little shop," he said. "I'll help you all I can."

That very week he and Mom came over to our house to stay. Beulah, the kids, and I enjoyed having them. We bought an old upright piano so Mom and Dad could play their music, which they did almost every evening. Dad started fixing up the old machines and soon we had our shop running. Then he started teaching Gene and I how to run the machines. Gene picked it up very fast. I was slower learning, but got pretty adept at running the engine lathe. Soon I was marketing some of the tools I thought would sell.

Dad had talked to some people at the Preheater Plant in Wellsville. They told him there was a need for men with his knowledge and skills, and they would farm out work to him, as he could make some of their special tool needs cheaper than they could. The Worthington said they would like to give some jobs to Dad, but couldn't. It would bring about too many Union problems.

One tool I was making was a magnetic nail holder. I was selling them as fast as I could make them. The tool was used to hold very small heat-treated nails that were driven into concrete. It took the place of a wire clip holder that was slow and awkward. I was making the tool on the engine lathe.

"What you need is a turret lathe, Bob," Dad told me. "Then you could make the tool in one setup, you could shuck them out like peanuts."

"There's a nice little turret lathe down at the scrap yard. I'll buy it, but you'll have to make the shop longer. We don't have much room ," Gene said.

Before I could object, Gene changed the subject. "George, I need to cut a left hand thread on this shaft I'm making. How do I do that?" he asked. "You cut a left hand thread the same way you cut a right hand thread. All you have to do is stand on the other side of the lathe." For a fraction of a second, Gene started to walk around to the other side of the lathe. My mother also had a good sense of humor. There was always laughter in Mom and Dad's home.

July 29, 1965, when I got home from work, Beulah and the kids were standing in the driveway. She was crying, the kids were looking down at the ground.

"Bob, your father had a heart attack, he's gone."

Like all men my Dad had his faults, but the good in him far outweighed all his faults. He worked hard for his family, and never asked much for himself. He always wanted a new car, but never bought one "The kids need things more than I need a new car," he would say. He enjoyed dressing up and he liked new clothes, but he never owned more than one suit at a time. He had a sense of humor and he had compassion for both animals and humans. He also had a short temper at times. On a couple of occasions he came at me like a rampaging bear, but he never hurt Mom or me or any of the rest of the kids. I never heard of anyone who had met my father say one bad thing about him. Even the Union officials at the Worthington whom he sometimes had friction with said he was fair, and they respected and liked him. He had a natural grace and charm. So did my mother. They didn't know they had it. It was just there. It wasn't the charm that some people are able to turn on and off at will when they want something from you, their's was natural and it was there all the time.

After Dad went, I never heard my mother play the piano again. When Dad's heart gave out so did the heart of our little machine shop. Without his expertise, the shop was too much for Gene and I, so we gave it up.

There seemed to be a void in my life. I felt like stealing some rich guy's sailboat and sailing the hell away from Horseheads. Not fighting the wind, or using a compass, just letting the wind take me wherever it had a mind to. Sometimes a man can get restless and can long for a little adventure and a change of lifestyle so badly he can hardly stand it. I'm sixty-five now, and that feeling I had back then is starting to come back into my life. I feel like running away. But I know I won't, I love my wife too much to do that.

Back there in the sixties, when I got that feeling, I found a remedy for the problem. The best cure for me was to create a challenge; a challenge so difficult for me to do there was a good chance I may not be able to accomplish it.

"Bob, your father had a heart attack, he's gone."

The New Stone House

"By God, I'll build a house, that's what I'll do." Then I won't have to steal a sailboat and sail away. This time I won't have to follow Gene's brainstorm. I've got my own darn brainstorm smoldering away in the back of my head. I'll build the house across from the shop. "First I have to clear the spot off," I thought. I cranked up the old bulldozer. Ten minutes after the brainstorm was born I was putting it into reality.

Beulah came home from work at the dry-cleaners and walked up to where I was clearing off the land. I shut off the bulldozer so we could talk.

"What are you doing, Bob?"

"Clearing some land to build a house on, Beulah."

"Oh, don't you think you ought to get a building permit first, do you want fried potatoes, or mashed for supper?" she said in one sentence. That's the way Beulah was and still is, no matter what hairbrained scheme I wanted to try, she never tried to stop me. In fact she always broke her neck to help me. At the supper table that night, we talked about the house we were going to build. Everyone wanted their own bedroom. That was foremost in their minds. That night I made a floor plan of the house. Rectangular in shape, 86 feet long by 28 feet wide, it would have four bedrooms, two baths, a large kitchen. Beulah insisted on a dining room big enough for lots of company. The living room would have a fireplace. It would be a Spanish-style ranch, with arches and hued beam ceilings with textured plaster walls and ceilings.

The exterior was to be all hand-picked fieldstone. Well now, it requires a hell of a lot of stone to build a house that big so many evenings weekends and holidays were spent scouring the nearby creek beds for suitable stone. Often while taking a Sunday drive one of the kids would spot some "really good stones" for the house, and we would stop and throw a few in the trunk of the car. After we accumulated quite a pile of stone, it was time to start the house.

The lot was leveled with the old bulldozer and the footers dug out by hand. Barbie and I hand mixed the concrete for the footers and floor with a Sears & Roebuck cement mixer, which was totally worn out when we were through. Once while sitting at the supper table, everyone complimented Bonnie on her first chocolate cake.

"When she's married, she will make her husband a good cook," my mother remarked.

"Yes," Barbie cut in, "but I bet she won't be able to mix her husband a good batch of concrete like I can," she bragged.

We built the walls over twenty-five years ago, and never spent an hour maintaining them. They look the same now as they did then.

I continued building the house weekends. It was slow going. The Lath and Plaster industry was being replaced by drywall. I was spending most of my time working out of town, sometimes as far away as Atlantic City. I was chasing after work that was getting more elusive every year.

"What are you doing, Bob?"
"Clearing some land to build a house on, Beulah."

Boatswain Kelly

Beulah, the kids and I had never taken a vacation except for going someplace on a weekend or holiday, so we decided to buy a boat. Our first boat was a home-built kit boat. It was very well made, but the engine wasn't too good. The transmission slipped a little and it had a bad fly wheel that caused the starter to lock up.

We planned to take the boat on a trip from Watkins Glen to Lake Ontario, by the way of the Erie Barge Canal. About half-way up Seneca Lake, the boat started losing speed even though the engine was running fine. We turned around and headed back to our dock on the south end of the lake. By the time we reached the dock we were barely moving. The transmission was slipping so badly that the prop was barely turning.

The trip was called off. We were all disappointed. We had planned the trip for a long time. To cheer the kids up, Beulah and I decided to take the kids to the drive-in. The movie *Bonnie and Clyde* was playing. It didn't cheer any of us up much. The movie was kind of sad.

I was determined to take Beulah and the kids on the boat trip, but couldn't find anyone who knew how to fix the transmission. Finally someone told me to talk to a man who owned a marina on Keuka Lake called Kelly's Marina. Beulah and I loaded the kids in the car and drove over to Kelly's Marina. I went inside the marina and asked a young lad working there if the owner was about.

"Yeah, he's working on a boat. He's out back at the dock, just go out there and you'll see him."

I walked down to the dock. A man was working under the dash of a large slick runabout, installing a stereo speaker. He had his back to me and was mumbling something about "people living high on the hog." At that instant, it hit me. I knew the man without even seeing his face. I had a flashback of a man wearing a white hat, blue shirt and dungarees. He had a Bos'n's pipe hung around his neck. I was dumbfounded for a few seconds. After I regained my composure I asked the man,

"Were you in the Navy?"

"Yeah," he answered, still not turning around.

"Were you on the *Arkab*?" I asked.

The man froze for a second. Then he finally faced me and answered my last question.

"Yeah, I was on the *Arkab,* but I don't like to brag about it. Who are you?" he asked.

"I'm Bob Broughton. You're my old Bos'n." I must have had a big grin on my face. I was really happy to see him. Kelly extended his hand, and we gripped each other's hand for a long time, Kelly studying my face all the time.

"I'm sorry, I know your an old shipmate, but I just can't place you." He had a kind of hurt look in his face.

"I wouldn't wonder," I told him. "I was a skinny seventeen-year old and it's been nearly thirty years. Besides, you had a lot of sailors under you. No way could you remember all of them."

Kelly dropped his tools and invited us in his office in the Marina Building. He broke out a bottle of Burgundy, and we talked about the *Arkab* until the bottle was empty.

We talked about Lt. Roland and Johnny Carroll. We talked about Marley and Manion, another boatswain. We talked about a lot of the officers and crew, but neither of us mentioned the Captain or Executive Officer of the *Arkab.*

Kelly was a good boatswain. He knew his job and was respected by all the officers and most of the crew. When he restricted me for falling in muster out of uniform, I didn't hold it against him. He was just doing his job and a couple of other times he chewed me out, I didn't like it, but I didn't take it personally.

I remember one time Kelly asked if anyone could letter well. No one said anything, so I said I took art in school and could letter pretty good. Kelly gave me some cardboard and told me to make some stencils and paint the numbers on the life rafts. It was a soft job, a lot better than chipping paint, and I took my time. A day or two after I finished the job, and just before Kelly told the Second Division to fall out from morning muster, he called out, "Broughton, the Captain told me to tell the Seaman who painted the numbers on the life rafts, 'Well Done'." Kelly didn't have to mention it in front of the whole Second Division, but he did and it was just what a young insecure sailor needed. It was just a little thing, but it still gives me a warm feeling when it comes to mind.

There were a few who didn't like Kelly. I remember some called him King Kelly, but they were mostly the screw-ups who didn't like anyone in authority. I think it was men like Kelly who were the glue that held things together on Navy Ships. I think if half the officers on the *Arkab* jumped ship, the Petty Officers and the Chief Petty Officers could have kept the *Arkab* on an even keel with their absence hardly noticed.

Kelly and I talked and drank Burgundy half the afternoon. He never did remember me, but that didn't matter. We had been shipmates many years ago. That in itself creates an unbreakable bond. He didn't have to remember me.

"The kids are getting restless," I told Kelly, "I better go."

"Don't you want me to see if I can fix your boat?" Kelly asked. I had forgotten why I came over in the first place. Kelly asked me what kind of engine my boat had. I told him. He reached for a manual on a shelf, thumbed through it for a moment, found my engine in it, flipped a couple more pages.

"Here's your problem," he said. "Confidentially, you can fix it with a big screw driver and hammer in about ten or fifteen minutes." I thanked him and we shook hands again and then we left. I hoped to see him again soon.

Boat Trip

Shortly after we got back to our dock, the boat was fixed. It was simply a matter of tightening some bands where the drive shaft was connected to the engine. I took the boat out on the lake and opened it up. It went like a bat out of hell. Our boat trip was on. We loaded up and we were off.

From Watkins Glen, we headed north for some forty miles before reaching the Erie Barge Canal near Waterloo to the first lock. While chugging through the channel through the Montezuma Swamps we came up with a name for our little boat. We christened it "Swampstomper". There's a total of thirteen locks before you reach Lake Ontario. The last lock is at Oswego. From Oswego we headed Northeast diagonally across lake Ontario to a little vacation spot called Sandy Pond where we met up with Maggie and her husband, Harley, and Jim and his wife, Gloria, as well as a few other relatives.

No need to go into all the little details of our boat trip. I'll simply say a trip to Europe wouldn't have been as enjoyable or memorable. With a great cook, four terrific crew members and a proud skipper on an old wooden boat, cruising some of the nicest waterways any where, need anyone say more?

We kept that boat just one season, sold it and bought a very nice twenty-six foot Chris-Craft Cavalier. It was ten years old, but in excellent shape, and it had enough room to sleep six people, somewhat comfortably, in the cabin.

One night we were coming back from a trip to Rochester. We were about halfway down Seneca Lake. The kids were sleeping in the V bunks in the bow. It was a clear, but dark night with no moon. Beulah was sitting in the seat next to me. The lake was calm, and I could see the glow of Watkins Glen ahead. We were moving right along with the throttle about two-thirds open. The shore was about a mile and half to either side of us.

Suddenly I knew something was wrong. I knew we were in danger. I instantly killed the throttle and the boat settled in the water and stopped. I turned on the spotlight. Less than a dozen feet ahead, the light shined on a large steel square shaped buoy. It had a light mounted on it but the light was out. If we had hit that buoy, it would have smashed in the bow where the kids were sleeping. The boat would have sunk in an instant in two hundred feet of water, a mile and half from land.

I swear I never saw the buoy and neither did Beulah. It was one of the strangest and most haunting things that ever happened to me. Call it a sixth sense, or a guardian angel watching over us, I don't know, but whatever it was that saved us, I will be eternally grateful for it. We finished the trip to Watkins Glen very, very slowly. "I should start going to church," I thought.

The buoy belonged to the Army Corp. of Engineers. I told the owner of the marina to contact them and inform them the light on their buoy was out.

Our 26 foot Chris-Craft, the Limb II.

The Limb II about 26 years after we sold it. Time had taken its toll and it was ready for the scrap heap. Its a shame because with a little care it could have lasted indefinitely.

Remembering Kelly

After we took our first boat trip I had good intentions of going back and thanking Kelly for telling me how to fix our boat. Well a couple of years went by, and I didn't go see him; then twenty years went by. Each year I kept telling myself to go see Kelly.

Finally one bright, early spring day in nineteen ninety-five, Beulah and I decided to go to Branchport to see Kelly. While driving along the lake, I told Beulah I had never seen the water so blue. March in upstate New York is pretty blah. The trees are bare and the hills and fields are kind of a dull, bland, brown color, but the lake was calm, blue and beautiful with a few early boaters out on it.

When we arrived at the marina it looked like it was closed. I was thinking about going back home, when Beulah got out of the car and tried the door. It was unlocked. She went inside and after a short while came back out with a young lad who was working there.

"Bob, he wants to talk to you," Beulah said. He told me his name, then told me Kelly died two or three years ago. It was quite a shock to me, and yet the thought had crossed my mind that Kelly may have died. On the way over, I mentioned to Beulah that Kelly must be getting up there in age, maybe he isn't with us anymore.

Driving back home I was melancholy and about as blue as Keuka Lake. I scolded myself for not going to see him all those years. Kelly really wasn't a good friend of mine, he was just someone I truly liked and respected. He was a shipmate. I guess in this day and age you would say that, for me, he was a role model. I don't ever recall ever hearing that phrase when I was young.

I felt a real loss. One of my last links with the past was gone, but I can send my thoughts back in time to the *Arkab*, and see myself standing at attention with my mates in the second division; Kelly standing in front of all of us with a clipboard in his hand, his white hat squared on his head, his faded, clean shirt and dungarees giving him what we used to call a "salty" look. His black shoes were shiny and he had a Bos'n's pipe hung around his neck. We all knew who the boss of the second division on the *Arkab* was, no doubt about that.

***

The light cruiser *USS Trenton* was commissioned in April, 1924 and earned her battle star serving in the South Pacific during World War II. Kelly was on her before he was transferred to the *Arkab*. After talking to Kelly's son and wife I found out Kelly was real disappointed when he was transferred off the *Trenton*. He was proud to serve on the *Trenton* and loved the skipper he was serving under. But with all the rigging and gear it took to run an auxiliary ship like the *Arkab*, it took a knowledgeable boatswain, and Kelly was the man for the job, like it or not.

From the boat deck, Aft of the stack to the end of the fantail was Kelly's turf. It was his domain. Kelly knew this half of the ship better than any of us. Kelly knew how to rig the cargo booms, run the winches and how to load and unload the cargo. Kelly knew how to tie the ship to the dock. He could splice line and wire cable. He knew seamanship from stem to stern. Kelly was also gun captain on the five inch thirty-eight, our biggest and most important gun.

He knew how to handle the men in the second division, even the ones who didn't want to be handled. When Kelly was angry with you or wanted your attention, he could stare at you in a stern and forbidding manner and you did his bidding in short order. But despite his somewhat tough exterior, there was one young seaman who had his number. He knew Boatswain Kelly had a streak of compassion in his heart. The young seaman had seen the compassion slip out on occasion.

One time Kelly was teaching us the art of knot tying and line splicing. I was having a hard time learning...

"Broughton, let's see you tie a bowline," he ordered.

I was like a little kid trying to tie his shoes for the first time and I couldn't tie the bowline. Some of the guys started laughing

"Knock it off!" Kelly growled at them. "Just remember, there's things Broughton can do that you guys laughing may not be able to do."

His remark helped cut the hurt and embarrassment of their callous laughter. After that little incident, how could I not help liking and respecting Boatswain Kelly. Well, after a spell I learned to tie a bowline; and I learned to tie a square knot, clove hitch, half hitch, timber hitch, sheep shank, and even learned to tie a hangman's noose, which I never had occasion to use.

I learned how to splice line. The young Indian lad we called Chief taught me. He could do anything with a line. When I went on watch up in the crow's nest, I would stash a short piece of line in my pocket and practice tying knots and splicing while on watch. The officers could only see the back of my head up there.

One time Kelly and some of the crew were sitting on the hatch taking a smoke break.

"I can tie a bowline now ," I casually mentioned to Kelly.

"Good," Kelly said.

I took out the short piece of line I had stashed in my pocket. With my hands behind my back, quick as a wink, I tied a neat bowline and tossed it down on the hatch in front of the guys. It tickled Kelly to no end, none of the other guys would even try to tie a bowline behind their back. To this day I can tie a bowline behind my back, but not quite quick as a wink.

We all knew who the boss of the second division on the Arkab was.

A Theory of a Lowly Wheelsman

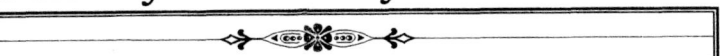

Located along a ship's sides inside the hull are huge ballast tanks. When the boat has no cargo the ballast tanks are filled to varying depths, enabling the Captain to lower his vessel deeper into the water, thus keeping the boat's screw and rudder submerged for better steering and propulsion. The ballast tanks also can be utilized if the boat has too much cargo weight on one side, causing a list. Water is pumped in the light side of the vessel until the boat is on even keel; this is called trimming. When a boat is fully and correctly loaded it needs little or no ballast, but sometimes a boat will get an extra light cargo like oats and the Captain may want his boat a little deeper in the water to make it behave better.

"We're running water in the ballast tanks, Bob, let me know when we have twenty-four inches in all tanks," Mickey, the Second Mate ordered. I broke out the sounding gear, consisting of a slate, chalk, and a long slender steel rod graduated in inches with a line attached to one end. I chalked the rod and lowered it into the well of the ballast tank. After the rod hit bottom I pulled it up. Two inches of chalk washed off, meaning two inches of water in the tank. Be quite a while before I get twenty-four inches. I went about my other duties.

OH, NO! I forgot about the ballast tanks. I quickly chalked up the sounding rod and lowered it down the well. When I pulled it up, sixty inches of chalk was gone. Damn! When I told Mickey what I had done, he quickly notified the engine room to start pumping the extra water out of the tanks. Then he told Cap Hanson we had sixty inches of water in the ballast tanks. Cap Hanson was furious. He cursed Mickey and called him a dumb bastard. I told Cap Hanson, "It wasn't Mickey's fault, it was my fault. Mickey told me to run in 24 inches and I forgot." Cap Hanson paid me no mind. He took all his wrath out on poor Mickey.

For two days all Mickey would do when he saw me was glare at me and yell, "For crying out loud, Bob." Mickey had good cause to be mad at me. Making a mistake like that was breaking an unwritten code on the lakes, a mistake that could put your shipmates in danger. Any more like that and I would lose their trust, I thought. I felt like hell, and I vowed to myself never to get lax again. I kept my vow.

Years later, after I had been off the boats for a long time, I was watching the nightly news on T.V. I was shocked when they announced a boat called the *Edmund Fitzgerald* had sunk on Lake Superior, in five hundred-thirty feet of water, taking her entire twenty-nine member crew with her. No survivors, and no bodies recovered. To this day, no one knows why the *Fitzgerald* went down in the storm. Gordon Lightfoot wrote a very sad song about the sinking, *The Wreck of the Edmund Fitzgerald*.

From what I have read of the many theories that have been published about why she sank, most don't make sense to me. The *Fitzgerald* was a relatively modern vessel. One theory was metal fatigue, but there were much older boats in the same storm, undoubtedly not as seaworthy as the *Fitzgerald*. Another theory was she struck a shoal and put a hole in her bottom. But I'd bet Captain McSorley, Master of the *Fitzgerald*, knew where he was, besides Lake Superior is so deep there's little chance of that. Another theory was a large wave came crashing through the pilot house windows disabling the Captain, Mate, and Wheelsrnan. This makes no sense to me as the boat was fighting a "Norwester", the waves would be coming at her stern. She would be in a following sea as she was down-bound. Some say her cargo shifted; she was loaded with iron ore. Iron Ore just doesn't shift, it's so heavy it's almost like it's part of the boat itself.

After all the investigations, nothing was ever proved, only theories. Looking back to the day I ran too much water in the ballast tanks of the *Cuyler Adams*, leads me to think maybe the deck watch got careless, like I did, and completely forgot about the ballast tanks, or maybe there was a misunderstanding as to whether water should be going in or out of the tanks. Maybe the pumps were filling the tanks instead of pumping water out and the *Fitzgerald* was sinking an inch at a time as she was fighting her way through the thirty foot waves on angry Lake Superior.

Another boat, the *Arthur M. Anderson*, was following the *Fitzgerald*. The *Anderson* was in contact with the *Fitzgerald* and she also had the *Fitzgerald* on her radar scope. Captain Cooper noted that the *Fitzgerald* was slowing down. Could it be because the

Fitzgerald was getting lower and lower in the heavy seas? The lower she got, the harder it would be to make forward progress. Captain McSorley's last radio message was

"Big seas, I never saw anything like it in my life."

Shortly after the message Captain Cooper lost the *Fitzgerald* on his radio. No distress call, nothing. The *Fitzgerald* just disappeared. Maybe the reason Captain McSorley reported such big waves was because he was looking at the waves from a boat much lower in the water than it had ever been before. A boat on the verge of disaster. Maybe in the end as the *Fitzgerald* was fighting its way in the huge following seas, a monstrous wave came crashing over the stern and broke the back of the slow moving, heavily burdened vessel, giving her crew no time for a prayer, or to cross themselves. I think the final wave was only the coupe de grace.

Angry as she was, I think Lake Superior was very patient in claiming the *Fitzgerald* and her crew for her very own. I think it took her all day and into darkness before she did so. If she'd had the grace to give the *Fitzgerald* just a bit more time the *Fitz* would have been tied up at the approach to the Soo Locks and out of harm's way. There would have been twenty-eight sailors sitting around the crew's mess room table drinking hot fresh coffee and bragging about how well Cap McSorley handled the *Fitz*, and what a great boat they were on.

If by chance someone is able to dive down and get into the *Fitzgerald's* engine room they could check to see if the engineers had been running water in the ballast tanks by checking the pumps or whatever mechanism activates the water to run into the tanks. If its proved no water was being pumped into the ballast tanks, another possibility is that while working and bending so hard against the storm the *Fitzgerald* cracked a hull plate, small enough not to break her but large enough to let enough water into the ballast tanks so slowly her crew couldn't tell in the thirty-foot waves and sixty-knot winds until it was too late. She was so low in the water a good size wave was enough to finish her by breaking the stern section in two and the *Fitzgerald* went down like a stone.

Another speculation was the hatch covers failed. I don't think the hatch covers were a factor. Any hatch covers I ever saw on Lake boats were very strong and always clamped and pinned or locked shut so as not to open in heavy weather. If there had been a problem with the hatch covers it would have been noticed. The pilot house allows for panoramic view of the whole deck area. After dark the deck lights light up the deck area. The mate would be checking the hatches and deck with binoculars. Besides, if there was suspicion something was amiss topside it could be checked out by walking the passageway under the deck and on top of the ballast tanks, which would give a view of the under side of the hatches without going out on the weather decks.

When Cap McSorley radioed that his boat had a list, that could indicate there was water in the ballast tanks on the corresponding side of the list. If water was getting into the cargo hold it wouldn't cause a list. Water finds it's own level so water getting into the cargo holds would just cause the boat to go lower in the water with no noticeable list.

If a diver intrudes into the engine room of the *Fitzgerald* to inspect the pumps, it would be like invading a sacred place, a tomb where at least four brave men died manning the engine room of the *Fitzgerald*. The third assistant engineer, an oiler, and fireman. In a storm of that magnitude, the chief engineer would probably be there too.

Despite their fear and probable sea sickness, this old ex-sailor knows they stuck to their post to the end. It's the character of steamboat men. They stayed at their post until the engine room filled with water, until Lake Superior's icy waters replaced the air in their lungs and they ceased to struggle. Common decency dictates that the engine room, pilot house, and living quarters of the *Fitzgerald* be left undisturbed.

I don't think it's any great mystery as to why the *Fitzgerald* sank. It simply took on water, either by human error or by the forces of nature. If you ever have had the opportunity to be on watch in the pilot house of one of those long narrow boats and looked aft and saw how they twist, bend and agonize in a storm you'd get a much better perspective on the situation. Ask any old sailor who has weathered some of those blows on the lakes, or better yet, ask some of the survivors of the *Steinbrenner, Bradley,* or *Morell,* if there are any still living. They'll tell you their boats simply broke up on the surface and filled with water until they sank.

Back in the early fifties, when I was wheeling on the *Cuyler Adams,* we got caught in several bad blows, but we had an excuse, we didn't have the excellent weather reports we now have available, with satellites that can give you very accurate reports days ahead of time. In the early fifties weather reports would sometimes tell us where we would get strong winds, for example, from the north or the northwest. So the captain would plot a course along the north side of the lakes to keep out the heavy seas that would build up on the South side.

"Ve gonna take da North shore," Captain Hanson would say in his broken English. But sometimes halfway to our destination the winds would suddenly shift to the South and we would be exactly where we shouldn't be. Once when the *Cuyler Adams* was pitching and rolling and the wind and water was slamming against the pilot house windows in a storm on Lake Superior, it got pretty scary. In fact it was down-right terrifying when we lost our steering and the deck beneath our feet was shaking and the bow started swinging too far right, which would put us parallel with the big seas. If that happened we would have in all probability, capsized.

The *Edmund Fitzgerald*, at one time was the largest vessel on the Great Lakes, with a length of over seven hundred twenty-nine feet. She was launched at River Rouge, Mich. in nineteen fifty-eight and operated by Columbia Transportation. To this day, the remains of her twenty-nine member crew are entombed inside her in five hundred thirty feet of water near Whitefish Bay in Lake Superior.

The Edmund Fitzgerald - Drawing by Bruce R. Broughton.

The Waves Song

'Tis, my turn to man the wheel
Maybe, my last so I feel
The waves come at me like a devil's machine
The waves come at me tall and mean
One after the other, no end in sight
Nature showing off her terrible might
On they come through day 'til night
In my mind to me they say
In the end we'll get our way
Fight us if you can, steamboat man
But, soon we'll execute our plan
Best you weep and pray while you can
You belong to us, steamboat man
And when you hear our song no more
We'll not wash you up on satan's burning shore
You'll be one of us, a true and trusted mate
As one we'll gently flow through heaven's open gate

I can imagine being the wheelsman on watch the night the *Fitzgerald* went down:

***

Best I stay in my bunk until it's time to relieve the twelve to four watch. I'm gonna have a long four hours when I go on, I better conserve my energy. Besides, what could I do if I did get up? I would have to hang on to something just to keep on my feet. Good thing I didn't try going aft to the galley for dinner, I would have stood a good chance of being washed overboard in this sea, besides I bet they never served dinner. I bet the cook is in his bunk, seasick. If I had eaten, it would be gone by now anyway. I'm getting a little sick myself. I hope I won't be sick while I'm at the wheel, but I probably will be. I wonder why we sailors get embarrassed when we get seasick, some are just able to hide it better. Even the old salts get seasick. They don't kid me any. Oh God, is her bow going to come back up? There. She's stopped going down, but we're just sitting here, her bow must be way under. Now she's coming back up. Why am I worrying so? The Fitz can take it. Maybe I should get out of my bunk and put my lifejacket on or something. I'll be going on watch soon. I'll be busy, that will calm me down. I wonder how far down Superior we are? Let's see, it's nearly four p.m. Monday, we left the dock in Duluth Sunday about one p.m., about twenty-eight hours ago. The Fitzgerald does about ten miles an hour loaded, two hundred-eighty miles. About three-quarters of the way down Superior. But in this weather, I don't know. Time to go on watch. Damn, it's a nightmare out here, wish I could go back to my bunk. As soon as the bow starts coming back up I'll make a dash for the pilot house stairs. Got to time it right. Damn, the deck fencing is gone. We're taking green water completely over the hatches. I don't like this. Glad I'm not on one of those other boats out there. The Fitz will get us to Whitefish Bay. Then things will calm down, she'll get us there, she's the best, she's the strongest. We'll be okay, Cap McSorley knows how to handle the Fitzgerald. We'll be in the Soo locks in a few hours. This wind is going to blow me overboard, got to hang on. Two more sets of steps to the pilot house. Almost there, go in on the lee side. Hell, there ain't no lee side. The wind is everywhere. Just get in. Wonder why I expected it to be cold in the pilot house? Hell, it's warm in here. Glad it's warm, I hate being cold. What's that *smell? Looks like someone got sick and vomited on the deck. I'll probably do the same in a little while. Less than an hour until I'm relieved of the wheel, gonna go right to my bunk. Come around Fitz, come around, you've got all the rudder I can give you. Please stop shaking. Damn it, behave. God I'm so sick. Never saw a look like that on Cap McSorley's face. Such a sad...Oh God no, we're gonna go down, he knows it ! The water...it's...so cold, it's... so black, I wish...I wish....*

The Wellsville Dry Cleaners

Nineteen seventy-two. The year of the Big Flood. There was a lot of misery for a lot of people in June of that year. Whole sections of cities and towns were covered with water and mud. A lot of people lost everything. We were high and dry, the flood would've had to be on the magnitude of the Biblical flood, to reach the top of Broughton's mountain.

But we lost more than most of the people in the valley that year. My Mother, Beulah's Dad, my Uncle Nate, and Gene Conners were gone by September of nineteen seventy-two.

I continued lathing until nineteen seventy-seven. I liked the work, but didn't see eye to eye with the union. The union had too much control. One thing I found out - you can't be your own man, and be a good Union man at the same time. I wanted to be my own man, so I decided to give up my book; time to get the hell out, I told myself.

We had the stone house livable, so we moved about 300 feet further up the hill and into our new stone house. We only lived in the house about one year, but we loved it and had the satisfaction of knowing we did it all, with the exception of drilling the well. I would have done that if I'd had a drilling rig. Best of all, we didn't owe the bank a penny on it. But we also didn't have a penny in the bank.

Not owing the bank anything would soon change. Another brainstorm was smoldering away in the back of my head.

"Beulah, why don't you quit your job at the cleaners? I'll quit lathing. We'll mortgage the houses and buy that cleaners in Wellsville."

"You won't like dry-cleaning, Bob," Beulah warned. "But we can go talk to the owners."

Well, to make a long story short, we made a deal with Anna and Bill Babcock, a hard-working couple who taught us the business and treated us fairly. When we bought the dry-cleaners in Wellsville, there were two other cleaners in Wellsville, besides a drop-off station. We wound up being the only cleaners in Wellsville except for the drop-off station. But sometimes it took borrowing money at high interest rates. Hind-sight tells me we should have walked away from the place, gone back to Horseheads and built houses.

Beulah was right. I sure didn't like dry-cleaning.

Bob & Beulah Broughton.
Proprietors of the Wellsville Dry Cleaners.

Family

I've never made much money in my lifetime, never owned a brand new car, or taken my wife to Florida for the winter, never been out of debt (and probably never will be), never had a taste of the so-called "good life". But I'm richer than some millionaires I know. I have a wife of forty-five years who is the most caring and kind person ever. A while back, she took a bad fall on the ice and broke her arm near the shoulder. She also has a bad back so she's in constant pain and probably will be for the rest of her life. Sometimes I'll look at her, mixing cookies or baking a cake and her eyes will be wet with tears, but she keeps going. My Beulah is a remarkable gal. She loves just about everyone, and just about everyone who knows her loves her, too.

I have the best kids and grandkids anywhere, and I'm so proud of them all. I regret never having been able to help them much. They work hard and don't ask anything from anyone, and that includes the government.

Billy and his wife, Audrey, work long hours and are restoring a great old farmhouse that reminds me of my Aunt Bertha's place. Let me tell you, Billy was a handful when he was little, nothing like his Dad when he was the same age. He must have inherited his mischievous ways from his mother. If I were to write about Billy's antics it would take most of my book. The gals say that Billy is cute and sexy. Now that part must have come from his Dad's side of the family.

Barb and her husband, Mark, have a wonderful place in the country just across the valley from what used to be "Broughton mountain". Barb works her tail off at the post office. Mark had a bad stroke a while back. But he is a very strong-willed individual and he's doing better with each passing day. Things are hard for them right now but they love each other and they're getting along.

Bruce and his fiancé, Annie, live in Painted Post, they bought a nice house there. Bruce worked his way up to an engineering position at Corning Glass Works. I wish his grandfather had lived long enough to see his grandson become an Engineer.

Bonnie, Rich and Richie live just across the street from us. She bought her grandparent's house. They have remodeled the inside and are now starting on the outside. I would wager that Bonnie and Rich work about as hard as anyone in Wellsville.

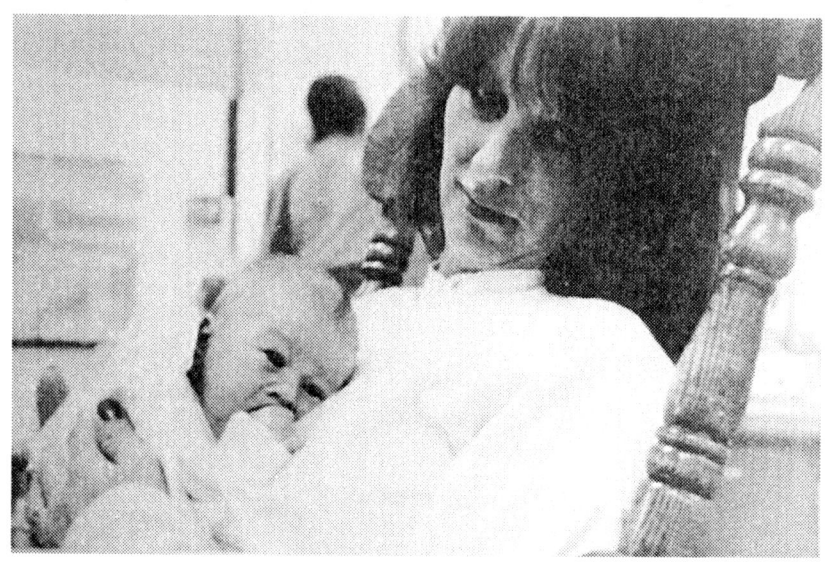

Several years ago Bonnie had a baby boy, Jeremy, who was born with a serious heart defect. A few hours after his birth, he was rushed to Children's Hospital in Buffalo by Mercy Flight. This picture of Jeremy and Bonnie was taken by Bonnie's husband, Rich, about the tenth day that Jeremy was in the hospital. Not knowing what was going to happen, they wanted to make sure that they had pictures of their baby. Of all the pictures that I have seen in my lifetime, none have had the effect on me that this picture has. Every time I look at this picture it makes me so sad. The picture tells a story that I can't put into words; the love, the sadness, the apprehension and exhaustion, it's all there in the picture.

Long before Jeremy was conceived, Bonnie's greatest desire was to have a baby. To have him taken away was such an unfair thing to happen. Jeremy died during heart surgery. We had five months to love and enjoy him. Now, Bonnie and Rich have another boy, Richie, to help wash away some of the hurt and bitterness. I've got to start spending more time with my grandson.

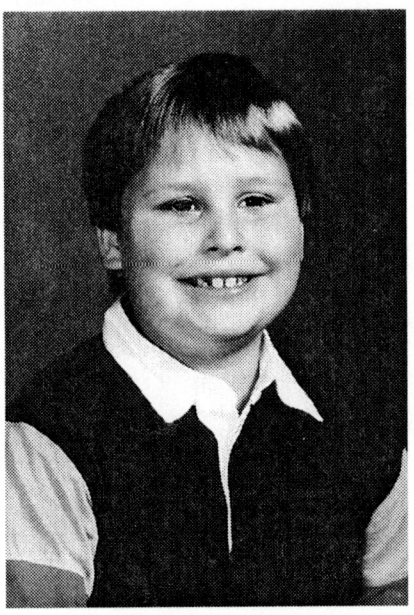

My grand-daughter, Becky, lives down in North Carolina. She and her fiancee, C.J., are getting married next year. Becky and I have always been great pals. Beulah and I don't see much of her, anymore. We miss her a lot.

One time I was bringing Becky to Wellsville from her house in Horseheads. Becky must have been about ten years old, or so. We were poking along the road, the other side of Addison, NY. I was driving my old restored Buick convertible, and we came upon a thunderstorm up ahead, bearing down on us.

"Stop the car, Grandpa, and put the top up," Becky yelled at me. I just grinned at her and told her to crank up her window. I tromped down on the accelerator, and we weren't poking along anymore. The big three-hundred-fifty cubic inch engine put a stop to the "poking along" in a hurry. Becky and Grandpa charged that on-coming thunderstorm in Grandpa's beautiful, powerful, white Buick convertible.

We plowed into the rain, wind, thunder and lightning. The slipstream rushed from the hood and windshield, forcing the wind and rain to roar over the top of the convertible. Only a little of the rain hitting the top of the back seat.

It all happened quickly. Soon we were back in the bright sunshine. Becky gave me a look of mock disapproval, then we both started giggling like two little kids who had done something mischievous and gotten away with it. Then we broke out laughing.

"There's a little store up ahead in Jasper, how's about we make a pit stop and get a Coke and candy bar, Becky?"

"I'll take a Pepsi Grandpa, Coke is for you old people," she snickered.

"I'll take a Pepsi Grandpa, Coke is for you old people."

The Pink House

In eighteen-sixty-eight, Edwin B. Hall designed and built this gorgeous home for himself and his family, but not without cost. The cost was not so much in money as cost weighed in sadness, regret and guilt.

A fountain pool graced the front lawn of the home. The precious little curly-haired granddaughter of the Hall's was unable to resist such a beautiful thing. She ventured too close, fell in the pool and drowned while the little girl's mother was distracted for a few moments talking to a neighbor. To make the tragedy even more horrifying, the little girl's grandfather, who no doubt worshipped her, witnessed the whole nightmare from the front porch. He was sitting there on the front porch unable to move or call out for help as he was paralyzed probably from the aftermath of a stroke. Shortly after the tragedy the grandfather died from a broken heart. The fountain pool was taken out and flowers and grass are now growing on the spot.

Photo courtesy of Marcile and Dr. Julian Woelfel, present owners of the Pink House

Little Beatrice Carpenter

In the summer of nineteen forty-one, we left my Grandma Pitts' house in Almond, and moved to Wellsville. What a transformation it was. The house in Wellsville was small for a family of nine plus Grandma, but we managed quite well, and we took a lot of pride in the place, and kept it clean and neat. I remember we had a new living room suit, new dining room furniture, and a new kitchen set, we had a washing machine and refrigerator.

Our back yard joined the back yard of an elegant, gorgeous mansion, known throughout the area as the Pink House. Though half a century has passed, neither the modest little house on Whitney Ave., nor the mansion on the corner of Brooklyn Ave. and State Street, has changed much. Both places have been maintained to perfection.

Whenever we were giving directions as to how to get to our house, we never gave the street name or number. It's the white house right behind the Pink House, we proudly would say. A few years back, my sister, Maggie, told me about an incident she had kept secret all those years, since the summer of forty-four when Maggie was fourteen:

"One of the neighborhood's young boys came up to me and told me they had found a secret space under the floor of the old tool shed behind the Pink House. I was curious, so that evening just before it got too dark, I sneaked over and went inside the tool shed. Sure enough the boy's had opened a trap door that revealed a small compartment under the tool shed. The only thing in there was a letter. I reached down and picked it up and took it home with me. I have forgotten what the letter said, but I remember there were two pages. The last page was signed by a gentleman by the name of Abraham Lincoln. I got scared and took the letter back and put it where I found it. That is about all I can remember of the incident."

Though Ronnie was younger than Maggie by four years, he remembers more vividly what took place. Ronnie and his friends were playing in our back yard, when one of the boys decided to climb over the wire fence that separated our back yard from the Pink House property. After all, isn't that why they build fences, so young boys can climb over and discover what the heck's on the other side? And if they discover an unlocked tool shed there naturally they walk in. Why the heck do you think they left it unlocked, if not so young boys can get in and see what is in there?

"When we got inside, we started raring around. While doing so, one of us discovered some loose boards in the floor," Ron said. "The loose boards were sort of a trap door affair. When we opened the door there was a compartment under the floor." Ronnie said he remembers the joist was lined with tin protecting two small bundles of letters.

"I took the letters home," Ronnie said. "Mom caught me with them. When she looked them over, she was upset and told me to take the letters back where I got them and never tell anybody about them, and never step foot on the Pink House property again. I did what she told me to do, I put the letters back and put the boards back where they belonged."

For many years now the fence and tool shed have been gone. I never learned if the owners of the Pink House ever recovered them, or if the person or persons who hid the letters took their secret to their grave.

Maybe when they tore down the shed the letters were still there, but went unnoticed and were burned up or destroyed in the process. One thing was obvious; who ever placed them there must have thought them important or they didn't want anybody to see them. They must have thought a tool shed would be a safe place to hide them, their reasoning probably was 'who would ever think of anything of great value in a tool shed?'

The present owners are the third generation. If they have no knowledge of the letters, probably the letters are gone forever.

Maybe, just maybe, old Abe had a secret lady friend, who had some connection or lived in the Pink House. Maybe the letters were hidden by a lady friend. Ronnie told me when he found the letters they were all tied in pink ribbon. The letters must have been sent to a woman, the macho men back in old Abe's day would never tie anything up in a ribbon, say nothing of a pink ribbon. When my sister and brother told me about the letters I was intrigued. I asked so many questions, it's a wonder they didn't lose their patience with me. After they had told me everything they thought they could remember, Ronnie came up with one last tidbit. He told me he heard our mother telling our oldest sister Alice about one of the letters, telling about her husband visiting the President.

Ronnie said, "I took one bundle of the letters, I don't know who took the other. Fact is I'm not sure who was with me, it was a long time ago. I was only nine or ten years old at the time."

The one letter Maggie found with Lincoln's signature must have come loose from one of the bundles or maybe wasn't tied with the two bundles the boy's took.

"It's the white house right behind the Pink House."

Baby Drowned

Sad Accident Brings Death to
Little Beatrice Carpenter
-Fell in Fountain in E.B. Hall's Yard.

A frightful accident occurred today when baby Beatrice Carpenter, a little over two years old, the youngest daughter of Mrs. And Mrs. J. Milton Carpenter, was drowned a few minutes before 1 o'clock in the fountain in the front yard of the E.B. Hall residence on West State street. Mr. And Mrs. Hall are Mrs. Carpenters parents, and Mr. And Mrs. Carpenter have lived with them since their marriage. The lawns about the residence are very beautiful and spacious and a semi-circle path goes from the street to the house. Mrs. Carpenter had walked out this path towards upper West State street, leaving the child near the house. The fountain is directly in front of the main entrance to the house and is 20 feet in diameter and contains fully two feet of water. It is generally spraying but was not today, thought the basin was full of water. It is not known whether little Beatrice started after her mother or whether the child went near the fountain and fell in.

The mother on returning to the house after a few minutes absence, saw the child had fallen in the fountain. Mrs. Carpenter shrieked for help and she herself pulled the baby from the water. But it was too late. The little one was dead. Porter H. Torrey, F.E.Richart, E.L. Rice, Will Kelsey and others went to the aid and

Dr. Roos and other physicians were quickly telephoned to. All speed was made in attempting to resuscitate the baby. A nail keg was brought from behind the house and the child rolled on this. Dr. Roos, Mr. Carpenter, the baby's father, and Drs. Witter, Kinney and Collar soon arrived and every possible means known to science was brought to bear to bring back the life of the little one but all to no avail. The doctors worked their hardest and did not even cease in their efforts after they knew there was no hope.

The anguish of the fond mother and father, and the grandparents is most pitiful and there is many a heartstring that feels as if it would break over the sad accident. The baby was an unusually pretty little girl and had everything in the world before her that the most fortunate of babies could have. Today she was dressed in attractive little whit dress with pink shoulder straps and white shoes and stockings and with her light hair and beautiful complexion it seemed an added blow that so fair a child should be taken.

The community is shocked by the awful news and the parents and sister Florence have the sincerest sympathy of all.

(Article from the Wellsville Daily Reporter)

Texas Hot

Most of my days start out eating breakfast at the Texas Hot. I'll have a hot cake and maybe an egg and drink about three cups of coffee. I sit at the counter and talk to anyone who happens to sit next to me. We talk about current events, complain about the weather, brag about the Buffalo Bills when they win a football game. If they lose a game we know why and go into great detail as to how they could have won, if the coach would just listen to us. In general, we go over a wide range of subjects.

Sometimes we swap stories about the war we were in or maybe tell something that happened to us when we were kids. The counter at the Texas Hot isn't off limits to the gals, but it's mostly a male domain. The gals seem to prefer the comfort of the booths and most of us guys kind of like it this way. Most of us love the gals, but it's kind of nice to have a place where we can get away from them for a little while and talk "man talk" without the fear of saying something a woman might think was sexist or maybe putting them down. Seems these days the gals are darned awful touchy about some things!

The stories told at the counter are sometimes a little far fetched and a few just plain outlandish lies, but most times you know which ones are true. You learn to sort them out.

One of my favorite stories is one told by a real sharp old gent, by the name of Dow Standards. He told me a story about when he was a little boy living one house up from the Pink House:

***

"When I was little we used to play hide and seek," Dow started in with his story. "One night while playing hide and seek, I spotted what I thought would be the perfect spot to hide. Some workmen had taken down one of the two statues that graced the entrance to the Pink House as it needed some repairs," Dow went on. "The base that held up the statue was made of wood; it had a chamber inside. I climbed the fence that ran up to the base and lowered myself feet first into the chamber. It was a tight fit but I managed to squeeze my body into the chamber. It was a lot further down than I thought. When my feet touched the bottom I could barely reach the top of the statue base with my finger tips. Then it dawned on me, it was easy to get in the chamber, but how in heck was I going to get out? After a while I started to panic, I started hollering for all I was worth, but my yells were so muffled no one heard me. I was afraid the kids would go home and leave me there all alone."

"Holy cow, I can't get outta here. I'm gonna be in here forever. My hiding place is too good. Maybe I'll fall asleep and the workers will put the statue back up on top of me. I'll be in here a hundred years, I'll die in here and they won't find me for a hundred years, and all they'll find is a bunch of bones."

"After what seemed forever one of the kids finally heard my muffled yells and discovered where I was. He ran across the street to get my neighbor, Tom Stiles."

"Dow's inside the statue and can't get out, we need help," the kid yelled. "Mr. Stiles reached down, grabbed me by the wrist and unceremoniously hauled me out of my self-made hell, shaken but unhurt. A little while after I got out, I discovered my pant's pocket was torn and my prize pocket watch was gone. I got a flashlight and shined it down the chamber, there it was at the bottom. 'I guess I lost my watch for sure,' I thought. 'I sure ain't gonna go back in there!' Then someone got a bright idea."

"My Dad's got a big magnet, we can tie a string on it and lower it down and get the watch out," one of the kids said.

"We did just that,"

Dow said. "But alas, the watch was not running. I wound it, but it wouldn't run. I tapped it gently on the sidewalk. Not a flick. The magnet had magnetized the gears in the watch stopping the action. I sadly walked home. When I crawled into my bed that night I was real glad I was there. My bed never felt better. I had a very bad day, but my safe comfortable bed made up for it all."

"I'll never go near that darn statue again. Maybe tomorrow I'll climb that big old pine tree beside the Pink House, but this time I won't get scared and stop halfway up. I'll climb clear to the top."

"The next day, that's just what I did," Dow said.

Sometimes the stories swapped are of a more serious nature. A friend of mine, Robert Owen kept a diary of his adventures while serving in the Navy on a Destroyer Escort during World War II. Following are a few excerpts from Robert's "Diary and Memoirs":

Nov 10: We heard a loud explosion and then a terrific explosion. The whole ship rocked from the concussion. The debris was falling on our ship. Sounded like hail. The U.S.S. Mount Hood, an ammunition ship. Lost all crew but one officer and seventeen enlisted men which had gone ashore. We were about 4,800 yards on the windward side. Walked out on deck and debris was still falling all around us. Even mattress covers! Then a fine film of oil began raining on us. They launched the whale boat to look for survivors. All they saw were parts and the men returned sick. A tanker standing nearby was badly hit. A large hole had been blown in her side. They took some wounded men off. I never knew whether anyone was killed. The "Hood" was only 1/3 loaded. If it had been loaded it would have gotten us too. Had a beer party in the afternoon. We are seeing too man movies to mention.

Nov 13: We are now going out everyday and in at night - sub practice. We found out later that a DE was alongside of Mount Hood. There was a total of 1300 casualties.

***

Steve opens the doors at six a.m. One can imagine what time he must hit the deck to get the Texas Hot ready for an always busy day. Steve used to own Cretekos Ice Cream Parlor, a family business that operated on Main Street for many years. I remember on my first real date I took my girl there for a Coke and a sandwich.

Beulah tells me she can remember Steve sitting on a barrel dipping candy in chocolate for his father. Steve still makes delicious candy around the Holidays.

During World War II Steve was a Commander on a B-17 bomber and flew several missions. He doesn't like to talk much about the war, about all he'll say is "I darn near got killed." I'd like to hear about his experiences flying B-17's but I don't push the issue.

"Mornin' Steve, How ya doing?" - "Fannntastic."

You never know who you may run into at the Texas Hot. That's one of the things that makes it so great. The Texas Hot is owned and operated by the third generation of two of Wellsville's prominent families, the Rigas's and the Raptis's. Evidence of their Greek heritage can be found by sampling their famous "Texas Hot Sauce" flavored with garlic, onion and special seasonings, the identity of which are a better kept secret than the combination to Fort Knox. Several people have claimed to know the recipe, but no one that I know of has every been able to duplicate the taste of one of the Hots off the grill at the Texas Hot.

Gus and John Rigas of Texas Hot Fame. Oh, and John is also owner of the Buffalo Sabers Professional Hockey Club. Perhaps you heard of them? Perhaps one day John will bring the Stanley Cup to Little 'ol Wellsville, imagine that.

The Greatest bunch of Gals anywhere!

House Number Three

There's a realtor in Wellsville, whom I happened to have a speaking acquaintance with. One time I ran into him on the street and told him I had a handyman special I would like him to list if he would.

"Sure," he said.

I told him I had a picture and would drop by his office so he could see it. Well, when I dropped by his office and showed him the picture, he changed his mind, in fact he got a little miffed, he didn't see any humor at all in my little joke.

Back in the thirties, a house like the one in the picture would have a family living in it. They would cover the windows with cardboard, patch the roof with some old boards, rig up a wood stove with the chimney sticking out a window frame and the place would be home-sweet-home for them.

I think the house we lived in, in Canisteo, was a little better than the one in the picture. I can't remember much about the house, but I do remember it had black tar paper on the outside, and I remember once I got a large sliver in my foot from the rough wood floors.

We bought a village lot from Beulah's brother and a book of house plans. I told Beulah to pick a house and I would build it for her. She chose an A-frame. It was a hard house to build, with lots of large windows, and it took a lot of lumber.

When I started the house in Wellsville, I was sixty years old, but I had a lot of energy. I did nearly all the work alone, except for the excavating, the roof and the wiring. My brother, Ronnie, did most of the shingles with some help from an old lather friend from Elmira, Jimmy Sproule, and his son, John. I found out that this old sailor who used to paint steamboat spars high off the deck from a Bo'sun's chair didn't like to climb much anymore.

When it came time to put the plywood on the roof, I built a scaffold inside the house. The house sits back from the street, and you couldn't see the scaffolding inside. It gave the appearance of me working out on that steep, high pitched roof, when in reality, I was working off of a six-foot step ladder. One morning while sitting at the counter of the Texas Hot, eating my breakfast, two young carpenters sat down next to me.

"Have you seen that A-frame someone is building up on Farnum Street?" one asked the other.

"Yeah," his friend said. "I went by there the other day, and some white-haired old bastard was out on that steep roof putting on plywood, all alone. That roof must have a twelve -twelve pitch roof!"

"I've seen that house," I cut in. "That roof is pretty high. That old son-of-a-bitch will probably break his damn neck."

The two young carpenters nodded their heads in agreement. I never told them I was the old son-of-a-bitch.

I started the house in June of nineteen eighty-seven and moved into the bottom floor eight months later, but I still have work to do on the place. Seems like I never do quite finish anything I start, anymore.

Beulah picked out an A-Frame design.

Where Did All the Trains Go ?

Wellsville was a great town in the late thirties and up through the fifties. We had the Sinclair Oil Refinery that processed oil from our own area oil wells. The refinery paid good wages, and did a lot for the area's economy. We had the Moore Steam Turbine, now Dresser Rand. The Moore Steam Turbine made the finest turbines in the world. Once when we all were sitting at the supper table, Dad told us about a turbine they had just disassembled for inspection. The turbine had run thirteen consecutive years without stopping.

"There wasn't anything wrong with it," Dad said, "we just put it back together and sent it back to the customer."

During World War II the factory was proudly flying the Army and Navy "E" under Old Glory, an award for Excellence for helping the war effort. We had the Air Preheater, another fine factory that provided goods for the war effort and paid wages equal to or better than other factories. I wonder how it did that without a Union?

We even generated our own electricity, and had enough steam left over to heat our school and library. I wonder what the real reasons for losing all that was?

Back in the thirties and forties you could hop an Erie Passenger train in Wellsville and go to Chicago or Jersey City. Wellsville had two passenger trains daily. The freight station was alive and well. Now the rails are rusty and you don't hear the throbbing of the trains anymore. But what I miss most is the lonesome wail of those old steam train whistles. Late at night or in the morning, before dawn, I could hear that sound as far away as Scio or Andover. I could relate to their call, they let me know I wasn't the only fish in the pond who was lonesome. I thought that there must be a lot of people out there in the night that grew melancholy when they heard that whistle, as they lay in their beds in the dark. There just never has been a sound quite like them, even the steamboat whistles didn't sound like that. Maybe the sound was akin to the sound an old timber wolf might make on a cold, moonlit, winter night, all alone after having lost his mate to a younger, stronger wolf.

Now I wonder where all the trains have gone, and what was the real cause of them leaving? I worry that they will never come back to Wellsville. Wouldn't it be something if one of those old one hundred fifteen-foot-long, nine hundred thousand pound steam locomotives came thundering through Wellsville unannounced, riding tall and proud on her six and a half foot high driving wheels, causing the ground to tremble and windows to rattle, black smoke and cinders belching from the stack? Plumes of white steam would be blowing from her relief valves, her whistle blowing loudly at the road crossings demanding the cars and people get the hell out of her way. Then it would stop at the station, panting like a sweaty, shiny, black, monstrous war horse, getting it's second wind, escaping steam hissing like a thousand angry serpents. Her bell would be clanging, the engineer's elbow out the open cab window, looking straight up the track, proud and aloof, knowing all the little boys and some of the big little boys, like me, were envious, and wishing they were he.

Oh, how my grandson and a million other grandsons would love it, be awed and frightened at the same time, if they could see and hear one of those majestic steam locomotives.

Wars, depressions, hard times, no matter, the year nineteen twenty-six was a great year for a boy to be born in small town America. I should know.

Dreams

Sometimes I dream about going back in time and doing things all over again. I'd like to go back in time and wheel the *Cuyler Adams* from Duluth to Oswego. I wouldn't want to wheel a modern lake boat with all the new technology, making the boat smarter than it's crew and all the regulators laying down the law. I'd want to wheel an old boat like the *Cuyler Adams*.

We used to call the *Cuyler Adams* a 'Ma and Pa Kettle Boat', you had to know where to hit it with a hammer or kick it to make it go.

I'd like to build another house similar to the one I built in Horseheads. This time I would have other people do the hard work.

I'd like to go to San Francisco and visit the *Liberty Ship*, the *Jeremiah O'Brien*. It would take me back in time to the *Arkab*. The *O'Brien* is the only liberty ship left in running order. I'd like to climb back up in the crow's nest and walk through the crew's quarters and maybe have a cup of Joe in the crew's mess, then climb the ladder to the bridge where my number four gun was and strap myself in, just for the hell of it and reflect back when I was a kid. I was proud they made me a gunner instead of an ammunition passer or some lesser station, knowing I had an important job helping protect my ship and shipmates.

I would want to pause a little while, hat in hand, at the 'tween deck where big, handsome, good-natured Tony fell into the cargo hold. If I ever visited the *O'Brien* I would want to be all alone on her. My emotions would get the better of me, especially after climbing down from the Crow's Nest for the last time.

My son Bruce took this great picture of the Jeremiah O'Brien when he went to San Francisco on a business trip.

I don't know about other people, but the older I get the more sentimental I get; but I don't think that's all bad. I still have some dreams, and I guess I'm still kind of a romantic. I don't think that's all bad, either.

It would be great to go back to the late forties and once again go flying with my old friend, Woody Davis in his old, rickety, little aircoupe airplane. I don't think Woody was the best pilot in the world. I think he was a little scared of flying.

I remember one time while coming in for a landing at the Wellsville airport, I happened to glance over to Woody's face, his eyes were wide and his manner was of total concentration. He was leaning forward and his body was as stiff as a poker, his Adam's apple kept going up and down. Woody once told me he didn't mind taking off, but it was a son-of-a-bitch landing, especially at the Wellsville airport. In the forties the Wellsville airport wasn't much more than a cow pasture.

While taking off you damn well better be airborne by the time you were halfway down the single dirt strip or your aircraft would make a one-point landing in the tall willow trees at the end of the runway. I've always had a dream of getting a pilot's License and flying one of those old World War I biplanes.

Woody in the center standing next to his 'Air-Coupe.'

It would be great to go back in time and on a warm summer night sit on that big old porch on the house that used to be on the corner of Cusick and Pine and listen to my mother, my father and my uncles play their music. It seems it's hard to find what I think is good music, like Floyd Cramer and Chet Atkins.

Sometimes Barbie can find some tapes I like, she knows the kind of music I enjoy. Rap is crap, it's not music to me. I like Country, but not modern Country. They all sound alike when they sing, besides I like instrumental music, not vocals.

Oh! How my Uncle Harold could make music come out of a piano. I wish some of his genius had rubbed off on me. He was a great guy, my Uncle Harold, everyone loved him.

This house is where my Mother was born, in Friendship, New York.

One time Uncle Howard was playing his xylophone, and Grandma Pitts entered the house after her morning walk. "You know Howard, your music sounds real nice from way down the street," she said. Somehow her compliment didn't come out quite right.

It would be nice to go back in time, before Beulah and I were married and once more ask her to be my girl, and experience the thrill when she says yes. Then once more do a little gloating over all the other male fish in the pond who wanted her.

Sometimes Beulah and I take a drive to Almond and I show her where Al Palmer's pool hall used to be and where my Uncles had a bakery and where my Grandmother's house used to be.

The house and buildings are gone now, the seventy-two flood finally destroyed Grandma's house after it survived two other floods. A fire took out the block where Palmer's pool hall was, but most of Almond hasn't changed much. The old school where the dumbest kid in the third grade went is still there, it's a carpet store now.

I take Beulah around the Village Park where we boys played ball and did other more interesting things under the band stand.

On the way back to Wellsville, we drive by the Alfred-Almond School and past the house where Janie used to live. Except for a different color paint, it looks the same, and we go by the hill Janie and I once climbed on a bright October day. It's still beautiful there in the fall, it hasn't changed much except the trees are taller. But I guess they should be after fifty years.

I know that you can't physically go back in time, but if one unshackles their mind and lets their thoughts drift you can go back in time as far as you can remember. It's nice because you can block out the unpleasant things and just envision the things that gave you happiness and pleasure, and if you're standing in the spot where these events took place, it really enhances your vision of the past.

I guess when a person gets to be my age, you kind of have to use the past as a crutch. It's mostly down hill from here on out. I don't want to bust anyone's bubble, but the golden years are mostly fool's gold years. I don't like it when I have to use glasses to see, false teeth to eat, what few muscles I have left don't work too good and the girls don't give me a second glance anymore. To put it kind of crudely, I think old age sucks, but I guess I shouldn't complain too much, my health seems to be good and all things considered I'm getting along okay.

It would be nice to go back in time, before Beulah and I were married and once more ask her to be my girl, and experience the thrill when she said yes.

Florence

Sometimes you don't have to unshackle your mind to go back to the past; sometimes something happens and you're back in time instantly. Like the day my son, Bruce, called and told me he had read in the paper that Florence Chadwick had died out in San Diego. As soon as Bruce said the name Chadwick, my thoughts were back in time over forty years. I had flashbacks of a handsome, tall, young lady with broad shoulders. She was wearing a black one-piece swim suit and a white swim cap. She had the long flowing muscles that swimmers develop, her arms and legs shining from the glow of television lights reflecting off the swimmer's grease she had applied to her body to ward off the bone chilling waters of Lake Ontario.

It was near Labor Day weekend, nineteen fifty-four, when she dove off the dock at Old Fort Niagara. In my mind I can remember when we pulled Miss Chadwick from the cold Lake Ontario water. She was cold, crying, and exhausted. My heart went out to her, but I didn't say anything. There are times it's best you say nothing. This was one of those times.

Miss Chadwick swam over halfway from Youngstown to Toronto. She was sick all the way, and there's no doubt in my mind she could have reached her goal if see had felt better. She knew she could do it, and so did everyone on the Anna III; but sometimes things happen, sometimes you have bad luck.

The last time I saw Miss Chadwick, she was slowly walking away from Anna III, down the dock at the Toronto Yacht Club, her head low, with her manager Vic Christie's arm around her shoulder.

It's all there stored in my mind. I can go back to Labor Day, nineteen fifty-four anytime I want to.

Friends

I miss my friends Woody and Don. They were always there if I needed them. I think Woody and Don figured they kind of had to take care of me. They were older and wiser, always looking out for my interest and giving me advice.

In all my life, I think I have had only three friends, that is to say real friends. Jim Sproule in Elmira is a friend, though I don't see much of him anymore.

It seems I have outlived most everyone. Out of the four guys I joined the Navy with, three have died and I don't know where the other is. We all had something in common, but that never made us good friends. I know and like a lot of people, but I don't consider them all friends, fact is I must not want any friends. If I did, I would do something to cultivate some.

I guess I'm kind of a loner and I like it that way, although I don't like my lifestyle too well. I feel frustrated, restless and bored. About the only thing that holds my interest is my wife and kids. I wish Barbie and Becky lived closer. It's only an hour and half drive to Barb's house, but I don't drive much anymore, and Beulah's driving is worse than mine. If one wants a little excitement just, go for a ride with Beulah at the wheel and her foot on the gas.

An 'Ol Man's Chat with Time

Why are you so anxious to leave me?
I'm going to need more of you.
Can't you spare just a bit more?
I confess, most often I don't use you right,
But there are things I haven't done yet.
Don't you know?
There are things I haven't seen yet.
Don't you care?
There are things I haven't said yet.
Why are you passing so swiftly?
You're unfair.
You force me to slow down,
yet you move ever faster.
You're catching me off guard.
You're leaving me unprepared.
So many things left undone,
So many knots in need of tying.
You're passing me by.
I'm going to lose everything.
What's to happen when you're through with me?
Will there be eternal bliss and beauty?
Will there be damnation?
Will I become a frog?
Will there be nothing at all?
You don't know do you?
You don't care do you?

Someone Once Said...

Someone once said, "Every man should build his own home" and "every man should write his own story." If home is where the heart is, I guess for me home would have been on top of our mountain in Horseheads. Beulah says Wellsville is home, that's where her roots are. Me, I don't think I ever had any roots. When it comes down to it, I really don't give a hoot where I live any more. It's who you live with that counts, not where you live. I guess home is where ever my hat happens to be hanging.

The *Cuyler Adams* kind of felt like home. The Navy and the *Arkab* sure as hell didn't. I really miss that old steamboat at times. One thing I found out about writing. I can say things in writing that are hard for me to say out loud. Love is one of them. By writing I can tell my wife and my kids I love them, and it's just as sincere as if I said it out loud, and it's there in writing forever.

Thinking about my past experiences, I'm getting to know myself better. Things come out that I wasn't aware of, things like my weaknesses and my strengths. Like when I was a kid on the *Arkab*, naked except for a towel around me, strapped in my twenty MM cannon, and was sure we were going to do battle with a Japanese submarine. I never was so scared in my life, but I knew that I would do my job, no matter what. But on the other hand, I don't stand up to people like I should. Sometimes I let people intimidate me, and then when they push me too far, I don't try to reason with them. My Dad's short temper comes out, and I go at them like he came at me sometimes. No matter how justified I think I am, I'm always sorry after I blow up at someone, but it's a weakness I can't seem to overcome.

All and all, I think writing about myself has been advantageous, and caused me to like myself better. Looking back, I realize I never hurt anyone too badly, except for pushing Clayton Henry into the water. I appreciate my family much more. Sometimes I feel maybe I've missed something. I never cheated on my wife, except for having some lustful thoughts, which I still have at times, like most dirty old men. I'm glad the girls at the Texas Hot can't read my mind; or maybe they can, but aren't too concerned. An old dog with no teeth isn't feared too much.

Bringing up my past brings some regrets too. I regret I didn't show more love to my mom and dad. They were so appreciative of any little thoughtful thing one would do for them, and I never did do much for them. They were a much better father and mother than I was a son.

I tell how good my brother Jim was to me. Now I look back and see I wasn't too understanding when the booze got the best of my brother, and he was down about as far as a man can go. The same for my sister, Alice, who died of cirrhosis of the liver at the age of thirty-six. I was so upset with their heavy drinking, I showed no compassion or understanding. I avoided them, when maybe a little love and understanding would have meant a great deal to them.

Thinking of my past has me feeling a bit better. I've gotten some things off my chest. Some thoughts were anchored deep in my mind, now I have pried some of them out and faced up to them. It's sort of like asking Mom and Dad, and Jim and Alice, to forgive me for my callous treatment toward them. Now in my heart I feel they have. If they could come back for a little while, I'm sure they all would say to me, "Forget it Bob, it's okay".

Writing has caused an explosion of pictures of the past to flash through my mind like a runaway movie projector. I can't believe all of these things happened in what seems like a short span of time. My God, I've already lived more years than my father did. I'm getting old. Half the time I can't find my glasses, and I forget what shelf I left my uppers on. Beulah has to remind me to zip my fly before I leave the house. I tell her it really doesn't matter much anymore.

Yeah, a lot of water has passed under the bridge. Speaking of water, wasn't it just last week I pushed Clayton Henry in?

Well, third grade teacher, maybe I was the dumbest kid in your third grade class, but I think I made pretty good use of my life. I have an honorable discharge from Uncle Sam's Navy. I have Able Seaman's papers. I could wheel a five hundred foot steamboat from Duluth to Oswego. If I had made steam boating a lifetime career, I'm certain I would have been a captain before I finished. I have a document proving I was a journeyman lather and worked as foreman on many of the jobs I was on, helping to build homes, schools, churches, and hospitals. I owned and operated a sightseeing business, giving a lot of people pleasure. I know because they told me so. I have a U.S. Patent hanging on my den wall. I didn't make any money on it, but if you think it's easy getting a patent, try it. I built three houses with my own hands, one a very unique house. My wife and I owned and operated a dry-cleaners for fifteen years. We were often told we did the best job at the lowest price and with the fastest service.

The accomplishment I'm most proud of was being a faithful husband and a successful father for over forty-five years. Our children and grandkids are proof of that success.

Now I even have the audacity to write a book. Think about that, third grade teacher. When I stop to think about it, maybe if you had passed me, I might have taken an interest in school and gone to college on the G.I. Bill of Rights. I might have become a hot-shot lawyer. Maybe I could have been a politician. Maybe I could of gotten a job with the government working with one of their many regulatory agencies, scaring mom and pop businesses to the point where they close their shops.

No, I wouldn't want to be any of them. They can have it. So I'm not mad at you anymore, third grade teacher. Sometimes when the house is quiet and we're all alone, we get to reminiscing about what could have been, if we'd just done some things differently, or whatever. But some of us are lucky, we have our wives, kids and grandkids and that's about all we need. I'm not mad at anyone out there. This may sound kind of funny, and I'm not quite sure I understand it myself, but hell - I even like the people I don't like.

This ain't the end, 'cause I ain't dead yet. The fact of the matter is, I think I'm getting another brainstorm smoldering in the back of my old bald head. Darned if I'm gonna sit on my duff and wait for the undertaker. Maybe I'll go out and take pictures. There's lots of places around Wellsville that would make really nice photographs. Who knows? If I do a good job, maybe some of them might even sell, besides, Beulah and I could use the money. Every time I go by the cemetery, I tell myself to hurry up if I'm ever going to fill that inside straight, time is running out.

When a man is pushing seventy, he has to take stock and think about meeting his maker. If my maker sees fit to let me pass through the Pearly Gates after I kick the bucket, I sure would like a job wheeling one of those old steamboats, assuming God has any up there.

Cap Hanson must be up there someplace. You could check with him, I'm sure he will tell you I was a darn good wheelsman. There's one more favor I'd like to ask of you, God, if it wouldn't put you out too much. I sure would like to meet Mark Twain, if you could use your influence and set it up. He might even know me. For about twenty years, we lived just one hill over from Mark Twain's in-laws, the Langdon's, home in Elmira, Quarry Farm where Mark Twain wrote some of his best work.

Knowing how dear the place was to him, I'm sure Mr.Twain kept track of all the comings and goings in the area. Besides, ,Mr.Twain and I would have something to chat about. We both loved old steamboats and had a lot of adventures wheeling them.

I sure would like a job wheeling one of those old steamboats, assuming God has any up there.

Photo by Bruce Broughton and Saint Peter

The Langdon's (home in Elmira) Quarry Farm where Mark Twain wrote some of his best works.

Quarry Farm

For one hundred twenty-nine years autumn leaves have fallen around the old marker stone in front of the house at Quarry Farm. I'm thinking it won't be many more seasons and the names Langdon and Clemens, chiseled in the old stone, will disappear into oblivion.

If left alone nature always wins out, patience and time are her allies. If she wants the names she'll take them in her own way, minute specks of dust at a time sending them helter-skelter through the air, and I for one think that's the way it should be.

Nothing lasts forever including us egotistical humans, and that fact doesn't bother me. I'm ready to go whenever nature is through with me. I'm getting a little weary, and when my turn comes, if there's anyone out there who loves me a little, don't shed any tears for me. Weep a little for yourself and all the others still living and waiting their turn to go.

I keep asking myself, why was I born? What was the purpose, if any? One would think with all the self-proclaimed geniuses out there, at least one could answer my question, but not one can. Maybe they should have flunked the third grade same as me.

The End